THE ORPHAN SCANDAL

THE ORPHAN SCANDAL

Christian Missionaries

and the Rise of

the Muslim Brotherhood

BETH BARON

STANFORD UNIVERSITY PRESS

STANFORD, CALIFORNIA

Stanford University Press
Stanford, California

©2014 by the Board of Trustees of the Leland Stanford Junior University.
All rights reserved.

Printed in the United States of America on acid-free, archival-quality paper

Library of Congress Cataloging-in-Publication Data

Baron, Beth, author.
  The orphan scandal : Christian missionaries and the rise of the Muslim Brotherhood / Beth Baron.
      pages cm
  Includes bibliographical references and index.
    ISBN 978-0-8047-9076-5 (cloth : alk. paper)--ISBN 978-0-8047-9138-0 (pbk. : alk. paper)
  1. Missions--Egypt--History--20th century. 2. Missions to Muslims--Egypt--History--20th century. 3. Jam'iyat al-Ikhwan al-Muslimin (Egypt)--History.
4. Orphans--Services for--Egypt--History--20th century. 5. Public welfare--Egypt--History--20th century. 6. Islam--Relations--Christianity--History--20th century.
7. Christianity and other religions--Islam--History--20th century. I. Title.
  BV3570.B37 2014
  266.00962--dc23
                    2014007328

    ISBN 978-0-8047-9222-6 (electronic)

Typeset by Bruce Lundquist in 10/15 Minion Pro

For Talya and Neta,
and all the Turkiyyas of the world

CONTENTS

Illustrations follow page 96

PREFACE

One hot summer morning in June 1933, an orphan girl named Turkiyya Hasan failed to rise in a show of respect for a visiting Protestant missionary at the Swedish Salaam Mission School in Port Said, Egypt. The defiance of the fifteen-year-old Muslim girl infuriated the Swiss matron, who rebuked and then began caning her when she answered back. News quickly spread from the Mediter-ranean port city to Cairo that a matron of the "School for Peace" had beaten an orphan in an attempt to convert her to Christianity. The story fed into a stream of reports on conversions, or attempted conversions, touching a deep nerve among Egyptians and creating a national uproar with international repercussions. The scandal marked the beginning of the end of foreign mis-sions in Egypt and the simultaneous take-off of Islamist organizations such as al-Ikhwan al-Muslimin (the Muslim Brotherhood).

The Orphan Scandal uses the Turkiyya Hasan affair in the summer of 1933 as a lens to examine the dynamic among Christian evangelicals, Islamists, and officials of the semi-colonial Egyptian state. It details the passionate efforts of American and European missionaries, many of whom were single women with little more than their faith to guide them, to look after orphaned and aban-doned children. Their attempts to convert their wards aroused the concern of Muslim activists, for whom the beating of Turkiyya Hasan at the Swedish Salaam Mission served to communicate the need for Muslim social welfare to the wider public. In battling missionaries for the bodies and souls of Egypt's children, Islamists appropriated evangelicals' tools to fight them, and in the process created their own network of social welfare services. State officials viewed the expanding anti-missionary movement as a threat and moved to crush it by cutting off its ability to fundraise, to assemble, and to publicize its views. At the same time, the state tightened control over private social welfare institutions and extended its own, sowing the seeds of a Muslim welfare state.

Facilitated by the British occupation, Christian missions reached their height in the 1920s, the exact decade the Muslim Brotherhood, among other Islamist organizations, was founded. The British had unilaterally bestowed independence on Egypt in 1922 after thirty years of occupation, and oversaw the writing of a constitution that was promulgated the following year. Egyptian independence was incomplete, however, and a semi-colonial regime continued to operate in tandem with the Capitulations inherited from the Ottomans that gave foreigners certain privileges. The Muslim Brotherhood was born in Isma'iliyya in 1928 as a response to concerns about the power of colonialism (the British army had a base there), the ability of evangelicals to operate freely in the vicinity, and the weakness of Muslims in confronting the West. Launching some of their first branches in cities and towns along or near the Suez Canal, the Muslim Brothers sought to revitalize Islam. At the same time, they organized resistance against the missionaries and formed the vanguard of the anti-missionary movement.[1]

With a trail that winds through the Arabic press and leads in and out of different missionary and state archives, the Turkiyya Hasan affair allows us to read the histories of missionaries, Muslim Brothers, and the semi-colonial state together. This in turn gives a new perspective on the early years of the Muslim Brotherhood, beyond a stress on the Brotherhood's antagonistic relations with British colonial authorities or Egyptian state officials. Richard Mitchell, Brynjar Lia, and Gudrun Kraemer, have extensively researched this early history.[2] *The Orphan Scandal* maps out the connections they have briefly noted between missionaries and the Muslim Brotherhood, taking us into the small cities, towns, and villages in Egypt where some of the most intense contests between evangelicals and Islamists occurred. Focusing on contact points, tracing struggles at particular moments, and identifying specific missionaries and missions—such as the Swedish Salaam Mission or the Egypt General Mission—becomes critical in detailing these encounters.

This approach of concentrating on events in the Canal Zone and Upper Egypt (where an important missionary orphanage was founded) has the advantage of decentering Egyptian history.[3] In so many works (my own included), Cairo becomes synonymous with Egypt. Here the emphasis is on linkages between the periphery and the center: events in Port Said, Asyut, and other cities and towns have important implications for politics in the capital. *The Orphan Scandal* traces how the anti-missionary movement started in the provinces—specifically in the Canal Zone—and only then migrated to the center and elsewhere in the country. This focus on the provinces also helps to shift the spotlight away from Hasan al-Banna, the Muslim Brotherhood founder and general guide, to illuminate the activities of branch members in places such as al-Manzala, Port Said, and Suez.

This book also shows semi-colonialism in action. What did it mean for Egypt to be independent and yet have British army bases and British police commanders and advisors working for the Egyptian government? How did this work out in practice, where did power lie, and who made the important decisions? Calling this period in Egyptian history a failed liberal experiment and putting the blame on Egyptian politicians ignores the extent to which Egyptians were constrained in their actions. This chapter of British imperial history has not gotten the attention it deserves, at least lately, perhaps because Egypt's status was so unique: it was not a formal colony like India nor a mandate like Palestine nor even a protectorate, as it had been during World War I. The manipulations of Sir Alexander Keown-Boyd, British advisor in the Egyptian Ministry of Interior, in the course of the orphan scandal reveal the complexities of semi-colonialism. Pushed by Keown-Boyd, Egyptian officials moved to suppress a peaceful protest movement against missionaries, which in the long term only fueled the Islamist opposition.

Under the watchful eyes of the British and protected by the Capitulations, Protestant missionaries found great liberty to proselytize in Egypt from the time of the occupation in 1882. Yet the armies of European and American evangelicals that descended on the Nile Valley had to do more than preach in order to reach the population. To win converts, they opened schools, clinics, hospitals, and orphanages, and sent Bible women into the homes of Egyptians to read the gospel to illiterate girls and women. A few came over unaffiliated with a church or board, but most came with missions. The largest of these was the American (Presbyterian) Mission, whose converts launched the Egyptian Evangelical Church. They had plenty of company in, among others, the Nile Valley Mission, the Assemblies of God Mission, the Church Missionary Society, the Egypt General Mission, and the Swedish Salaam Mission, all of which are discussed here.

Scholars have only recently started to explore this critical chapter of American and European forays in Egypt, with Heather Sharkey and Paul Sedra leading the way.[4] Their works have emphasized evangelicals' involvement with Orthodox Coptic Christians. Indebted to these scholars and not wanting to retrace their steps, *The Orphan Scandal* focuses on missionary interactions with the Muslim population and Islamic activists' responses to foreign missions.

In discussing some of the larger missions, including the American Mission and the Egypt General Mission, this book pays particular attention to Pentecostal and other evangelicals from non-mainline churches. Their brand of "muscular Christianity," aggressive proselytizing, and attempts to convert Muslims often got them into trouble with locals and state authorities.

What did conversion mean in a semi-colonial context and in sites where power was unequal on multiple levels, such as an orphanage or school? Did these encounters constitute "conversations," that is, dialogues between evangelists and locals, or between adults and children, as some have theorized? Or were they part of a regime of "coercion," that is, where undue pressure or excessive force was designed to force transformation?[5] The answer may well lie in the distinctions between the notion of religion as belief, which cannot be forced, and of religion as a set of practices, which can be prescribed. Christian missionaries stressed belief and faith; Muslims saw practice as central. There is also a third possibility, that religious conversion meant not just a shift in belief or practice but in legal identity. At what age could this occur, who counted the years, and what constituted force? These all became critical questions in contestations over conversion.

This work suggests that the number of converts cannot be taken as a measure of the success or failure of missions, which is relative in any case, and not necessarily germane. That missionaries did not "succeed" at converting a large number of Muslims does not mean that missionaries did not leave a large footprint in Egypt. Just as those who carried the call and those who were converted were "mutually transformed,"[6] those who fought conversion and those they fought against were both changed as well. In short, American and European missionary actions had unintended and unforeseen consequences, generating ripples with deep reverberations in Egyptian society, culture, and politics.[7]

While accounts of United States involvement in the Middle East generally take World War II as a starting point, a new body of work has begun to address the legacy of American missionaries in the region over a century before. These works seek to deepen the history of American imperialism by showing how profoundly earlier engagements touched local populations.[8] Yet Americans tend to see their history as apart, rather than a part of struggles in places where their predecessors sojourned, and to see Islamists as extremists who have no possible connection to their own past. In the story told here, American missionaries clearly had a hand in exacerbating tensions between Christians and Muslims and in mobilizing Islamists in Egypt.

In a recent renaissance of work on European evangelical missions to the Middle East, historians have attempted to shift interpretations away from ones that see missions as the "religious wing of imperialism" to ones that stress their contributions to social work, health care, education, and science. Part of the argument is that missionaries themselves made a shift from attempts to Christianize the population to attempts to modernize and secularize it.[9] *The Orphan Scandal* suggests that the religious imperatives of missionaries to save populations and their social welfare work cannot be neatly separated, and that missionaries, at least in Egypt, used social services to try to convert locals. At the same time, rather than promote secularism, missionaries may well have helped to derail a movement in that direction on the part of local Egyptians that was already under way. The missionary model of education fused secular/scientific education with religious indoctrination; while the Christian content of that education did not appeal to Islamic activists, the model did.

Missionaries, Muslim Brothers, and Egyptian state officials fought their battles over the bodies and souls of orphans, who are the real protagonists in this story. The "orphans" here came from a variety of backgrounds: they were abandoned, disabled, motherless and/or fatherless, or did not have relatives who were able or willing to care for them. *The Orphan Scandal* moves youth lacking parental care, such as Turkiyya Hasan, from the shadows to the light, showing that they were not only pawns in a struggle between foreign evangelicals and local Islamists, but also formidable actors in their own right. Their exceptional histories, and those of orphaned and abandoned children in general, have the potential to tell us a great deal about family, society, and the state.[10]

Re-creating the world of orphans, who are so often marginalized, is not easy. In *Orphans of Islam: Family, Abandonment, and Secret Adoption in Morocco*, the anthropologist Jamila Bargach chronicles the lack of choices for pregnant women in a North African country where single mothers are unknown and legal adoption does not exist, writing movingly about the dilemmas and stigmatization of orphans and abandoned children.[11] Nazan Maksudyan, Andrea Rugh, and Amira Sonbol, among others, have explored the history of orphans in the Ottoman Empire and Egypt.[12] How did those who were the recipient of missionaries' orphan care experience it? What did their everyday lives look like? How were they impacted by custody battles between missionaries, Islamists, and the state? This work seeks, in humanizing its subjects, to enrich our understanding of the social history of early twentieth-century Egypt.

Missionaries generally documented their work carefully, yet missionary archives present certain methodological challenges. Scholars are often overwhelmed by the sheer volume of material produced by evangelicals, who left letters, diaries, minutes, reports, magazine articles, and other papers. Much of this material was meant to record their successes and struggles overseas, part of an effort to raise funds at home. By contrast, the populations among whom they worked seemed to have little to say about their encounter with missionaries. Residents in orphanages, pupils in schools, or patients in clinics and hospitals often have no names or voices. This has sometimes led to the assumption that evangelicals had a minimal impact on the societies in which they worked.

Looking at a specific event in a fixed period of time—the summer of 1933—punctures this image. The Turkiyya Hasan affair generated a paper trail of press stories, confidential consular reports, government files, and missionary records that help to document the relationship of Muslims and missionaries. The Arabic press, including Muslim Brotherhood and other Islamic publications, heatedly discussed the orphan scandal, capturing the intense local reaction to proselytizing in Egypt. Hasan al-Banna had quite a lot to say about the fight against missionaries in his newspaper and memoirs. The United States and British National Archives detail behind-the-scenes government machinations, particularly in some fascinating confidential files. The archives of the Presbyterian Historical Society, the Flower Pentecostal Heritage Center, the Friends Historical Library, and Yale University Divinity School also document the lead up to the Turkiyya Hasan affair and its aftermath.[13]

The Orphan Scandal starts with the story of the Turkiyya Hasan affair, telling it from the perspective of the international cast of characters involved and, where possible, in their own words. The multiple vantage points reveal the intractable dilemma at the heart of missionary-Muslim encounters in Egypt. The kaleidoscope of contending views demonstrates that missionary understandings of their project were often vastly at odds with the understandings of those they had come to save. While many Egyptians saw the beating of the Muslim teenager as a criminal act, some European and American observers considered it an overblown "missionary incident." Yet the views did not simply polarize along a Muslim-Christian or Egyptian-foreign axis. Egyptians had multiple perspectives—with some joining the foreign attempt to quiet the noise around it and contain the damage—as did Americans and Europeans who became caught up in the drama.

ACKNOWLEDGMENTS

Writing a book is a journey, and the trails taken can lead in many directions. This book started as a history of orphaned and abandoned children in Egypt. When it became clear that missionaries not only ran orphanages but kept unparalleled records on them, the book became a history of missionaries and orphans. Research in missionary archives uncovered materials on the caning of a teenage Muslim orphan girl named Turkiyya Hasan in Port Said in 1933. This launched a search for Turkiyya through archives and libraries, which led surprisingly to the Muslim Brotherhood, the Islamist organization that stood on the frontlines of the anti-missionary movement. This is not, then, the book I started out to write, but it is the one I finished.

Many helped at different stages of the journey. Special thanks go to those who shared moving stories about adoptions, their own or ones in their family. Their stories affirmed the importance of the gift of care and of giving orphaned and abandoned children homes and histories. Mine Ener was there at the start, with her infectious good spirit and questions about social welfare. I am saddened that she could not see this journey through, but her own book has become a compass. I am also saddened that I did not get the chance to know Amy Johnson better, having met her only once (and that at a memorial for Mine). This book honors the memory of both women.

Many other colleagues helped in innumerable ways. Heather Sharkey paved the way with her own pathbreaking research, painstaking editing of two volumes on missionaries, and patient reading of parts of this work. Eve Troutt Powell unsettled certain assumptions about Egyptian history and showed me how to listen carefully to the stories our subjects tell. Nefissa Naguib accompanied me every step of the way, pressing me to tell this story and sharing many of her own. Inger Marie Okkenhaug and her Scandinavian colleagues helped me to see the missionary women who sojourned in the Middle East in a different light. Muge Gocek demonstrated how to tackle hard topics and not be afraid to speak up. Akram Khater inspired me to write a narrative history and then encouraged me to finish it and find new mountains to climb. Many others have shared their company and counsel, among them Malek Abisaab, Iris Agmon, Nadje Ali, Yesim Arat, Febe Armanios, Ami Ayalon, Ergene Bogac, Mehmet Ali Dogan, Ellen Fleischmann, Emad Hilal, Rudi Matthee, Negin Nabavi, Arzu Ozturkmen, Leslie Peirce, Lisa Pollard, Barbara Reeves-Ellington, Mona Russell, Holly Schissler, Omnia El Shakry, and Zeina Schlenoff.

Throughout the past decade when this book was researched and written, Anny Bakalian, "Umm MEMEAC," has been a steady presence at the Middle East and Middle Eastern American Center and a real support: her warmth and multiple acts of kindness have created a home away from home for so many. Colleagues at the center—Ervand Abrahamian, Ammiel Alcalay, Simon Davis, Alex Elinson, Mandana Limbert, and Chris Stone—have helped create an exciting environment in which to work. Special thanks to Samira Haj for always being honest and nudging me out of my comfort zone, and to Dina LeGall for always being there. For commenting on more chapters of this book than they would care to remember, colleagues at City College—Craig Daigle, Greg Downs, Emily Greble, Danian Hu, Andreas Killen, Adrienne Petty, Cliff Rosenberg, and Judith Stein—deserve special appreciation. So, too, do colleagues who helped in the last miles—Lale Can, Jennifer Johnson, and Barbara Naddeo.

During this journey, my teachers and friends continued to impart important lessons: Annette Aronowicz offered a model with her intellectual integrity and curiosity; Gene Garthwaite provided a sanctuary and sustenance in the north; Nikki Keddie gave good advice; Mary Kelley showed the way forward; Kitty Sklar affirmed the importance of educators and reformers; and Robert Tignor always asked good questions. Selma Botman gave one of the greatest gifts of all—time to write. Gary Yizar got me to where I needed to go with great humor, and Lu Steinberg made sure that I got there healthy and intact. Chase Robinson diverted me from the book by agreeing to host the *International Journal of Middle Eastern Studies* at the CUNY Graduate Center. Although editing slowed down progress on this book, it made it a different, and I hope a better, one. Thanks to all those who shared in that amazing journey.

I have learned far more from my students than I ever imparted and look forward to sharing in their journeys in years to come. Sara Pursley, stalwart partner in the enterprise of churning out an *IJMES* issue every three months, contributed intellectually at every stage and saved me from making too many mistakes here; Jeff Culang, also a partner at *IJMES*, gave critical comments, researched special topics, and helped with the art program; Secil Yilmaz made teaching fun and completing the book possible; Melis Sulos reinforced the significance of the history of children; Mohammed Ezzeldin helped to locate and contextualize cartoons and articles in the Arabic press; and Spencer Bastedo and Andrew Alger chased down books and lightened my load on the last leg. At the beginning, critical assistance came from Aleksandra Majstorac-Koblinski and Cemal Yetkiner, who pursued their own American missionaries in the Levant and Anatolia, and Kutlughan Soyubol, who knew when to abandon them; Zach Berman, who copied British records; Ceren Ozgul, who shared her own work on the reconversion of Armenians; and Merja Jutila, who recovered one of the few extant copies of a Finnish text on the Swedish Salaam Mission and translated parts of it.

The search for Turkiyya has been facilitated by a number of archivists and librarians. I would especially like to thank the staffs at the Flower Pentecostal Heritage Center, Friends Historical Library at Swarthmore College, Library of Congress, Mina Rees Library at the CUNY Graduate Center, Presbyterian Historical Society in Philadelphia, University of Chicago Library, Yale University Divinity School Library, as well as the United States National Archives and Records Administration and the National Archives of the United Kingdom. Financial support from a number of sources made this book possible, including a fellowship from the Carnegie Corporation of New York and grants from the PSC-CUNY Research Awards Program.

Just as I thought my journey was ending, the production of the book was beginning. Kate Wahl set a quick pace and provided thoughtful advice at every step of the way. Frances Malcolm and Mariana Raykov patiently moved the manuscript along, and Richard Gunde edited with a perfect touch. It has been a delight working with the production and publicist teams at Stanford University Press. The anonymous readers remain anonymous, and I thank them.

This is, in many ways, a book about family, the families we are born into and the ones we create. My parents, Zelda and Stanley Baron, have taught me the meaning of love and commitment. My siblings, Lisa Carlton and Ben Baron, and circle of cousins—Larry and Aaron Cohen, and Michael, Sandy, and Marc Baron—and their spouses, have opened their hearts and homes. My own children, Neta and Talya, have been there every step of the way, graciously sharing their teenage years with Turkiyya. This book is dedicated to them and to all the Turkiyyas of the world.

CAST OF CHARACTERS

American Mission. The largest mission in Egypt, with headquarters in Cairo, hospitals in Asyut and Tanta, schools throughout the country, and an orphanage in the capital. Started in 1854 and affiliated with the Board of Foreign Missionaries of the United Presbyterian Church of North America (UPCNA).

Charles Adams. Chairman of the faculty of the Theological Seminary, Cairo.

Ellen Barnes. Succeeded Margaret Smith as head of the Fowler Orphanage.

Egyptian Missionary Association. Group administering the affairs of the American Mission, reporting back to the Board of Foreign Missions of the UPCNA and the Women's General Missionary Society.

Evangelical Church. Autonomous Egyptian Presbyterian church started by American missionaries.

Esther Fowler and John Fowler. Quaker couple who funded the girls' orphanage in Cairo named for them.

Margaret (Maggie) Smith. Moving spirit behind the founding of the Fowler Orphanage in 1906 and its first head.

Samuel Zwemer. Loose affiliate of the American Mission, prolific writer, and field referee of the Swedish Salaam Mission.

American Diplomats

William Jardine. Minister of the Legation of the United States of America.

Horace Remillard. American consul in Port Said.

Assemblies of God Mission. Came to oversee Pentecostal missions in Egypt, which were initially unaffiliated with a board or church.

Lillian Trasher. Pentecostal founder of the faith-based Asyut Orphanage in 1911.

Body of Grand 'Ulama'. Council of senior clerics at the al-Azhar mosque-university complex.

Shaykh Muhammad al-Ahmadi al-Zawahiri. Rector of al-Azhar.

British Officials

W. J. Ablitt Bey. Commander of the Suez Canal police, special branch, Port Said.

Judge Arthur Booth. British legal advisor in the Egyptian Ministry of Justice.

Sir Ronald Campbell. Acting British high commissioner.

Sir Alexander Keown-Boyd. Director general of the European Department, Public Security Division, in the Egyptian Ministry of Interior.

Church Missionary Society (CMS). British Anglican mission founded in 1825 that ran schools and a large hospital in Old Cairo.

Egypt General Mission (EGM). The second largest mission in Egypt, with headquarters in Zaytun and stations in the Delta and Canal Zone. Started in 1898 by an interdenominational band of Protestant laymen from England and Northern Ireland.

Hayat Ibrahim/Kawkab Kamil. Teacher in the EGM girls' school in Suez who converted to Christianity and fought her uncle's attempt to gain custody of her.

George Swan. Head of the EGM and chairman of the Inter-Mission Council of Egypt.

Egyptian Journalists

Sulayman Fawzi. Editor of satirical weekly *al-Kashkul.*

'Abd al-Qadir Hamza. Editor of pro-Wafd daily *al-Balagh.*

Muhammad Husayn Haykal. Editor of Liberal Constitutionalist daily *al-Siyasa.*

Inter-Mission Council. A body made up of representatives of evangelical organizations, which served as a liaison between the Egyptian government and Protestant missions.

Islamic Benevolent Society. A Muslim charitable organization founded in 1893 by nationalist leaders and Islamic reformers.

al-Sayyid Ahmad Mustafa 'Amir. Main donor for an orphanage for Muslim children in Asyut.

League for the Defense of Islam. A coalition started in June 1933 to combat proselytizing.

Shaykh Muhammad Mustafa al-Maraghi. President of the league and ex-rector of al-Azhar.

Muslim Brotherhood. Islamic revival organization founded in 1928 in Isma'iliyya.

Labiba Ahmad. President of first Muslim Sisters branches and editor-owner of the monthly journal *al-Nahda al-Nisa'iyya.*

Hasan al-Banna. Founder and first general guide.

Shaykh Mahmud Jum'a Hilba. Member and Port Said cleric.

Ahmad al-Misri. Founder of the Port Said branch.

Ahmad al-Sukkari. Boyhood friend of al-Banna and head of the Brotherhood branch in al-Mahmudiyya.

Dr. Muhammad Sulayman. An Islamic activist in Port Said.

Nile Valley Mission. Methodist mission started in 1905 that eventually sponsored schools in Upper Egypt and a girls' orphanage in Ramla.

Viola Light Glenn and Lewis Glenn. Founders of the mission.

Sha'b Party. Ruling political grouping in the summer of 1933.

'Ali al-Manzalawi. Minister of religious endowments.

Fahmi al-Qaysi. Minister of interior.

Hasan Fahmi Rifa't. Governor of the Canal at Port Said.

Muhammad Shafiq. Acting prime minister.

Isma'il Sidqi. Prime minister, in Europe in the summer of 1933.

Swedish Salaam Mission. Faith-based mission started in Port Said in 1911, with a girls' school and Home for Destitutes, and stations in al-Manzala and Dikirnis.

Anna Eklund. Finnish co-founder of the mission.

Maria Ericsson. Swedish founder of the mission.

Turkiyya Hasan. Teenage Muslim orphan beaten at the mission.

Alice Marshall. Acting principal of the mission.

'Ayida Na'man/Martha Bulus. Teacher in school and convert to Christianity who contested her brother's attempt to gain custody of her.

Helmi Pekkola. Finnish author of a history of the mission.

Alzire Richoz. Swiss matron who beat Turkiyya Hasan.

Young Men's Muslim Association (YMMA). Islamic association started in Cairo in 1927 and modeled after the Young Men's Christian Association.

Muhibb al-Din al-Khatib. Founding director of the Muslim Brotherhood newspaper *Jaridat al-Ikhwan al-Muslimin.*

Dr. 'Abd al-Hamid Sa'id. Founding president.

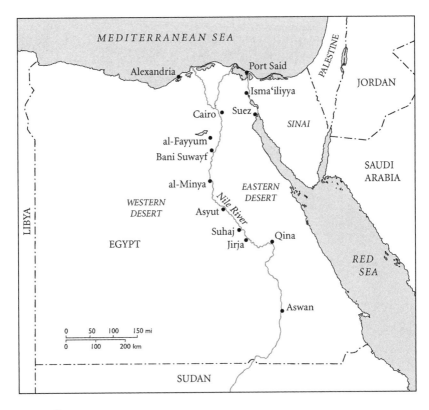

MAP 1 Egypt

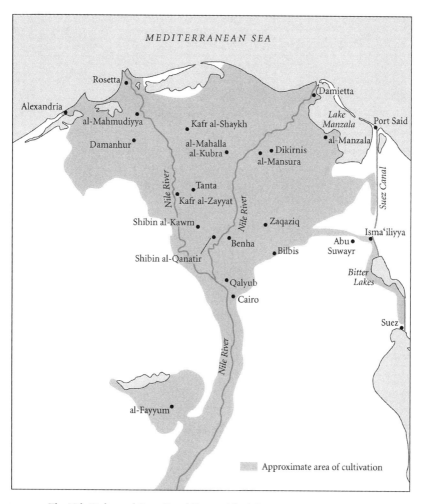

MAP 2 The Nile Delta and Suez Canal Zone with al-Fayyum

PROLOGUE

The Turkiyya Hasan Affair

THE STORY OF THE TURKIYYA HASAN AFFAIR is told here from the perspectives of ten characters who were directly involved. The aim is to give insight into the diverging ways participants experienced, remembered, witnessed, or heard about the beating of Turkiyya Hasan in the Swedish Salaam Mission on the morning of June 7, 1933, and its aftermath. The narratives will revisit some of the same terrain, retracing steps and recounting conversations, to get at the heart of this explosive encounter between orphans, missionaries, Muslims, and officials of the semi-colonial state. An attempt has been made to give the points of view of all the major characters involved in the affair, but the Swiss missionary who caned Turkiyya is surprisingly silent. Alzire Richoz seemed to leave little record of her voice, only bruises on the body of a teenage girl.

At the Eye of the Storm: Turkiyya Hasan

Turkiyya al-Sayyid Hasan Yusuf remembered her arrival at the Swedish Salaam Mission in Port Said in a part of the city known as "Arab town" at the age of nine or ten. Her father had died (or vanished), her mother had been unable to care for her, and an older sister and brother were not able to raise her.[1] Upon her entry, the Finnish matron Anna Eklund told her, "Now you are our daughter in God," and gave her a doll and chocolate, which she enjoyed, and images of a strange man. She realized it wasn't Muhammad, for Muslims did not depict their prophet. Who was it? Only later did she learn that the images were of the man the missionaries called Jesus Christ.[2]

During the school year, Turkiyya studied with upwards of four hundred other day students in the mission girls' school. At night, the day students returned to their homes and parents; she stayed with the twenty or so female boarders at the mission, finding some distractions there. Encouraged by the Swedish founder of the mission, Maria Ericsson, she tried to teach the stream of adult visitors who came to visit how to speak some words of her native tongue. She made them repeat the Arabic words just as her teachers made her repeat words in the English language that they taught in the school.[3]

As the months grew into years, Turkiyya realized that living in the home came at a price: pressure to accept Jesus. She looked up to an older Muslim girl named Fathiyya, who clung to her faith in spite of extreme measures to convert her like placing a Qur'an in the girls' bathroom to make the Muslim girls boarding in the home ashamed of their religion. Turkiyya was happy to help Fathiyya get out of what she called "this desolate prison" in the spring of 1931. One night, Turkiyya kept watch while Fathiyya escaped, taking sanctuary in a local police station.[4]

Turkiyya missed the older girl and wished she could tell her about the disturbing letter she had received from Maria Ericsson over a year later: "My dear Turkya, will you be among those who are washed in the BLOOD of the LAMB?" the letter dated September 8, 1932, from Flint, Michigan, asked. "Are you ready when the Lord your Saviour comes? He is coming soon." Miss Ericsson then warned her, "Do not fight against Him any longer. Do not try to silence His voice speaking in your heart. The dear Lord is coming back very, very soon, and oh, what cries of agony there will be from all who rejected HIM. . . . For then the great day of HIS wrath is come; and who shall be able to stand? . . . Even the mighty kings on earth shall not know how to escape from His judgment."[5] Turkiyya hid this intimidating letter and another from Finland, hoping to show them to someone, anyone who could help, as proof that the missionaries were frightening the Muslim girls in the home into becoming Christians.[6]

The pressure on Turkiyya increased until her last Sunday at the home, when the acting principal, Miss Marshall, gathered the girls and asked for a sign from those "who want to be washed by the blood of Christ." Conversion appealed to some of her classmates, but it did not appeal to Turkiyya, so she kept quiet. Miss Marshall then told her privately to get "ready to travel to Zaytun," where the British Egypt General Mission had a home for female Muslim converts, "for it is time to wash you with the blood of Jesus, and we want to baptize you next Sunday."[7] Turkiyya said that she was a Muslim and did not want to travel to Zaytun to be baptized. At that, Miss Marshall slapped her across her face. Turkiyya ran out of the dining hall, refusing to eat with the missionaries that day or on Monday or Tuesday.[8]

On Wednesday, Turkiyya was pulled aside by Miss Richoz and was forced to listen to the missionary speak about Jesus for a quarter of an hour. Having had enough, Turkiyya ran up to the building roof. "Oh God, I am a Muslim," she shouted out, calling for salvation from "these tyrannical people." She knew Richoz, who had followed her up, had heard her and saw that the American missionary John Afman, who headed the Salaam Mission boys' school, was there on the roof as well. She sat down, preoccupied and angry, and when Afman left, she refused to rise. When Miss Richoz asked her why she hadn't risen, she replied, "I forgot." Richoz admonished Turkiyya for her bad manners, to which Turkiyya retorted: "These are the manners that I learned here at this school."[9]

Turkiyya was surprised by the intensity of Miss Richoz's reaction and un-prepared. First the missionary attacked her with a sharp pen, and when she screamed out in pain, Miss Richoz dragged her inside a sitting room on the roof and closed the door. Richoz then began hitting her with both hands on her head and face, telling her not to scream like a Muslim, "because we are not Muslims here." The missionary next picked up a cane and beat Turkiyya with it in a frenzy, and then threw Turkiyya down on a sofa, sat on her back, covered her mouth with her hand to muffle her screams, and continued to beat her. With great effort Turkiyya lifted herself off the couch to ask, "Are you trying to kill me?" to which Miss Richoz replied, "I won't kill you, but I will kill the devil that keeps you from Jesus."[10] When Turkiyya had finally stopped screaming, Richoz told her she believed she had been chosen by Jesus, to which Turkiyya replied that she wasn't chosen, that she was a Muslim from a Muslim family. She fled, retreating into the room that she shared with other girls, and fell into a deep sleep from exhaustion.[11]

The next day, Thursday, Turkiyya's nephew came by the mission to ask after her. She told him to tell her sister Amina to come quickly, because they wanted to take her away the following day. When her sister came, Turkiyya showed her the marks on her body from the beating and cried. Angered, Amina went to talk to Miss Marshall and Miss Richoz, but they refused to let her take Turkiyya out of the orphanage. They did give her Turkiyya's birth certificate, which they had wanted to keep in order to baptize the girl. Turkiyya then asked her sister to find someone, anyone, who could get her out of the orphanage, for she was worried that the next morning she would be forced to leave for Zaytun.[12]

That night her brother appeared to ask for her release. Still, the missionaries refused to let her go. Only when her sister and brother-in-law showed up with a Port Said police officer who said he had orders to have Turkiyya released into his custody did they relent. On her way out, Turkiyya grabbed a bag containing the letters from Maria Ericsson and other missionaries. At the police station, she told the story of Richoz beating her to make her accept Christianity and showed the medical examiner the cuts and bruises on her arms and legs, and the gouge close to the spine that really hurt. She listened as he said that she was going to be put under observation at the hospital for a few days.[13]

Instead of undergoing a baptism in Zaytun that Sunday, as the missionaries had planned, Turkiyya appeared before the Parquet. She told the officials from the Port Said office of the Department of Prosecution in the Ministry of Justice investigating the case that the matron had beaten her for refusing to embrace Christianity. The prosecutors then cross-examined her on statements they had already taken from Richoz and Marshall that she had been ill-behaved and impolite. Turkiyya admitted that she had made a scornful remark to the matron, yet she insisted that the missionary's desire to convert her was the reason for the beating. As evidence she pointed to four other Muslim girls who had been converted at the school—half of the eight who lived in the home. As further proof of the pressure brought to bear on her, she pointed to the letters she had slipped into her bag when she left the home.[14]

Overnight Turkiyya's life changed, as she was catapulted from anonymity in the orphanage to the public limelight. Her picture at the public prosecutor's office appeared prominently on the front pages of Egypt's largest daily newspaper, *al-Ahram*, as well as on page one of *al-Jihad*. Other newspapers—*al-Balagh*, *Kawkab al-Sharq*, and *al-Siyasa*—carried stories about her ordeal.[15]

"All of you must have heard of the sad incidents which the missionaries commit behind a veil," she told a crowd of some sixty people gathered at the Port Said home of a local merchant, Muhammad Effendi Sarhan, a week after the beating. "It is not my intention to relate to you any of these incidents as you have already read a great deal about them in the newspapers." Rather, she said, "by standing before you tonight, I mean to warn you against the grave danger menacing our sacred religion as a result of leaving Muslim boys and girls in these dangerous schools." Seeking to help those she had left behind in the Swedish Salaam Mission, Turkiyya exhorted her audience: "If you knew the fate which would inevitably befall these boys and girls if you allow them to remain in these schools, you would sacrifice money and soul to rescue them from the certainty of becoming infidels."[16]

Turkiyya continued, "The events of today and yesterday have proven that there are Muslims who will not accept seeing their religion insulted." Imploring listeners to do "everything in your power, promptly and firmly, to establish an orphanage in which these tortured victims can seek refuge," she stressed that the children "are looking forward to your efforts with hearts full of hope."[17] Turkiyya's words sparked attendees to donate three hundred pounds toward a new orphanage, and her new guardian, Dr. Muhammad Sulayman, helped to organize the effort. She was pleased that those friends she had left behind in the orphanage would not be forgotten.[18]

Basking in her newfound freedom, Turkiyya was now being looked after by a concerned circle of supporters who were impressed by her standing up to the missionaries. But there were others who saw the affair through completely different lenses.

All Hell Is Breaking Loose: The Governor's Predicament

On Sunday, June 11, four days after the beating of Turkiyya, the governor of the Canal at Port Said, Hasan Fahmi Rifaʿt Bey, telephoned the British advisor in the Ministry of Interior, Sir Alexander Keown-Boyd, to discuss what Europeans were euphemistically calling "the missionary incident." He told Keown-Boyd that the affair had "taken a serious aspect," and that he was expecting a large delegation of Muslim protestors in his office. Keown-Boyd tried to dismiss the matter as an ordinary case of punishment, suggesting that the girl's story was being taken up by local politicians who wished to cause embarrassment. The governor replied that there was more to it than that.[19]

"You know me well enough to realise that I have no personal feelings in the matter. I do not care if the whole of Port Said or Egypt embraces Christianity or any other religion," Rifaʿt Bey told Keown-Boyd. But he did care about the escalating protests under his watch. The statements the Parquet had taken from the acting principal of the Swedish Salaam School, Alice Marshall, about disciplining the girl may have been true, "but at the same time I must point out that the affair is really serious. It is admitted that the girl was beaten." The Swedish Salaam School had already been in trouble, he said, referring to a recent controversy surrounding a young woman (Nazla Ghunaym) who had converted to Christianity, quickly renounced her new faith, and then renounced that renunciation. Now "99% of the population honestly believe that the girls are forcibly

Christianised and feeling is running so high that I receive complaints not only from Moslems but also from Copts and the school has become a menace to the peace and security of Port Said."[20]

Rifa't Bey reluctantly greeted the delegation of six prominent Muslim men who arrived at his office at noon on Monday. The visitors included Dr. Muhammad Sulayman (an ophthalmologist), Muhammad Sarhan and Hamid Tira (local merchants), 'Abd al-Halim al-Shamrawi (an editor of *al-Balagh*), and Shaykh 'Abd al-Wahhab al-Issawi and Shaykh Mahmud Jum'a Hilba (Muslim clerics). The men handed him a petition against the Swedish Salaam Mission School with five hundred signatures, an impressive number given the short time frame, requesting "His Excellency" to remove all the Muslim students from the school immediately and close it down.[21]

But the governor was not a man to be pressured, even by a group that appeared to be well organized and that included members of an Islamic reform organization called the Muslim Brotherhood of Port Said. He told the men visiting his office that "if they wish to prevent girls from going to this school, they should first establish a mission, where the orphans and the poor can find food and clothes." Trying to stop the protest from expanding, Rifa't Bey ordered the men to stop writing about the "missionary incident" in the press and to be "men of deeds and not words."[22] Yet his order came too late, or it was ignored, for a petition submitted to the king from the Muslim Brotherhood of Port Said appeared in *al-Jihad* that day and another was published in *al-Balagh* the following day.[23]

To add insult to injury, a group of women in Port Said was planning a protest, too. According to intelligence provided to the governor by William Ablitt, the British police commander in Port Said, the women intended to send a telegram to King Fu'ad to voice their opposition to the activities of local evangelicals. Rifa't Bey realized that "Hanim" (Lady) Turkiyya's case gave the female activists a prime example of inappropriate missionary zeal. (Given the girl's economic background, he thought, she was hardly a lady.) Yet there was little he could do until he received instructions from Cairo. His earlier phone call to Keown-Boyd only produced instructions to write a report. Maybe the petitions would force those in the capital to realize that something needed to be done quickly to quell this storm.[24]

On Tuesday, word finally came from Cairo that the matron who beat the girl was being expelled from Egypt, which was a great relief to Rifa't Bey. He also received instructions to take custody of the remaining Muslim children in the Swedish Salaam Mission. His commander of police escorted four girls and two boys to Cairo, where amidst great publicity they were turned over to the Ministry of Interior to be placed in government institutions. Others were handed back to their families.[25]

Yet even the exit of Richoz and the removal of the Muslim children from the orphanage did not subdue local anger. That Thursday, Miss Marshall telephoned his office, concerned about the veiled threats the mission had received about an impending attack. Rifa't Bey agreed to Ablitt's plan to place a police detail outside the building, giving inhabitants round-the-clock protection, and he informed the American consul that he had taken the necessary precautions to ensure the safety of the mission and its teachers. The governor hoped that calm would finally prevail in Port Said, "that the whole matter would be dropped by all concerned and allowed to die a natural death."[26]

Between a Rock and a Hard Place: The Minister of Interior

Egyptian minister of interior Mahmud Fahmi al-Qaysi Pasha had been dismayed by the disturbing reports coming from Muslims and Copts in Port Said during the second week of June. Having been notified of an upcoming protest to the king and agitation by the head of al-Azhar, al-Qaysi Pasha was worried about the widening storm.[27] The interior minister didn't need special intelligence to tell him about the troubles brewing in the northeast of the country. He could read of the beating of the fifteen-year-old Muslim orphan in Port Said in the daily press, which blamed the government for leniency in dealing with Christian missionaries and negligence in defending the official religion of the state.[28]

Al-Qaysi Pasha admitted that the government had little to show for its promises to the public in the wake of previous missionary scandals. Yet he recognized that the Egyptian ministers could do little: their hands were tied by British advisors who watched their every move and a British occupation that protected Christian evangelical activity. They were impeded, too, by the Capitulations— fiscal and legal privileges enshrined in treaties inherited from the Ottomans— giving extraterritorial immunities to Europeans and Americans in Egypt. This made it difficult, if not nearly impossible, for al-Qaysi's government to prosecute missionaries (though those who beat young girls might be an exception). Matters were further complicated by the fact that Egyptian law protected freedom of religion, which the missionaries took to mean freedom to spread the gospel and change religion, and Muslims took to mean freedom to protect Islam from proselytizers and to practice minority religions.[29]

Yet the truth of the matter, as al-Qaysi Pasha had to admit, was that the government had little desire to crack down on missionary activity. Even before Prime Minister Isma'il Sidqi Pasha had left for Europe to recuperate from a heart ailment, its attempts had been pretty dismal.[30] From an economic point of view, the missionaries provided social services on the cheap, and as interior minister he knew Egypt needed the hospitals, schools, and refuges for the destitute that they had opened.

On Monday, June 12, after the beating of the teenage girl, al-Qaysi Pasha met with the Council of Ministers to discuss strategies to deal with the affair and to counter opposition attacks. The council resolved that whatever the Parquet in Port Said concluded, the government would deport the matron involved in the beating and extract the Muslim girls still in the Swedish Salaam Mission. After the meeting, al-Qaysi Pasha informed Keown-Boyd of its decisions and asked him to contact the proper consular authorities so the matron could be quickly deported.[31]

When al-Qaysi Pasha received the report from the Parquet that Monday afternoon, he found the alarming letter that the founder of the orphanage had sent to the Muslim orphan girl, Turkiyya. "Mr. Keown-Boyd—you have told me often that the missionaries do not press or incite Moslem children to change their religion," he told the British advisor. "Here are documents which prove that they use both cajolery and intimidation."[32] With further proof that the missionaries had overstepped their bounds, the council resisted some of Keown-Boyd's pressure to tone down the official statement. Al-Qaysi Pasha obtained the advisor's grudging approval of the Arabic statement he proposed reading in Parliament the next day, which the British judicial advisor in the Ministry of Justice had already approved.[33]

That Wednesday, June 14, al-Qaysi Pasha stood in front of the Chamber of Deputies to read the Council of Ministers' statement summarizing the Parquet report on the Turkiyya Hasan affair:

> As soon as the police learned of this incident, before the newspapers published the story, they began an investigation, which the Parquet completed. The inquiry revealed that Turkiyya al-Sayyid Yusuf testified that the matron of the home beat her for her refusal to embrace Christianity. When medically examined, she was found to have contusions requiring her to be placed under observation in the hospital for three days. The matron and principal of the home admitted that the first had beaten Turkiyya because she was ill-mannered and rude

to her. But they denied that they asked her to embrace Christianity and stated that they gave the students their choice in religious beliefs. When Turkiyya was questioned on the matron's and principal's statement, she answered that she in fact had been rude to the matron but she insisted that the desire to induce her to change her religion was among the reasons she was beaten.[34]

Al-Qaysi Pasha then informed the Chamber of Deputies of the actions the government had already taken. First, the matron of the school had been forced to leave Egypt. Second, the remaining Muslim girls in the refuge were in the process of being sent to government institutions or those of Islamic associations to be cared for and educated at government expense. Third, the government had allocated 70,000 pounds for new institutions and refuges to provide orphans and destitute children with a sound upbringing. The interior minister hoped that the plan he had put together with Keown-Boyd would quiet the affair.[35]

Reading the organ of his party, *al-Sha'b*, al-Qaysi Pasha found some peace of mind. The paper reported that the government was taking adequate measures in response to the missionary incident. It also suggested to other papers that rather than criticize the government, they ought to urge Muslim parents not to send their children to missionary schools and to establish alternative educational institutions instead. It added that the government could not close missionary schools in the absence of proof of coercion to embrace Christianity.[36]

Yet much to his dismay, al-Qaysi Pasha's remarks in Parliament drew a mixed response. While many applauded the deportation of the matron and the allocation of funds for Islamic institutions, others viewed the actions as insufficient. The opposition press continued to assail the government. When al-Qaysi Pasha returned to Parliament eight days later to present legislation on allocating the funds to build orphanages, he came again under heated attack.[37] The matter would not go away so easily. Yet he had begun to see ways the government might be able to take advantage of the matter, pushing back against the British occupation and becoming the champions of Egypt's children.

Pulling Strings: The British Man on the Spot

In his twenty-six years of serving British imperial interests in the Sudan and Egypt, Keown-Boyd had never seen anything quite like this. As director general of the European Department of the Egyptian Ministry of Interior and the man meant to protect foreigners in Egypt, he had his work cut out for him. Although Egypt had technically gained independence in 1922 and had its own constitution and Parliament, Keown-Boyd and his British colleagues preserved imperial interests with behind-the-scenes maneuvering: a show of force here, a word or piece of timely advice there. The Egyptian notables who wanted a slice of the pie knew the game, which Keown-Boyd had mastered.[38]

Yet the Protestant missionaries had really put the British in a tight spot this time. It was on the morning of Saturday, June 10, that Keown-Boyd first heard from Ablitt that a girl in the Swedish Salaam School had told the police that she had been beaten in order to accept Christianity. After instructing the police commander to ascertain the facts directly from Miss Marshall, he waited to hear the missionaries' defense. Shortly thereafter Ablitt informed him that the "beating was not denied" but, according to the missionaries, had been inflicted on the girl for "rudeness and disobedience" by a Miss Richoz.[39]

The next morning, Keown-Boyd learned that the case had been handed over to the Parquet to investigate. Concerned that it could easily go against the Europeans, he instructed Ablitt to ensure that Miss Marshall and Miss Richoz gave statements to the public prosecutors and that a police officer was sent to the court so that "statements were properly taken." Next he called Zaki Hamza Bey, a deputy in Port Said who sat on the Parquet, to tell him not to close the investigation without these statements and those of corroborating witnesses. His instructions were meant to lead to a favorable report and the desired outcome—the dropping of the case.[40]

At first Keown-Boyd thought that the incident had been overblown and anticipated that the strategy he had set in motion in Port Said would quiet the storm. But late Sunday morning, he received the medical examiner's report and realized immediately that it "alter[ed] the whole aspect of the question." The report described Turkiyya's abrasions: contusions of nearly two inches length on both calves, three contusions of the same length on her left arm, and smaller cuts on her forearm and left wrist. There was also a two-inch contusion on her back. She obviously had been beaten badly. "If the contusions were in fact caused by Miss Richoz's blows, there is to my mind no justification for that lady's behavior and she will have placed us in a very difficult position," Keown-Boyd admitted to his British colleagues. "Egyptian sentiment is strongly opposed at any time to the beating of girls in schools and such indiscriminate hitting does not conform to the accepted ideas as to what the behavior of a Christian teacher should be."[41]

From his experience directing the European Department, Keown-Boyd knew that only designated personnel had permission to cane students in foreign schools, and only within certain bounds: the principal had the authority to cane Turkiyya but Alzire Richoz did not, and a caning was to be administered in a prescribed way. Neither had the right to use the sort of force Richoz had used that day.[42] Egyptian law was quite clear on that: a 1902 law on school regulations (Number 898) had restricted corporal punishment, outlining what was accepted and unacceptable for different aged school children.[43] Keown-Boyd awaited the Parquet's report to see whether it confirmed that Miss Richoz had inflicted the injuries. If she were found responsible, "then I think the Missionaries in Egypt will be well advised to see to it that she takes herself as soon as possible to her native country where she can practice her muscular Christianity on hardier maidens."[44] Keown-Boyd had clearly lost patience with aggressive Protestant proselytizers who were now breaking laws.

When the minutes of the Parquet's inquiry arrived in Keown-Boyd's office in Cairo on Monday afternoon, June 12, they confirmed that Miss Richoz had beaten Turkiyya, inflicting some eight or nine blows. Keown-Boyd's job now was to arrange for the quick exit of Miss Richoz from the country.[45] Early the next day, Tuesday, Keown-Boyd admitted two compatriots, Alice Marshall and George Swan (who headed the Egypt General Mission and chaired the Inter-Mission Council) into his office. After listening to Miss Marshall's bare-bones account of the case, he asked his colleague Judge Arthur Booth, the British legal advisor in the Ministry of Justice, to join them. Keown-Boyd then told the missionaries that the actions of Miss Richoz had "placed the government in a very difficult and embarrassing situation." Complaints had "poured in" from different directions, articles had "flooded" the newspapers, and most Egyptians now believed the girl had been beaten to force her to become a Christian. He emphasized that "corporal punishment in schools was forbidden in Egypt, and a beating of the nature indicated ought never to have occurred." Keown-Boyd then conveyed the government's position that Miss Richoz should leave Egypt at once and that the home should hand over any Muslim girls living there to the authorities right away.[46]

Keown-Boyd allowed Swan to consult the Inter-Mission Council, a group comprising representatives of evangelical organizations in Egypt, while he updated the minister of interior and consulted with legal authorities. In the midst of this shuttle diplomacy, Marshall and Swan returned with a delegation that included the heads of the American University in Cairo and the British Church Missionary Society. The evangelicals said that they would accept the government's proposal, but they wanted a declaration that the enquiry had established that the incident at Port Said was a beating for disciplinary purposes and not an attempt to forcibly convert the girl. Keown-Boyd then went back to the minister of interior with the desired change to the proposal.[47]

While the Council of Ministers considered the new text, Keown-Boyd returned to his meeting with the missionaries. This time, his patience stretched very thin, he repeated the government's ultimatum. Marshall agreed to hand over the Muslim children in the school to their parents or guardians and to send Miss Richoz to Palestine that night. At that point, the head of the British Church Missionary Society asked Keown-Boyd whether Miss Richoz would be permitted to return to Egypt, at least to Cairo if not Port Said. Keown-Boyd, who could not quite believe the man's audacity, replied that while he would not blacklist her right away, it was best to leave this matter alone.[48]

With little room to maneuver, Keown-Boyd accepted the final Arabic draft that al-Qaysi read to him. After concluding the marathon negotiations, he assessed the affair. The evidence—the medical report and Maria Ericsson's letter to Turkiyya—had opened his eyes to the culpability of the missionaries. "This letter, I think you will agree, quite possibly may have caused a girl at the susceptible age of 15 mental torture vastly greater than any physical pain caused by the beating," he wrote to his British colleagues. "This and similar attempts at conversion might I think quite possibly account for the unruly and exasperating frame of mind in which she now appears to be. It seems far from impossible that these good ladies have actually driven the girl to take refuge in Islam."[49]

Keown-Boyd was not "favorably impressed" by Alice Marshall and affirmed that "certain disclosures as to missionary methods made in connection with this case have considerably shocked us." Although he realized that his mandate was to protect European nationals and British interests, he thought that immediate steps were needed to rein in independent or semi-independent missionary bodies.[50] He agreed with the words of the acting high commissioner: British officials could not be at the "mercy of the unwise or fanatical among the missionaries."[51] They could not keep putting out fires, particularly one that had spread all the way to the British Parliament, where the opposition was questioning the response to the affair.[52] Obviously, Keown-Boyd saw the situation quite differently from those affiliated with the Swedish Salaam Mission.

Unfortunate Absence: The Acting Head of the Home

How unfortunate to have been out of the school Wednesday, June 7, when Turkiyya chose to act up, thought Alice Marshall. Perhaps Turkiyya had thought she could test the diminutive Alzire Richoz, who had filled in for her that day. The girl must have really acted out for Richoz to so lose her temper. Still, Marshall thought she had contained the matter, for when Turkiyya's sister and brother stopped by the school for an explanation, they "seemed to be satisfied that the punishment had been justly administered."[53] But then a police officer came to remove the girl, and two days later the commander of police in Port Said notified her that the matter was being investigated.

Now Marshall had to sort out this mess. On Sunday, she gave a statement, saying that although Turkiyya had been beaten—how could she deny it, given the marks on her body?—it had been for disciplinary reasons. Marshall stuck by that line and instructed Richoz and Nafisa, an Egyptian resident in the orphanage who witnessed the event, to do the same.[54]

On Tuesday, she had to give an explanation of the event to Keown-Boyd. She told him that Miss Richoz had been anxious about Turkiyya, a girl who was "not clever, apt to be bad-mannered and at times unruly," and who had set a bad example for the other girls. Richoz, she suggested, wanted to "reduce Turkia to order" before she went on leave. That day the girl had "failed to stand up to show respect to some distinguished American visitors." Given the location of the roof chapel, "exposed to the curious gaze of the neighbours," Richoz had ordered Turkiyya "into a room for private chastisement." The girl was "rude and aggressive," and "showed fight and seized the cane." Richoz, though smaller than Turkiyya, was tough, and "regained mastery of the situation and clearly by this time considerably roused, hit the girl with the stick where she could."[55]

Marshall had expected Keown-Boyd and Judge Booth to be more sympathetic to the missionaries' point of view than they were. Instead, they gave her an ultimatum: either the mission would send Miss Richoz out of Egypt and immediately hand over the Muslim children in the orphanage to the government or the authorities would prosecute Richoz for administering corporal punishment.[56] The hastily convened Inter-Mission Council, of which the Swedish Salaam Mission was a member, advised Marshall to accept the government's proposal. Since she could not let her colleague stand trial, the acting principal agreed.[57]

Rushing from the capital to Port Said, Marshall took charge of the mission. Richoz had left for Palestine, where she was certain to find sanctuary in a friendly mission, and Marshall began to arrange for the transfer of the Muslim girls back to their families. She hoped that things would now quiet down. Unfortunately, some young men were hanging about the mission making veiled threats, which Marshall reported to the Swedish legation, the governor, and the police.[58]

When the American consul in Port Said requested a statement from Alice Marshall via one of the Americans in the mission two weeks after Richoz had caned Turkiyya, she balked.[59] By now she had already told the tale, or enough details of it, to the police, the Parquet, British advisors, the Inter-Mission Council, and the Swedish legation. Following the advice of the legation, she gave a simple statement: "I do not feel free to commit myself to giving any written details about the matter, except just to say that the girl Turkia Yousef Hassan, was caned as a last recourse for insubordination, by the Swiss lady left in charge during my absence."[60]

Cat and Mouse: The Head of the Inter-Mission Council

George Swan attempted to comfort Alice Marshall when she arrived at the Egypt General Mission headquarters in Zaytun Monday, June 12. Having lived in Egypt for thirty-five years, Swan had seen attacks on missionaries before. Missionaries had prevailed and continued on with their work, and they would overcome this challenge, too. His mission, like the Swedish Salaam Mission, targeted Muslims. It had started with a band of seven men from England and Northern Ireland who together with the female missionaries who came later built a network of schools and a hospital in the Delta region and Canal Zone. They had even established a home for female Muslim converts to Christianity.[61]

After the interview with Keown-Boyd, Swan received a packet from him that included a copy of the letter Maria Ericsson had sent to Turkiyya. Keown-Boyd challenged him to explain it, telling him that the Ericsson letter "has done your cause more harm with responsible and reasonable Egyptians than any of the calumnies published against you."[62] What could Swan write in response? This and the other letters that Turkiyya had saved had become critical evidence in the investigation.

Trying to shift the discussion away from the letters, Swan pointed to a conspiracy behind the scandal. He told Keown-Boyd that the missionaries had abundant evidence "to show that the incidents at Port Said were originated and continued by a malicious and evil-minded man, who was seeking to satisfy thereby his own personal aims, and have since been exploited for political purposes."[63] He accused the ophthalmologist Dr. Muhammad Sulayman of plotting to destroy the Swedish Salaam School "partly from bitterness of soul caused by the light morals of his German Christian wife and perhaps partly to fill his clinic."[64] But Keown-Boyd was not convinced. Other evangelicals proved more receptive to the theory.

Keeping Watch: A Member of
the American Mission Tracks Events

As chairman of the faculty of the Theological Seminary in Cairo and a member of the American Mission, Charles Adams kept a close watch on the Turkiyya Hasan affair, concerned about its widening repercussions. Adams knew that the American Mission stood to lose a great deal by the mushrooming anti-missionary movement. The Presbyterian mission had grown to become the single largest Protestant evangelical enterprise in Egypt, with hundreds of evangelicals running a vast network of schools, hospitals, clinics, and refuges, including the Fowler Orphanage for girls in Cairo.

The affair disrupted work on his book, *Islam and Modernism in Egypt*, which examined the Islamic reform movement launched by the religious scholar Muhammad 'Abduh. Adams viewed Islamic reform as analogous to Protestantism, seeing Muslims as striving to free their religion from a rigid orthodoxy, just as Protestants had broken free from Catholicism. Evangelical missionaries could help in this process, he thought, but the growing anti-missionary movement threatened to undermine a partnership.[65]

A couple of weeks after the caning of Turkiyya, Adams wrote to the head of the United Presbyterian Church of North America's Foreign Board in Philadelphia to update officials there. "The trouble began with an unfortunate incident in the Girls' Orphanage of the Swedish Salaam Mission, at Port Said," recounted Adams. "One of the Muslim girls, named Turkiyah, refused to stand up as usual to join in the daily prayers of the school." Adams connected the initial infraction to Christian prayer, which was obligatory for all students in missionary institutions, rather than to visiting missionaries. "When the head mistress, a Swiss lady, a member of that Mission, remonstrated with her the girl became unmanageable and broke out into disrespectful language and screaming and created such a scene that the missionary, perhaps in exasperation, used a small rattan cane on the girl's legs." Adams told the story of a naughty girl exceeding the bounds of good behavior, and of a matron, pushed beyond her limits, using minimal force. He sympathized completely with the matron. What else could she do when faced with an insubordinate child? "The girl struggled to get possession of the cane and in doing so received some scratches."[66]

Emphasizing the girl's responsibility for the punishment and minimizing the extent of her injuries, Adams suggested that the "discipline which was administered for disobedience and insubordination was thoroughly deserved." He had little problem with the caning of Turkiyya. Yet he acknowledged that "the manner of it was unwise. . . . And the unfortunate part about it was that it all arose because of the refusal of the girl to take part in Christian religious exercises and has given color to the charge which is now being broadcasted indiscriminately against all mission work of an attempt at forcible conversion."[67] Adams objected to the interpretation of events: forcing a girl to participate in prayer was not akin to forcing her to convert.

"In the meantime the attention of the neighbors had been attracted by the uproar and the police informed," Adams reported. Once the police became involved, the Parquet investigated, but it dismissed the case, "on the ground that the case was one of school discipline and not of use of force in religion." He told of Miss Marshall's trip to Cairo to meet with the chairman of the Inter-Mission Council, and their meeting, in turn, with the head of the European Department of the Ministry of Interior. The latter had "informed them that he had received instructions from those higher up to present the mission with two alternatives: either that the missionary who had beaten the girl should at once leave the country or that she should stand trial before the Mixed Tribunals for having contravened the law forbidding corporal punishment in schools." The Inter-Mission Council met, deciding that it was "wiser to accept the first alternative than to fight the case before a court that is French in its outlook and not too sympathetic towards mission work."[68]

In the end, the threat of facing French Catholics on the Mixed Court undid the Protestant missionaries' resolve to oppose the move to deport Miss Richoz. At that point, Adams recounted, the Parquet dismissed the case against her in a plea bargain. In his letter to Philadelphia, Adams included one more tidbit: "The members of the Swedish Mission now suspect that the girl may have been instructed by parties outside to make such a scene in order to bring about what has happened."[69]

Confidential: The American Consul Reports on the "So-Called Missionary Incident"

The American consul in Port Said, Horace Remillard, had watched with both fascination and alarm as the incident at the Swedish Salaam Mission grew into a full-blown scandal. It concerned him because the interdenominational Protestant mission had American links: its founder, Maria Ericsson, lived in the United States as an American citizen; Americans staffed and frequently visited it; an American headed the girls' school; and American dollars, along with British, Swiss, Swedish, and Egyptian funds, kept it afloat.[70]

About a week after the caning, Remillard received a phone call from the governor, who assured him that the necessary measures had been taken to protect the mission and that everything was quiet.[71] But two weeks after the caning, with public outrage and press furor in full swing, the American legation in Cairo sent Remillard instructions to report on the "so-called missionary incident."[72] To comply with the directive, Remillard sent a request through one of the four Americans in the compound, asking Alice Marshall for a written statement. She agreed to stop by his office to answer questions on the condition that their conversation be kept confidential.[73]

Remillard welcomed Marshall to his office nearly three weeks after the caning of Turkiyya. He took notes of her version of the incident, or more precisely, the version she was now telling: that Alzire Richoz had reprimanded Turkiyya "for not standing up in the presence of visitors as she had been taught to do and as was done by the other pupils with her at that time." Her response to the reprimand, Richoz told her, was to use "violent, abusive and blasphemous language," for which Richoz threatened Turkiyya with corporal punishment. The girl "dared her teacher" and "refused to hold out her hand to receive the blows," which was the expected response when physical punishment was meted out. Turkiyya struggled with Richoz, who struck the girl "with the stick over one shoulder while holding her wrists."[74]

Remillard's own assessment was that assertions that the girl was beaten "because she refused to be baptized" were without foundation. But he admitted that the mission "appears embarrassed" and saw Richoz's actions as "unwise."[75] As a result of the affair, he noted that local Christian missions were clearly losing influence with the Muslim population. He had it on good authority, for example, that Muslim attendance at the Sunday service of the American Peniel Mission, one of an array of Protestant institutions in town, had declined drastically, down from fifty or sixty worshippers to two or three.[76]

In his report about the incident, Remillard revealed one last curious detail: the Swedish Salaam Mission believed that "a secret influence was used . . . to distort the facts and make it a national and religious issue."[77] The incident might not have drawn attention were it not, Marshall said, for a certain Dr. Sulayman, "who is inimical to the Mission for reasons of personal jealousy."[78] Although the members of the mission had no definitive proof against him, "they feel morally certain of his responsibility in the matter."[79] Remillard found Marshall anxious about divulging the doctor's name, for "it would lead to certain trouble, with the Mission at a disadvantage from lack of tangible evidence."[80] That is why he filed the report as a confidential one, to be hidden after the head of the American legation read it.

Conspiracy Theory: The Finnish Historian

From Finland, where many supporters of the Swedish Salaam Mission of Port Said lived, Helmi Pekkola tried to make sense of the scandal. Writing a history of the mission in the wake of the affair, she drew upon a Swedish manuscript written by a teacher in the mission, Erica Lindstrom; a book by Maria Ericsson; and oral histories, letters, and lectures by Anna Eklund.[81] The result was the Finnish book *Jumalan Poluilla Islamin Eramaassa* (On God's Path in the Desert of Islam). In the book, Pekkola claimed that Dr. S (whose full name she did reveal) had been deeply implicated in a conversion controversy in the winter and spring of 1933 that set the stage for the Turkiyya Hasan affair.

According to Pekkola, after his German wife left him, Dr. S developed an interest in a Muslim orphan named Nazla, who had converted to Christianity and taken up a teaching post in the Swedish Salaam School in Port Said. There she joined the Egyptian Evangelical Church where local Protestants worshipped and married an Egyptian evangelist, renting an apartment with him in a building that Dr. S owned. Pekkola claimed that in spite of Nazla's existing marriage and her pregnancy, Dr. S was "knitting a web" to entrap her, and conspired with her mother, who informed the police that Nazla's marriage was illegal due to her age. Nazla was brought in for questioning in late March 1933, and after being subjected to threats and a few sleepless nights in detention, she signed a paper—"not knowing what she did," renouncing her faith in Christ.[82]

With her marriage to a non-Muslim whose baby she was carrying now void, Nazla quickly sought to undo her renunciation. Writing an appeal to the governor, she filled out documents and obtained signatures from witnesses. "For Nazla the way was paved with agony, but she walked through it in God's strength," recounted Pekkola, for "she had gained peace and joy in her Savior." Nazla then fled to a mission in Cairo, where she gave birth in early June and where her baby died a few days later. She subsequently fled the country with her husband and help from mission friends rather than be forcibly returned to her grandfather in Damietta as ordered by the Islamic court.[83]

In Pekkola's telling, the failure of local Muslims to block Nazla's original conversion or her re-conversion set the stage for an attack on the mission. "Doctor S's plans in regards to Nazla hadn't worked out, and in his rage he decided to bring down the whole hated Mission." He found an unexpected ally:

THE TURKIYYA HASAN AFFAIR

"One of the pupils at the Salaam Mission girls' orphanage was to become a very helpful henchman to him."[84]

That pupil, T (as the mission historian called Turkiyya) was a "difficult-to-educate bad-mannered girl" who had always been "a source of grief and sorrow at the Mission." She visited Dr. S often in the spring of 1933, and "with his advice she secretly collected photographs and letters that her friends had received from the missionaries."[85] T then staged a premeditated act, when "one day in the beginning of June, she threw a fit. She got mean, and got even more upset from the scolding, until she was physically punished." Turkiyya then "ran away, taking with her the photographs and letters she had collected." With Dr. S, "she went to the other enemies of the mission and told them that she had been hit because she did not let herself be forcefully baptized."[86]

For the Finnish historian, the affair sparked by T was not a total debacle. The press published Turkiyya's evidence, which spread the gospel message and "testimonial of Jesus Christ . . . for all the people to hear." Pekkola believed in an ultimate victory, that God, "in his grace," would "let the light of gospel shine in the darkness of Islam for the salvation of many."[87] Her perspective on the Turkiyya Hasan affair contrasted greatly with that of the man she accused of being behind it.

The Man behind the Mystery: Dr. Muhammad Sulayman

Dr. Muhammad Sulayman did not care about the rumors making the consular and missionary rounds about him and his German ex-wife.[88] His Islamic activism did not grow out of malice toward her but rather out of a concern for young, vulnerable orphans like Nazla and Turkiyya. He was thrilled to work with members of the Port Said branch of the Muslim Brotherhood to try to rescue such girls from the Swedish Salaam Mission. The Brotherhood branch in Port Said with which he had become affiliated had been started by a young native son—Ahmad Effendi al-Misri—after he returned from a sojourn in Isma'iliyya, where Hasan al-Banna, the general guide, had launched the Muslim Brotherhood in 1928. The Brotherhood promised to rejuvenate Islam and fight the British, causes the doctor endorsed. Its branch office sat right across the street from the Ophthalmology Hospital where he worked.[89]

Lately the Muslim Brotherhood had taken a keen interest in combating evangelical activities, which was important to Dr. Sulayman given the inroads missionaries had made in Port Said. There had been a whirlwind of letters, visiting delegations sent by the general guide, and discussions within the organization.

A Muslim Brotherhood branch in nearby al-Manzala had alerted the Brothers in Port Said of the impending conversions of girls from Port Said in Swedish Salaam Mission institutions.[90] The Brothers in Port Said had watched the mission closely for months, but even when a girl who was an acquaintance of Turkiyya asked Dr. Sulayman for assistance in leaving, he could not extricate her from "that hellish place," for she had no family to claim her, and state officials would not intercede on her behalf. He also had had no luck thus far in rescuing Nazla from the clutches of the missionaries, in spite of his ongoing attempts to work with her mother and grandfather to return her to the fold of Islam.[91]

But the luck of Dr. Sulayman and the Islamic activists of Port Said had turned, for they found the perfect heroine in Turkiyya. On Monday, June 12, five days after her caning, Dr. Sulayman joined the delegation that met with the governor of Port Said, giving him a petition against the mission, and it sent one to the king.[92] On Wednesday, June 14, he attended a gathering in the home of Muhammad Sarhan, where Turkiyya gave a moving talk. He was elected to the executive committee of the Jam'iyyat al-Nahda al-Islamiyya (Society of Islamic Awakening), which had been formed to rescue poor Muslim boys and girls from missionaries by establishing an orphanage. Muhammad Mustafa Tira, who represented the Muslim Brotherhood branch of Port Said, was also at the meeting. On Friday, the Muslim Brotherhood convened their first conference in Isma'iliyya, dedicating it to a discussion of the threat of missionaries to Islam and Muslims.[93]

The whirlwind of activities undertaken to publicize the beating of Turkiyya and turn her into a symbol for the movement to fight missionaries continued. Dr. Sulayman headed the delegation that took Turkiyya to Cairo the following week, paying the costs with Muhammad Sarhan. He escorted her to the launching of the League for the Defense of Islam, a coalition that had come together to combat conversion and that included members of the Muslim Brotherhood, and was elected to the league's higher committee.[94] He took Turkiyya on a circuit of press interviews, during which he became a subject of interest as well, appearing in a photograph with Turkiyya and members of the staff of *al-Balagh*.[95]

A reporter at the weekly *al-Fath* praised him for gaining knowledge of what happened to Turkiyya and having the merit "to lift the curtain" on the brutality committed by male and female criminals under the name of "peace" at the Salaam School.[96] With his newfound fame, Dr. Sulayman gained access to national luminaries. He and Muhammad Sarhan stopped by the House of the Nation for a meeting with Mustafa al-Nahhas Pasha, head of the Wafd

Party. Afterward, they made a call at the Saʿdist Party Club to visit party leader Mahmud al-Nuqrashi Pasha. Although the Shaykh al-Azhar refused to give them an audience, they learned from contacts that King Fuʾad sympathized with their fight against Christian conversion. Others supported their efforts and donated funds to build a new orphanage.[97]

Upon his return from Cairo, Dr. Sulayman faced questioning by the commander of the Port Said police, Ablitt, whose special branch of the Suez Canal police kept him under close surveillance. Still, he continued his activism, for he wasn't going to let the police stop his efforts. Keeping up his pressure on the Swedish Salaam Mission, he pushed for information on the whereabouts of orphans such as Nafisa, the friend of Turkiyya who had given testimony to the Parquet and seemed to have disappeared. He developed international contacts, welcoming an Indian activist into his home to discuss strategies for fighting missionaries. He tried to drive members of the Evangelical Church of Port Said out of town, arranging for their transfer from government jobs. And when young men gathered to start a local chapter of the Young Men's Muslim Association, he was elected president. The "Mission case" may have been causing him to lose clients, as Ablitt asserted, but it was well worth it. For him and his Islamist associates, the beating of Turkiyya presented an opportunity.[98]

I THE BEST OF INTENTIONS

Evangelicals on the Nile

1 FORGOTTEN CHILDREN

Caring for the Orphaned and Abandoned

CHRISTIAN MISSIONARIES AND ISLAMIC ACTIVISTS battled in the 1930s over the bodies and souls of Egyptian children on the field of social welfare. The tug of war was most pronounced in the efforts to "save" or "liberate" the orphaned and abandoned. The struggle, which shaped the Muslim Brotherhood, seeded the welfare state, and sealed the fate of missionaries in Egypt, was a long time in the making. Tracing its roots, and the reasons missionaries came to have a near monopoly on orphan care, is critical to understanding the confrontation that culminated in the 1933 Port Said orphan scandal.[1]

Among those who were considered the deserving poor, orphaned and abandoned children stood out in Muslim societies, but there were very important differences in their legal status and place in the social imaginary. According to Islamic law, an orphan (*yatim*; pl. *aytam*, *yatama*) was one who had lost a father. Foundlings (*laqit*; pl. *luqata'*), or abandoned children, in contrast, were often presumed to be the result of illicit sexual relations, though children were also abandoned due to penury. Islamic inheritance law, which Copts followed, set the parameters for caring for these children, with the law clearly distinguishing between those whose paternity could be established and those whose paternity was unknown or contested: one was to be specially protected, the other ostracized for their unknown pedigree.

Islamic law has a great deal to say about the care of orphans, encouraging kind treatment, detailing the responsibilities of guardians, and protecting inheritances. The child's mother, if still alive, was not responsible for supporting the child financially; and she had no rights over the child's upbringing or claims to his or her property after the child had passed a certain age. Inheritance was set by fixed Qur'anic shares and could only be assigned to those in the blood line. By regulating and assigning guardians, usually a male family member, the law sought to protect the inheritance of orphans.[2] The law prohibited adoption, barring admission into a family to those outside the male bloodline, and did not allow the giving of a new paternal name to a child. These rules effectively excluded orphans from becoming legally knit into a new family on the same terms as other offspring. Fostering and giving the gift of care, in which children without parental care were taken into other families but kept their own names, existed. Hidden or secret adoption was also practiced, but these unsanctioned arrangements ran the risk of becoming undone at critical moments.[3]

The regulations surrounding orphans shored up the notion of the family as a set of blood relatives with a shared pedigree and patrilineal descent. The social and legal emphasis on biological as opposed to adoptive parenthood created challenges for those who were infertile and could not reproduce.[4] And it left those without a patrimony—abandoned children—in a social wilderness. Bearing the stigma of the act of illicit sex and carrying the stain of a misbegotten birth, they were sometimes perceived to have "tainted" blood. Whether the sexual act through which they were conceived was voluntary or forced, their mothers were considered to have dishonored the family by having premarital or extra-marital relations.[5] Stigmatizing children born out of wedlock and branding the mothers was obviously not unique to Egypt, but it meant that single motherhood was not an option, and it left illegitimate children on the margins of society. They were not legally orphans, which would have given them certain protections.

In practice the "orphans" in the story presented here came from a variety of family situations and did not adhere to a strict legal definition: they were abandoned, disabled, motherless, fatherless, or simply had no relatives who were able or willing to care for them. They were, in short, children without parental care. The Ottoman-Egyptian state strove to build up a social welfare network that would help orphans who lacked resources or family members willing to raise them; abandoned children, who had no knowledge of their families at all; and all others who fell through the cracks of family networks. Its work was interrupted by the British occupation of 1882, after which state investment in social welfare declined. Here is where missionaries found a special calling and a niche. Protestant missionaries had begun arriving on the shores of Egypt in the mid-nineteenth century with the gospel in hand and a vision to save Egyptians. When the locals did not turn out in large numbers to hear their message, evangelicals started building schools, hospitals, and later orphanages to guarantee a captive audience. Partaking of social welfare came with an obligation to study the Bible, sit in on services, and listen to prayer. Egyptians initially took this to be a small price to pay for services which were in short supply.[6]

"Managing" the Poor: The Ottoman-Egyptian State

Social welfare in premodern Egypt had been a prerogative, or responsibility, of religious authorities, with each religious community taking care of its own poor and establishing trusts for this purpose. The modernizing state under the Ottoman viceroy Mehmed ʿAli (r. 1805–49) eyed the assets of Islamic religious endowments and began assuming administration of them. The state gained oversight over institutions set up to serve those who were not sufficiently provided for by the safety net of the family or by other forms of religious charity.[7] The latter included large multifunctional complexes established by sultans and other wealthy donors, which had previously operated autonomously from the state. The Maristan Qalawun, a medieval mosque and hospital complex, was one such institution. It came to have an orphanage and foundling home, which took in abandoned children found on the streets of Cairo and those whose parents could not properly care for them.[8]

The Ottoman-Egyptian state was interested in "managing" the poor, whether those in need were widows, sick, elderly, or orphans. In addition to taking over administration of religious endowments, the state started its own social welfare operations. Prominent among these was the Madrasat al-Wilada (School for Midwives). Established in the 1830s in the Civilian Hospital of Azbakiyya, the school contained a home for foundlings and orphans, becoming the first rudimentary state-founded orphanage. The refuge served as a recruiting ground for students for the midwifery school, which initially had a difficult time filling its rosters.[9]

There was obvious demand for a home for abandoned and orphaned children, as borne out by police records, which for the eight-year period 1846–54 reveal an "extensive discussion" of abandoned infants and their admission to the Madrasat al-Wilada. Parents, neighbors, and others brought infants they could not nurse or care for to the police for placement in the new home, with numbers of foundlings entering the home ranging from one to three per month. The state turned to wet nurses, who in the days before the use of baby bottles were essential in supplying infants with sustenance.[10]

In the mid-nineteenth century, the abandonment of infants seemed to occur most frequently near religious institutions, or at least that was where they were most often reported to be found. One infant boy brought to the police station in November 1846 by an unnamed peasant woman was discovered at a mosque in al-Jamaliyya, a neighborhood in Cairo.[11] The British Arabic scholar Edward Lane noted that when a mother died leaving an infant, and the father and other relatives could not hire a nurse, the infant was sometimes left at the door of a mosque, usually during Friday prayers.[12] Newborns may also have been left directly at the door of a wet nurse, who would then receive a subsidy to breastfeed the infant until it could be weaned and placed in an institution.[13]

The poor pursued distinct strategies for obtaining relief, seeking aid when necessary from the state. Orphans were among those who petitioned for entry into Takiyyat Tulun, a mosque which was transformed into a poor shelter in 1847–48 and successfully operated in this capacity for over thirty years. Children sought admission when a parent passed away: when the father of a girl named Khadra died, she asked to be admitted into the refuge, for she had no one to take care of her. Mothers, whether they were divorced, separated, widowed, or army wives, petitioned for admission into the shelter with young children when they had no means of support.[14]

The Ottoman-Egyptian state may have unwittingly sponsored a home for unwed mothers at the refuge. In one year alone, forty-nine babies were born in Takiyyat Tulun to women who seemed to use the refuge "for the sole purpose of having a safe place to give birth." Many of these women stayed afterward for months nursing their newborns; others used it only as temporary refuge when they were ready to deliver. These women may have come to the refuge in the mosque complex to give birth away from the watchful eyes of villagers or urban neighbors.[15]

The Ottoman-Egyptian state increasingly took the role of guardian, investing itself with greater responsibility for the protection of its most vulnerable subjects. This paralleled moves by the Ottoman state in Istanbul, which from the 1850s set up an authority to administer a central fund for orphans—the Supervision of Orphan Properties—as part of a series of reforms to strengthen state control over the courts and the judges who presided over them. The authority managed the property and money that orphans would inherit at majority.[16] Going even further than the Ottoman reform in secularizing the law pertaining to orphans, Khedive Isma'il (r. 1863–79) established the *majlis hasbi* (a probate or guardianship court) in 1873 to protect the well-being of minors. For the first time, the new regulations fixed the age of majority (which under Islamic law had been fluid depending upon the individual youth) at eighteen.[17] He also established the Ministry of Religious Endowments, claiming the mantle of the guardianship of the weak and vulnerable to legitimize his rule.[18]

The Ottoman-Egyptian state recognized the limits of religious endowments and state resources in meeting the demand for social welfare services. Hoping to expand the range of educational, medical, and social services available to the population, the state tentatively welcomed missionaries, who were provided with access to land and other benefits. Missionaries appealed as providers, for their projects seemed to match those of a modernizing state that sought to teach minds and discipline bodies.

In the field of orphan care, French Catholic orders sponsored the first foreign orphanages in Egypt. When priests found two infants (most likely twins) abandoned on the doorsteps of their church in Alexandria in 1850, they handed them over to the sisters, who commenced their work with foundlings. Shortly thereafter, the Dames de la Charité started a home for the orphaned and abandoned. Expanding their efforts in response to regional crises, they took in forty orphaned refugee girls from the Levant in 1860 and that same year started the Orphanage of Saint Vincent de Paul for boys. Subsequently, the sisters began a separate home for foundlings, christening it the Refuge of Saint Joseph.[19] French Catholic orders also established orphanages in Cairo, among them the Maison du Bon-Pasteur and the Maison des Soeurs Franciscaines. At the end of the century, the latter housed fifty-four orphaned children and supervised the care of thirty babies, the smallest of whom were with wet nurses in Bulaq under the watch of a sister.[20] Catholic orders set up orphanages in other cities, too. In Port Said, the complex of social welfare institutions of the community of Bon-Pasteur d'Angers included an orphanage. In the 1890s, it housed sixty-four abandoned or orphaned girls, who in the morning studied and in the afternoon produced handiwork to support the institution.[21]

Privatizing: British Policy, Colonial Wives, and Orphan Care

After the British occupation of 1882, colonial officials took control of the Ottoman-Egyptian state, running it as a "veiled protectorate," with shadow advisors in each ministry overseeing affairs. Sir Evelyn Baring, Earl of Cromer, Britain's agent and consul general in Egypt from 1883 to 1907, was the de facto ruler. Concerned with shoring up Egypt's European debt, Lord Cromer reined in state forays into social welfare, funding education and health care minimally. Dismantling state welfare institutions or starving them of funds, the British looked to religious foundations and privately funded secular enterprises to provide solutions to social problems.[22]

Under colonial rule, the British controlled some ministries (interior) more tightly than others (endowments) and sought to gain greater control over the Ministry of Religious Endowments in particular. The new khedive, Tawfiq (r. 1879–92), who replaced his father, Isma'il, countered by eliminating that ministry in 1884 and creating in its stead a General Administration of Endowments, which was directly responsible to him. British officials claimed that they sought to reign in khedivial corruption in administering the religious endowments and had the ministry reinstated under Tawfiq's son, 'Abbas Hilmi II (r. 1892–1914), who nevertheless retained a good deal of control over it.[23]

The Ministry of Religious Endowments oversaw the running of an array of mosques, hospitals, schools, and shelters, such as Takiyyat 'Abdin, a hospice started in 1904 that cared for twenty-five to thirty indigent single women.[24] It also administered the Cairo Orphanage for Boys and Girls at Bab al-Luq, which in 1918 housed ninety-six boys and thirty-five girls. According to a government report, children were accepted into the orphanage "when it is established that their families are unable to provide for their bringing up." The children received an elementary education, including instruction in reading, writing, math, health, and Islam. The boys and girls were then prepared for different professions: boys were taught industrial crafts and trained as shoemakers, blacksmiths, or tailors, and girls were taught domestic skills and trained in cooking, ironing, and sewing. Workshops connected to the orphanage supplied clothes and similar items to establishments run by the Ministry of Religious Endowments.[25]

Officials encouraged colonial wives, foreign missionaries, and local social reformers to launch private social welfare operations. To facilitate this, they handed out state subsidies in the form of exemptions from customs duties, train passes, and the like. In one 1885 venture, British abolitionists launched the Cairo Home for Freed Slaves, a refuge for liberated African and Circassian female slaves. Run by a British matron, the home aimed to prepare those who sought shelter there for lives in domestic service. Cromer turned to Protestant missionaries for help in caring for those placed in the home who were too young to stay, since it was designed for temporary refuge. American Presbyterians took in twelve African girls, raising them in the Azbakiyya Boarding School.[26]

British colonial officials in Egypt crafted certain social welfare policies and then turned to their wives, compatriots, and Protestant friends to provide services. In this way, friends of the late Lady Cromer established a refuge for foundlings, the Lady Cromer Home (or Foundling Hospital) in a wing of Qasr al-ʿAyni Hospital in 1898. The numbers of those taken in rose quickly: in 1902 the hospital admitted 85 infants; two years later, it admitted 131. Cromer took a special interest in the institution, noting in the annual report for 1904 that the mortality among children admitted to it was very high, and he ascribed their deaths "to the terrible condition in which the majority are brought to the hospital. The mothers abandon them, immediately after birth, on some piece of waste ground or in some deserted building, and they are seldom found until after they have been exposed, in a state of nudity, to the weather for several hours."[27] Cromer blamed Egyptian mothers for abandoning their newborns, showing little understanding for their plight, fear, or desperation, and ignoring social, and particularly paternal, responsibility for the situation of the mother and child.

Most mothers who ceded maternal responsibility for their children did not do so easily. Rather, they felt compelled to give them up knowing the impossibility of living in Egypt as single mothers. They simply had no alternatives: keeping the product of an illicit sexual encounter would have endangered their own lives. So why did they abandon them, at least according to Cromer, in such desolate places? In the nineteenth century an unwed mother may have had anonymity in leaving a newborn at a mosque, church, or the home of a wet nurse; but the options may have become more limited over time, for the British colonial state proved more efficient at policing public spaces than its Ottoman-Egyptian predecessor.[28]

The British saw the work of the Lady Cromer Home, which expanded to include dispensaries, as a model for future endeavors.[29] The Home for Babies, as it came to be known, grew by 1920 to include forty-two beds in three rooms, with an English matron and her assistant overseeing four nurses. An adjacent Birthing Home consisted of fifty-four beds, with two Egyptian and three English doctors rotating rounds.[30] When an American nurse visited the foundling home in 1924, she found sixty wet nurses living there, along with children up to four and five years of age. The babies "looked particularly well cared for," the nurse noted, pointing to suppers consisting of a large piece of "native bread" and a chunk of goat's milk cheese.[31]

The colonial state oversaw the passage of legislation in 1912 to clarify proper procedures regarding the handling of an abandoned baby. The new law gave the woman who found the infant the right to keep it, thus limiting state intervention and responsibility for feeding and caring for these infants.[32] The new legislation coincided with the founding of a number of missionary orphanages and meant that foreign missionaries would not face legal hurdles when keeping foundlings in their care.

The colonial state was also eager to get older children off the streets. Preoccupied by "street children," whom they suspected of criminality, British officials oversaw the passage of legislation in 1908 addressing what they defined as the problem of vagrant children. It is unclear whether there were more street children than in the past (British sources suggested the number increased from the late 1800s) or whether the state had simply become more attentive to them due to increased policing and concern for order in the streets. The "immediate effect of this measure," wrote Eldon Gorst, Cromer's successor as consul general, "was that eighty-one children in undesirable surroundings were taken off the streets in Cairo and Alexandria."[33] The children were packed off to a recently built reformatory in Giza. The Ottoman-Egyptian state had also been concerned with vagrants and public order, but the British colonial state paid particular attention to vagrant children and built a new "home" to discipline and resocialize them.[34]

Other homes for street children opened their doors, among them the Malja' Abna' al-Sabil, called by the British who launched it the Shubra Brotherhood Waifs and Strays Home for Boys. Dorothea Russell, wife of Russell Pasha, the British commander of the Cairo police, became a spokeswoman for the home. "We contend that . . . it is the truly destitute child whom it is the business of the State to look after. The State does not do it, hence the crying need for this Home," she wrote, noting that the class of the boys in the home was "a class that no other institution will take, the totally destitute."[35] Dorothy Russell's appeals for funds from the semi-colonial state seemed to fall on deaf ears. The public-private partnership between British colonial officials, who helped set state policy, and colonial wives, who launched and supported social welfare institutions, was not without contradictions.

By 1924, a few years after its founding, the Shubra Brotherhood Waifs and Strays Home was sheltering some 150 to 180 boys. Like boys in other homes, they learned industrial crafts, using the proceeds from sales of the items they made to cover the costs of materials and the wages of industrial instructors. In describing the lines along which the home was run, Dorothea Russell explained, "Nothing of this kind has before been attempted in Egypt. It is run on the most modern and up to date principles of self government by the boys, on character forming principles. It has been found in America to give results, to which nothing comparable is attainable under the old systems." The novelty was "an atmosphere of unofficialdom."[36]

The committee running the home investigated Egyptian charges of proselytizing in the 1920s but found that the accusations were unsubstantiated. Dorothea Russell explained that the "original impetus" to start the home came from religious-minded and pious people—the moving spirit was the business manager of the Nile Mission Press—but they were not, she adamantly asserted, missionaries. The boys were taken regularly to mosque or church services, whichever was appropriate, and attempts were made to give them Islamic or Christian religious instruction. Yet she also noted that the home had no funds to pay an Islamic instructor and al-Azhar refused to send one.[37]

Egyptian elites often supported foreign-run refuges. Sa'id Zulfiqar Pasha gave liberally to the Shubra Home, keeping abreast of news on the home with reports written especially for him.[38] The shelter received write-ups in the local press, including pieces in the monthly *al-Mar'a al-Misriyya* and pictures in the weekly *al-Lata'if al-Musawwara*, which showed the boys in the home as well as members of the orphanage committee.[39] Yet other Egyptians, recognizing a crying need, sought a nationalist and/or Islamist solution, calling on Egyptians to start their own social welfare institutions.[40]

A National Duty: Egyptian Social Reformers

As foreign women—missionaries and colonial wives—sought to collect orphans and abandoned children in hospitals and orphanages, some local women worked to place them in families. Egyptian elites established the Waqf Khalil Agha (Khalil Agha Trust) in connection with the Qasr al-'Ayni Hospital to, among other things, find private homes for the abandoned children given refuge there.[41] In 1902, a few years after the launching of the foundling home, a little over a third of the children—thirty-two out of eighty-five—had been placed with a family.[42] Twenty years later, an American nurse visiting the wing of the hospital that housed the orphans learned that most of the children had been fostered "while they were still small," though evidently some still sought placement: "One tiny brown baby attached himself to us and toddled along all over the department."[43]

Those placed were most probably girls, who were desirable for the household help they could provide; there were also restrictions against bringing a male into a family who was not part of the blood line and would have had to been segregated from female family members at some point. That the practice of fostering—giving the gift of care—existed among the elite in Egypt is clear: Safiyya Zaghlul, "Mother of the Egyptians" and wife of the nationalist leader Sa'd Zaghlul, visited an orphanage in the early 1890s as a thirteen-year-old and "adopted" a four-year-old girl who was raised in her family and married off at eighteen.[44] Ottoman elites often took in orphans as playmates for their children, providing for their needs, teaching skills to them, and arranging for their marriages. Secret adoption, hidden from public view and the historical record, may also have been practiced.[45]

Muslim activists called upon Egyptians to care for the nation's weakest members, augmenting royal benevolence and supplanting foreign ventures. As part of a national reform program to counter missionary and colonial patronage of social welfare and to plug holes in the social welfare system, Egyptian associations began to set up their own refuges. Members of the Islamic Benevolent Society, founded in 1892, started the Malja' al-'Abbasiyya ('Abbasiyya Orphanage), an industrial school and orphanage for boys in Alexandria, naming it after Khedive 'Abbas Hilmi II.[46]

Ten years after the founding of the Lady Cromer Home, Zaynab Anis, a member of the Islamic reform group Tarqiyat al-Mar'a (Woman's Progress), started Jam'iyyat al-Shafaqa bi-Atfal (Society of Compassion for Children) to help abandoned and orphaned children.[47] A similar social welfare group, the Jam'iyyat Thamarat al-Ittihad (Society of the Fruits of the Union), opened a school and home for orphans in Cairo in 1914, collecting seventy-five girls of various backgrounds and organizing them into a scout troop. Just as missionaries sought to imbue orphan girls with Protestant values, local social reformers pushed nationalist, Islamic, and, before World War I, Ottoman creeds.[48]

In the wake of the 1919 Revolution, Egyptian social reformers reiterated that locals needed to establish institutions to care for their own orphans and abandoned children. One strategy was to claim some of the institutions started by foreigners as their own. After Balsam 'Abd al-Malik, the editor of *al-Mar'a al-Misriyya*, visited the Malja' al-Atfal (Home for Babies) in Qasr al-'Ayni Hospital, she noted that it "had been previously known as the Lady Cromer Home. The truth is that there is no connection between the home and that name, for it is part of Qasr al-'Ayni Hospital and is funded by the Egyptian government."[49] In addition to subventions from the Egyptian state, the foundling home received donations from Egyptian female notables.[50] Where foreigners saw the hand of colonial wives and an English matron at work, Egyptians saw local funds, wet nurses, and children. The reality was probably a little more complex than Balsam 'Abd al-Malik might have wanted to admit, however, with the rotating English and Egyptian physicians symbolizing the entanglements of social welfare in a colonial state.

Nationalists started new institutions to care for the orphaned and abandoned, sometimes becoming mired in rancorous political debate. 'Abd al-'Aziz Nazmi's Malja' al-Hurriyya (Shelter of Freedom), an orphanage for boys in Cairo, came under attack by rival nationalists when the effort to launch it stalled. In the context of an anti-colonial struggle against the British occupation, the name signaled the connection many nationalists made between social welfare and national independence.[51]

Other social reformers targeted orphaned and abandoned girls for their projects. Jam'iyyat Nahdat al-Sayyidat al-Misriyyat (Society of the Egyptian Ladies' Awakening), an association with an Islamic nationalist vision started by Labiba Ahmad (1870s–1951) in 1919, took as its first project the founding of an orphanage. Labiba Ahmad and her colleagues gathered together 170 orphaned or abandoned girls from the area around Sayyida Zaynab, opening a home in 1920. Not all the girls were technically orphaned: one of the few profiled had been abandoned when her parents divorced and remarried. This spurred Labiba Ahmad to decry the ease of divorce, pointing to the price paid by children whose natal families came apart and who were excluded from new family formations.[52]

Social activists such as Labiba Ahmad challenged the stigmatization of orphans and abandoned children by promoting them as good citizens of the nation, whose responsibility it was to care for them, and by giving them a political purpose. As a sign of their nationalist spirit, the girls in Labiba Ahmad's orphanage marched in political demonstrations carrying placards. Given her desire to "elevate the nation," Labiba Ahmad, who was "inspired by God," vowed to raise the girls in the home as good Muslims. In the early 1920s, after the discovery of a ring that lured poor girls into prostitution, she added a workshop and institute to her social welfare complex to teach the orphans and other poor neighborhood girls sewing and similar skills.[53] She consistently argued in her journal *al-Nahda al-Nisa'iyya* that "the nation" should care for its weakest members and replace foreign enterprises, and she celebrated such local institutions as a refuge in Benha, where orphans whom "fate had prevented from knowing the affection of mothers or fathers" received good care.[54]

Tracing the girls who sought shelter under Labiba Ahmad's patronage and the care of a matron who ran the institution is difficult. Although their testimonies are not recorded, their images are captured in photographs, with two group photographs standing out: one shows a disheveled group of girls upon their entry into the orphanage and a subsequent one depicts them in ordered lines and neatly dressed.[55] These images illustrate the reforming impulse of the nationalists and their modernizing agendas, as order, discipline, and cleanliness were reinforced.

In harsh economic times such as the late 1920s and early 1930s, abandonment may have increased, and attempts to sell infants were also recorded. After police caught a man peddling a two-month-old in the Sayyida Zaynab district of Cairo in 1933, they arrested the infant's birth mother, who came from the town of Mahalla al-Kubra; she told investigators that she had decided to sell the infant because she was "hard up."[56] Lack of money spurred Lucette Lagnado's maternal grandfather to sell a newborn child against the wishes of her grandmother, who was devastated by the loss.[57] Islamist and other women's associations continued to identify foundlings and orphans as needing care but did not rush to start homes. This was due in part to the stigma surrounding abandoned children, which made it hard for female social reformers to take up this cause. Although foundlings formed a minority of the children in most orphanages, the ambiguity surrounding their births had an impact on other children.

"Saving Children": Called to Egypt

Late nineteenth- and early twentieth-century Egypt was awash in Protestant evangelical missions—large and small—which came from a variety of countries and were sponsored by a range of churches. These included but were by no means limited to the American Mission and Assemblies of God (American); the Egypt General Mission and Church Mission Society (British); the Canadian Holiness Mission; the Dutch Reformed Church; and the Swedish Salaam Mission. When one group "occupied" an area, or set up a station, others respected the claim and did not compete in the same village or town out of regard for "mission comity."

They could come because the British made it possible, protecting missionaries at the same time that they watched them. "British officials have always been hyper-nervous about the Moslem faith, and have kept a tight hand on Christian Missions, fearing that they would be a cause of arousing the Mohammedans to fanatical uprising," wrote George Swan, a leader of the Egypt General Mission and head of the Inter-Mission Council, who worked closely with

British colonial officials. "Anything of the nature of open-air work has always been prohibited and all the other work carefully watched, and often requests made for its modification."[58] Those looking for a free hand experienced limitations, whereas those who had encountered obstacles elsewhere in the Muslim world found the freedoms to proselytize in Egypt refreshing.

To reach as broad a sector of the population as possible, missionaries offered an array of services. Those who patronized their institutions encountered evangelicals as matrons in orphanages, teachers in schools, and nurses and doctors in clinics and hospitals. Although Egyptians were aware of their attempts to persuade others of the validity of their Christian message, those in need sought out social services that were otherwise in short supply. Missionaries arriving on Egypt's shores in the nineteenth and twentieth centuries identified a particular vacuum in the care of abandoned and orphaned children, and they saw an opportunity, because Ottoman-Egyptian and colonial authorities allowed them to build their institutions. Where others saw a stigma, missionaries saw the possibility of "winning souls for Christ": the child was a blank slate who could be saved.

Evangelicals did not generally start their careers with the plan of founding an orphanage—a costly enterprise that would not be self-sufficient—but rather stumbled into circumstances that allowed them to launch one. Sometimes a patron happened to appear: Margaret Smith, an evangelical with the American Mission who spent decades teaching, realized her dream of founding an orphanage when a couple willing to fund one visited Cairo. Sometimes it was an accident: Lillian Trasher was handed an infant by a dying woman and shortly thereafter launched the Asyut Orphanage. And sometimes it just happened: Maria Ericsson's Home for Destitutes grew out of the Swedish Mission's school for girls after a cluster of students took to boarding at the school. Of course, these evangelicals would have explained the emergence of their orphanages in other terms, seeing the hand of providence.

Most of the orphanages founded by missionaries were for girls, though a few, such as the Dutch Reform Mission's orphanage at Qalyubiyya, were for boys, and some, such as the Asyut Orphanage, were mixed (with boys and girls separated of course). The reason may be that more boys than girls were in orphanages run by the state or overseen by it. Consider the number of boys (96) to girls (35) in the Cairo Orphanage for Boys and Girls at Bab al-Luq in 1918.[59] It may well be that state social services favored boys just as state education did, and that missionaries found female orphans particularly underserved. It may also be that single female missionaries felt they were better suited to serving girls or preferred them.

Once the orphanage as an institution took root in Egypt—evolving locally out of multifunctional spaces that became more specialized over time or were planted by foreign missionaries—Egyptians may no longer have felt obligated to care for relatives' orphaned children. Rather than stretching resources thin, poorer families could now hand over the orphans in their midst to a mission, with the hope that the orphanage would offer training and job opportunities. That many orphans had relatives is clear from the records, which show the children visiting family members over school breaks, finding shelter with them during political crises, and being sent back to them when they misbehaved. Additionally, many of those in the missionary orphanages were not technically orphaned under Islamic law. Their fathers may have been alive but were unable to care for them due to work or, commonly, an inability to work. Or their mothers were alive but did not have the resources to raise them.

Evangelical Exuberance: The Nile Valley Mission

Every mission had its own narrative of trials, tribulations, and triumphs, with some of the smaller and lesser known ones having the most interesting tales. One such American enterprise, the Nile Valley Mission, provides a portrait of evangelical enthusiasm in the face of challenges and shows how social welfare work evolved in the field. The founders of the Nile Valley Mission, American Methodists Lewis Glenn (1874–1941) and Viola Light Glenn (1870–1939), came from the farmlands of Indiana and Illinois and were "born again" in late nineteenth-century revivals. Viola started preaching about the new doctrine of living without sin to Midwestern American audiences, "fiery messages which swayed the multitudes."[60]

The "spirit" moved them, and they went out on faith to take up missionary work in Egypt, recognizing it as the center of the Muslim world. They also recognized that their proselytizing was made possible by the British occupation. "Through the providence of God this land of wonders has been opened up for evangelization by the British occupation in our day," wrote Lewis Glenn, celebrating imperial protection. "The rattling sabre of their army has restrained the fanatical hordes from driving out the pale-faced messengers of the cross who come with glad tidings to these darkened sons of Adam."[61] Lewis Glenn's racist imagery arose from an American context of evangelical encounters with Native Americans and was transplanted to the Mediterranean.

The Glenns sailed for Alexandria in 1905, with an infant son and two single female missionaries, and upon landing searched for a destination not already "occupied" by a mission. Hearing from a friendly American of "a number of large inland towns without a missionary," the Glenns proceeded by train to Damanhur, where their objective was, in Elder Glenn's words, "to open work in one of the most fanatical towns of the fanatical Delta."[62] Seeing the landscape through the prism of the Bible and of a war between Islam and Christianity, Glenn used the military language common to missionaries of the period: they occupied, retreated, battled, faced sieges, and ceded territory. In Damanhur, while "mingling with semi-civilized hordes of lower Egypt at an inland town," Lewis Glenn became quite ill and was forced to relocate to the coast.[63] After his recovery, the Glenns moved their mission to the oasis of al-Fayyum, south of Cairo, where their personal trials continued, as two infant children died. Perhaps due to the void the loss of the children created, or to local circumstances, they started a girls' orphanage, which quickly became the centerpiece of the station. They later moved the orphanage to Ramla, a town on the coast near Alexandria.[64] "You women of freedom here under the Stars and Stripes and with church and social privileges your Eastern sisters never dream of, do you blame us for gathering in some of these little girls and giving them a chance for their lives and a hope of heaven hereafter?," Glenn asked potential donors on a church tour in the United States.[65]

The Nile Valley Mission grew into a community of some seventy individuals, counting the American missionaries, orphans, preachers, teachers, and Bible women. The latter were native women, often converts, who traveled in rural and urban areas to read the Bible to women and children in their homes, and were considered a crucial part of the attempt to spread Protestantism. With a collective effort, the Nile Valley Mission expanded its reach and started stations in the Upper Egyptian towns of Suhaj and Jirja, where affiliated missionaries opened day schools, visited villages and towns, and ran winter conventions.[66]

When Viola Glenn, who spent the last decade and a half of her life blind, was asked by her son whether the missionary life was worth the steep price she had paid, losing children and her eyesight, she answered in the affirmative: "As I closed my eyes there came before me the faces of those the Lord helped me to win for Christ," she told Victor. "I saw them. I saw them as they appeared before they were saved while still in their heathen darkness. Then I saw them after Christ had set them free, with the light of heaven on their countenance and a good, glowing testimony."[67] In spite of her loss of vision, Viola saw with clarity what she took to be the greatest benefit of missionary social welfare services—conversion of Egyptians—but was blind to the discord her mission and others caused in villages, towns, and cities throughout Egypt.

The care of orphaned and abandoned children became a growing concern to state officials and social activists in nineteenth- and twentieth-century Egypt. Ottoman-Egyptian officials had a multipronged approach to strengthening social welfare: establishing state facilities, tightening control of the administration of religious endowments, and allowing the development of missionary institutions. British officials formulated a colonial policy that cut back on the first track—state projects—and shifted responsibility for social welfare, including orphan care, to the private sector. They encouraged colonial wives, foreign missionaries, and local elites to fund and run social welfare projects such as orphanages, giving support in the form of subventions.

The cutting back on state welfare, or the lack of its development during critical decades, left a vacuum, which opened the door to non-state providers. These sponsors hoped to enhance their legitimacy as guardians of the poor, to earn social and political capital, and to "save" children. Each saw orphaned and abandoned children as open to proselytizing, modernizing, and nationalizing agendas. Orphans collectively received attention as some of them appeared in Egyptian press photographs in the first quarter of the twentieth century, moving out of the shadows and into the light. Although they rarely had names—only the name of the orphanage or school was given—some had faces and were now visible. For a moment, at least, they were incorporated into the newly emerging nation, if only rarely into specific families.

Yet the particularities of orphan care—its social and economic costs—made the starting up of orphanages by locals particularly challenging, and the number of orphanages started by Egyptians remained low. Egyptian elites preferred to support foreign orphanages than to start ones of their own, and allowed foreign missionaries to gain control of the care of orphans and abandoned children. Their desire to subcontract the care of orphans was due in part to the ambiguous status of abandoned children, in part to multiple demands on limited resources. The missionaries' free hand in taking over this niche was also made possible by a British policy that protected missionary activity. Having no intention of providing large public outlays for social welfare, colonial officials encouraged missionaries to build schools, hospitals, and refuges. The policy provided social welfare services on the cheap and at the same time enabled colonial officials to placate a large constituency of missionary supporters back home.

While the question of who would provide the care and cover the costs of social welfare—the state or private groups—might have been in contention, the shape of the institution to house orphans was increasingly clear. Orphanages emerged in modern Egypt as a specialized site for caring for orphaned and abandoned children. Group homes of various sizes were run, often rather strictly, by matrons, in an almost industrial fashion. The numbers of children in these homes varied, ranging from a handful to hundreds (and later over a thousand in the Asyut Orphanage). What children gained in security of (sometimes minimal) food, shelter, and clothing, they sometimes lost in affective ties.

Children ended up in orphanages for a variety of reasons: some were abandoned at birth; others were pushed out, the by-product of broken marriages or dysfunctional families or their own physical impairment; still others were placed in the home upon the injury, illness, impoverishment, or death of a parent. For these children, the alternatives of informal adoption or care by relatives had not materialized, and they remained at the margins of society. The orphan scandal of 1933—the Turkiyya Hasan affair—would bring them into the center of debates on conversion, social welfare, and the state.

2 WINNING SOULS FOR CHRIST

American Presbyterians in Cairo

AMERICAN PRESBYTERIAN MISSIONARIES noted the "disciplining" of Turkiyya Hasan in the summer of 1933: "a young girl was impudent and disobedient to her teacher. She was slightly punished and took revenge by saying she was punished because she would not become a Christian."[1] They could not understand the vehemence of the anti-missionary campaign that followed, as those affiliated with the American Mission experienced a backlash. "These are difficult days for us all and especially for the Moslem converts, because of the organised opposition against our work," wrote American evangelical Anna Criswell in late June. "Many of our missionaries and also their work have been attacked in the public press and in some places the work has been stopped for the present."[2] The local converts who worked on the frontlines, going out to read the Bible to women in Muslim homes, encountered the stiffest opposition. Criswell called upon her friends in the United States for prayers so that teachers and other evangelicals could all continue their work "in such a way as not to offend, but at the same time in such a way as to bear a faithful witness to Christ."[3] She herself prayed "that all this publicity may only bring the gospel message to the minds of thousands more of the Moslems."[4]

The first American Presbyterian missionaries arrived in Egypt in 1854, soon eclipsing the Anglican Church Missionary Society. (Having arrived in 1825, the CMS abandoned the field in 1865, returning only after the British occupation in 1882.) Evangelicals of what would become the American Mission of the Board of Foreign Missionaries of the United Presbyterian Church of

North America (UPCNA) established the seeds of the largest missionary outfit in the Nile Valley. With a board in Philadelphia, the UPCNA sent hundreds of missionaries to Egypt to oversee thousands of local assistants and provide services to tens of thousands of locals. They built an extensive network of missionary schools, hospitals, clinics, and other social services with the goal of evangelizing.[5]

The Women's General Missionary Society (WGMS) eventually took over the sponsorship of many of the single women missionaries, who by the late nineteenth century formed the majority of Protestant missionaries in Egypt.[6] Women missionaries served as the foot soldiers of the missionary movement, bringing evangelical Christianity into Egyptian homes: they started schools, worked as nurses and doctors in American hospitals and clinics, visited secluded women, and opened refuges for the orphaned and abandoned. Although the American Mission came to focus on Copts in the hopes that they would then take on the conversion of Muslims, it was not averse to proselytizing among Muslims and Jews.

Margaret (Maggie) Smith (1847–1932) landed in Egypt in 1872 as part of this army of American evangelicals. Like other Protestant missionaries, she came with what she thought were the best of intentions, carrying "light"—the gospel message—to a land engulfed in "darkness." After thirty-four years in the field, Margaret Smith realized one of her dreams: the founding of an orphanage for girls. The Fowler Orphanage became one of the most successful institutions of the American Mission. Many of those who walked through its doors walked out converts, joining the Evangelical Church (the new Egyptian Protestant church started by American Presbyterians) and going on to work for the American Mission, or other Protestant enterprises, in Egypt and the surrounding lands.

"The Last Rose of Summer": Bible Reading and Teaching

Born in Ohio, on the eastern edge of the American Midwest, the first of ten children, Margaret Smith moved at a young age to Kansas. There her father, a Presbyterian minister, helped to found the town of Berea, and attempted to prevent the new territory from becoming a slave state. Smith attended a public school and received religious training at home, uniting with the Church of Berea at the age of sixteen. She then started teaching at the Sabbath (Sunday) school, specializing in foreign mission. At the age of twenty-five she was selected by the Synod of Kansas to become a missionary in Egypt.[7] Accepting the challenge of "winning souls for Christ," Smith joined the quickly growing missionary family in the Nile Valley. The group included Anna Thompson (1851–1932), an unmarried missionary who had arrived earlier that year, also from Ohio. The two became lifelong friends: the tall and talkative Thompson and the petite Smith, whom Thompson described in her diary as "very humble and unpretending."[8]

When Margaret Smith arrived in Egypt, the country was bustling under the modernizing vision of the Ottoman viceroy Khedive Isma'il. The khedive had transformed the capital, building an opera house, parks, palaces, and wide boulevards after securing a series of European loans. He opened the Suez Canal in 1869 with a grand celebration, later selling his shares to the British, who along with the French came to control the strategic transit route. Isma'il looked north to Europe for approval and south to Sudan and Ethiopia to enlarge his empire, hiring American Civil War veterans for the effort. He had great admiration for the United States, which, unlike Great Britain and France, did not seem to harbor imperial designs in the region. So he granted American missionaries permission to start schools, giving them land in Cairo for their mission headquarters.[9]

Shortly after her arrival in 1872, Smith was assigned a young Muslim male Arabic tutor, a teenager named Ahmad Fahmi. The new missionary and her tutor read a selection of texts, including devotional books and chapters from the Bible, on a daily basis for months. Fahmi began asking Smith questions about "prophecies respecting Christ."[10] In October 1877, his interest piqued, Fahmi gave Smith a document professing his faith in Christianity, telling her that she was "the means of his enlightenment."[11] American missionaries saw Fahmi's newly professed faith—which turned out to be on again, off again—as a real breakthrough, for they had won few Muslim converts, and none from such an elite background as his. But intense opposition from his family, which steadfastly opposed the conversion and tried to induce him to recant, showed them just how difficult winning Muslim converts from an elite family could be. He was forced to leave Egypt and went to Scotland to study medicine.[12]

American evangelicals learned through this affair that battling a well-connected Muslim family for a son's soul presented many obstacles. Working with slaves, orphans, and abandoned children, whose families made few if any claims and who could stay on in Egypt to help the evangelicals, was less complicated for the missionaries and, in the long run, could be more productive. Still, Fahmi's conversion served the Protestant cause in Egypt, and in 1878, after years of negotiation and diplomatic pressure from the U.S. consul general in Egypt, Khedive Isma'il issued a decree recognizing the fledgling community of Protestant converts as a distinct Christian sect. This recognition gave Egyptian Protestants the ability to establish their own personal status laws apart from the Orthodox Copts and to negotiate directly with the Egyptian government (even if American Protestants still controlled the purse strings).[13]

Once her Arabic was up to speed, Margaret Smith began visiting women in their homes to read the Bible in the vernacular, a dimension of evangelical work that was considered critical to spreading Christianity. Evangelicals saw secluded women as key to the spiritual life of the larger household. "I visited at two Moslem houses today," Smith recorded in her diary on December 5, 1880. This was below her average of three to six households daily, but since one home was the palace of Ibrahim Khalil Pasha, whose harem women would have taken up more time, the low number was understandable. There she "read some to his lady" and granddaughter.[14]

The missionaries devoted a great deal of time and energy to reading the Bible to illiterate women in private homes. As Charles Watson, a second-generation missionary in whose home Smith resided, noted: "Miss Smith would go away from the house immediately after breakfast, going by donkey to her work," which was in Harat al-Saka'in. She "would come back late in the afternoon, dragging herself wearily upstairs, looking like the last rose of summer." Her body may have been frail "but her spirit was undaunted."[15] Smith was not just responsible for her own visits; like other female missionaries, she trained and supervised a team of native Bible readers. Her dedication to reaching out to the poorest of the poor earned her a reputation among fellow missionaries.[16] Visiting the poor, whose material circumstances contrasted with a missionary's modest comforts, tested Smith's faith. It may have tested her hosts' hospitality as well. In the days leading up to the 1882 'Urabi Revolt, when anti-foreign sentiment was on the rise, Smith "had to stand rebuffs, criticisms, and sometimes drenchings of dirty water thrown from some window overhead as she went about her work," Watson reported.[17]

Still, Smith found the work rewarding and sought to continue it. When she temporarily took over for her friend Anna Thompson at the Azbakiyya Girls' School in 1880, she wrote in her diary that it was "very hard to give up my interesting work [in Harat al-Saka'in] a part of which, visiting at Moslem houses, no one can take up."[18] Like many single women missionaries, Smith fused Bible reading with teaching. Charged with running the girls' school in Harat al-Saka'in in addition to visiting homes, she helped it develop into one of the largest schools for girls in Egypt. The school attracted the daughters of prominent Egyptians such as Ahmad 'Urabi Pasha, the colonel behind the 1882 revolt that bore his name.[19]

In spite of their prodigious work for the Protestant cause, single women missionaries had little voice in mission governance, until Smith led a protest in the early 1890s on the occasion of the founding of the Egyptian Missionary Association. The association, which in its heyday numbered well over a hundred men and women, administered the affairs of the American Mission, reporting back to the Board of Foreign Missions of the UPCNA and the Women's General Missionary Society. It met twice a year to vote on membership and tenure, review committee recommendations, bargain over finances and funds, and confirm assignments in schools, hospitals, and homes, among other matters. "Mission tradition has it that it was Miss Margaret Smith, a timid, new missionary, who when the mission association came into being, stuck by her guns," wrote mission historian Earl Elder, and she "asserted her right and along with it that of all unmarried women to sit as a member of the association."[20] Gaining a voice set the stage for female missionaries to endorse special projects.

Fulfilling a Dream: Quaker Patrons, Cairene Children

Margaret Smith's longtime dream of founding a home for homeless children began to take shape after Esther and John Fowler, a Quaker couple from Ohio, visited Egypt in 1895.[21] In John Fowler's words, the couple toured Protestant mission institutions, including Smith's school in Harat al-Saka'in, motivated by Esther's "concern for the people of that land."[22] They were struck, according to John, by the "sharp contrast in the countenances of the children in the mission schools and the destitute ones on the streets, many of whom were blind."[23] Their concern for street children came amidst a heightened effort on the part of colonial officials and Egyptian elites to remove beggars and street children from public view and sanitize public space as part of their modernizing drive.[24] John Fowler's time in Egypt profoundly shaped his experience of religion and expression of it. Later he recalled that toward the end of his trip, "a feeling of love for the people of that land [Egypt] so filled my heart as I never before had had any conception," and he desired "to rescue those poor people."[25]

After returning to the United States, Fowler entered into a formal agreement with the Presbyterian Board of Foreign Missions in Philadelphia, committing himself to raising funds for the establishment of an orphanage for destitute, abandoned, and orphaned children and a hospital for the blind in Cairo. The board pledged to help realize a plan that was in line with half a century of work in the Nile Valley. Retaining ultimate decision-making power and abstaining from committing funds to a project that was not self-sustaining, the board promised to consult with Fowler and contributors from the Quaker Society of Friends regarding the site and building of the institutions.[26] The agreement affirmed that "the Institution shall always be kept under the influence, care and superintendence of Protestant Christian officers and teachers, who shall endeavor to instruct the inmates in the precepts of the New Testament." In a nod to Quaker concerns, it noted that "war or military drill shall never be taught therein."[27]

Donations for the proposed project came from individuals, Quaker meetings, and Friends' schools, amounting to as little as one dollar and as much as five hundred.[28] By fall 1904, the Fowlers had raised nearly $9,000 in subscriptions, too little to buy land and build a home and hospital but an amount sufficient to rent space and accept children.[29] Perhaps because Dutch missionaries had earlier started a boys' orphanage nearby in Qalyubiyya, the Fowler Orphanage Committee in Egypt targeted girls. It won approval for its plan to house orphans at a girls' boarding school after Smith promised that she would run the orphanage as a faith-based institution. She was not permitted to approach the board or anyone else directly for funds, though she could solicit funds indirectly by asking for prayers and could cultivate ties with John and Esther Fowler and their Quaker Friends.[30]

More than a decade after the Fowlers had visited Cairo, the American Mission stood ready to receive orphans. The Fowler Orphanage for girls opened its doors in February 1906 when the first six orphans were placed in the Fum al-Khalij School under Margaret Smith's care.[31] The missionaries soon realized, however, that the location was not suitable due to the neighboring brothels and "drunkenness and every evil right near the school."[32] After a few months, the missionaries rented a more appropriate place, the home of a man whose wife had attended one of Smith's schools.[33] When that home proved too small, they moved to a larger house in northern Cairo. There the missionaries learned that traffic patterns in the area made sending the girls to the nearest mission school dangerous, so they started a school in the building.[34]

The first years of the Fowler Orphanage were marked by the search for a stable home. As head of the orphanage, Smith pushed for expanded quarters, petitioned and updated the Board and "Friend Fowler," pressed fellow missionaries into service, and utilized the educational and health services of the mission to help the girls in her care. She selected Sitt Habashiyya as matron of the home. (Sitt Habashiyya may well have been one of the twelve ex-slaves raised by Thompson and other American Presbyterian women missionaries in the mission's Azbakiyya Girls' School.[35]) As the home grew, Smith needed more administrative assistance and appealed to the Women's General Missionary Society Board to name Ellen Barnes, who was already in the field, a missionary.[36] A rotating coterie of American missionaries passing through the home filled in for one another while the older girls—the "daughters of the Home"—became its main workers, carrying out the chores of cooking, sewing, washing, housekeeping, and watching the little ones under the direction of the matron and American missionaries.[37]

Smith's project of finding a permanent home for the orphanage received a boost when a Mrs. Arnold of Pittsburg left it a legacy of $10,000.[38] In the end, rather than erect a new building, the American Mission purchased the Austro-Hungarian Hospital in 'Abbasiyya, which had been sequestered as enemy property at the outset of World War I, at a bargain price of $5,000. After renovations, the complex included a chapel, a day school, and living space for the orphans and missionaries who cared for them.[39] Finding a home of their own solved the problem of suitable accommodations, but the orphanage still needed operating funds. Since the money that the Fowlers raised "could be used only for a building or Home," as Smith explained, "and the foreign Board had no money to give for living expenses"—food and clothing—Smith was permitted "to begin trusting the Lord for these things."[40]

The most regular and continuous donations to the home came from Quaker acquaintances of Esther and John Fowler. Twenty years after the founding of the orphanage, after both of the Fowlers had passed away, a circle of their friends in Ohio formed the Fowler Orphanage Association. The group collected photographs and reports on the orphanage, corresponded with the directors, and met at the Yearly Meeting of Ohio Friends. For over half a century, they participated in a project that reaffirmed their own faith, giving regular annual contributions of hundreds of dollars to a home thousands of miles away.[41] Ellen Barnes, who succeeded Smith as head of the home, noted in 1923 that donations of clothing, toys, books, blankets, food, and money came from a variety of foreign sources, "from as far east as China and as far west as America," and no doubt had the Quaker association in mind.[42]

Yet the reality is that the bulk of funds came from inside Egypt. In 1922, for example, the split broke down into roughly 58 percent of funds from Egyptian sources; 32 percent from America, England, and other lands; and 10 from mission sources.[43] The proportion of support that originated inside Egypt came from individuals, schools, churches, and societies as well as through the sale of resident girls' handiwork, including silver shawls, bead bags, dolls, and garments. One year, in the midst of the Great Depression and declining donations, the girls sold 324 garments, 64 dolls, and 25 bead bags.[44] Just as they had received donations, residents of the home were socialized to give to others: the girls put money in a collection box for orphanages in Qalyubiyya and Khartoum, and other institutions in need. And, after graduating, many of the girls frequently sent gifts to the Fowler Orphanage.[45]

Saving Bodies: Residents of the Home

The first two children Smith received into her care were Greek girls whose widowed mother had limited resources. They left within a week, taken by Roman Catholic priests who demanded them.[46] Yet there was no shortage of girls needing a home. A couple of subsequent residents had blind mothers who could not care for them owing to their disability; in one such case the mother and daughter lived together in a room on the roof of the orphanage.[47] Another girl had epilepsy (and had been taken by her mother "to the tomb of some dead sheikh" for a ceremony, much to the chagrin of the missionaries.[48])

The Fowler Orphanage also housed a few girls whose mothers were prostitutes, and the missionaries hoped to save both daughter and mother. One of two Muslims awaiting baptism in 1909 was "praying earnestly" on behalf of a mother who was "living a bad life."[49] The next year, a woman "living a disreputable life" took her daughter out of the orphanage.[50] Although the missionaries publicized some of these stories to dramatize the need for the orphanage, or the need to move it to safer quarters, they did not want to identify the girls too closely with prostitution and used euphemisms to discuss a practice that was regulated under British colonial rule.[51] Some of the girls who came into their care may even have been the offspring of imperial soldiers. Others arriving at the home were the products of broken marriages and competing religious claims. The three- and five-year-old Syrian girls who quickly replaced the first two Greek girls came from such a background. Their Christian mother had remarried after converting to Islam and sent the girls to a Muslim school. Their father had taken his daughters from that school and brought them to the home to be raised as Christians.[52]

The Fowler Orphanage did not take in abandoned infants or accept newborns after the death of a mother, for it was unequipped to handle babies.

The sole exception to this rule was when, in 1910, according to Smith, "a dear, dirty, half starved, cross-eyed baby girl was given to us to bring up for the Lord." Trying to prevent the spread of any disease she may have carried, the missionaries stripped and cleaned her: "What little she wore, even the tuft of hair on the top of her head was cast into the fire. Nothing remained of her former trousseau except a few beads and two iron rings." The girl's beginnings—whether as cast-off daughter of a prostitute, product of an illicit relationship, or offspring of a dying woman—and how she came to the home are unclear. The iron rings and beads suggest that a mother or another relative gave her something to distinguish her, and she came with a name or was quickly given one: "Her name is Mitemina but we call her Timmy for short."[53] This seemed to be a singular episode in the records of the Fowler Orphanage: babies found abandoned in or near Cairo were secretly or informally adopted; placed in the Lady Cromer Home or some other refuge; or given to a wet nurse, who received a state stipend to feed them until they were ready to be placed in an institution.

Locals may have come to see the institution as more of a boarding house than an orphanage, with relatives (including infirm widowed mothers or fathers) delivering girls to the home for any number of reasons. The girls may have become a strain on a family's resources, or relatives hoped that the children would acquire skills so that they could support themselves. One girl, Fa'iza, who had lost both her parents by the age of five and a half, remembered vividly "how the relative who brought her and her small sister there, tricked them by sending them for a drink of water while he disappeared from the house." Although at the time she could not be consoled, she grew up happily to become a teacher and Bible reader according to the head of the home.[54]

Those applying for entry to the Fowler Orphanage were carefully screened, particularly after one young girl entered the orphanage with tuberculosis and had to be isolated on the roof. In the wake of this episode, the missionaries drafted a physician from the American Mission's Tanta Hospital to examine the girls.[55] Admission became increasingly selective: in 1920, six of twenty-one applicants were turned away for medical and other reasons.[56] The orphanage population fluctuated between forty and sixty residents, with only a limited number of openings annually. Once in the home, physicians checked the girls for eye disease, influenza, and other medical conditions. With so many youths living in close quarters at a time when epidemics still ravaged Egypt, health and hygiene were major concerns. At the same time, the missionaries turned stories of death from disease into spiritual victories: the girl with tuberculosis who was isolated on the roof "spent much time in prayer," according to Smith, "and death was a happy homecoming for her."[57]

Saving Souls: The Ones Who Got Away

Those accepted for entry into the Fowler Orphanage were subject to a contract outlining the terms, which stipulated a fine for the family if the girl was removed early. The missionaries wanted to keep the girls in the home for as long as possible, and at least until the age of eighteen, so that they would have time to shape them. The girls faced a steady stream of Protestant rituals and practices that were meant to instill an ethic of hard work. Their days were filled with a routine of lessons, homework, housework, and prayer, as they attended a day school connected to the orphanage or in the area and continued their post-elementary education at missionary secondary schools. Each girl had her own Bible and could find additional religious reading material in the children's library.[58] At regular prayer time and at times of special need, they joined Smith and the other missionaries in services.[59]

The evangelicals modeled charitable "Christian" behavior for the residents of the home, trying to transform them spiritually and guide them on the road to conversion. One day Smith brought home an old woman who had been beaten by street toughs, instructed that she be bathed and clothed, and gave her a small room where she rested. Before she died, the old woman confessed "her faith in the Saviour," which was portrayed both as a victory for the cause and a lesson for the girls in the home, who were exposed to multiple such lessons.[60]

Yet not all of the girls followed the enforced regime, and some barely passed the initial trial period. "One child of eight years of age was so vile in her example and speech that after we had tried every means to reform her it seemed necessary for the sake of the other children to expel her," Smith reported, attributing the girl's mischief to "Satan." The girl seemed to have deliberately misbehaved so that her mother would take her from the home. But the girl's mother "begged" the missionaries to give her daughter another chance and stayed away, at which point the child's behavior "changed very much," for her strategy to exit the home had not succeeded.[61]

Others rebelled or fled when they thought they were at risk: "There have been times of deep spiritual awakening and sorrow for sin, then again there has been a spirit of insubordination to the teachers by a few of the older girls," Smith wrote in 1910.[62] That was the year a consumptive girl who had shown signs of tuberculosis had stayed in a room on the orphanage roof, since no hospital would admit her at that stage due to risk of contagion.[63] Girls resident in the orphanage with relatives willing to give them shelter took flight, fearing they would contract the disease, which left only girls with no family members to shelter them in the home, "and some of them were plotting to get away," Smith noted. "The eldest girl got someone to write to her friends to come and take her quickly lest she should take the disease and die."[64]

Some girls may have made it through the trial period and epidemic scares only to be expelled later on. A report nearly two decades later (1927) notes that of the three girls who had left the orphanage that year, "one was of age" and ready to move on, but "the other two were dismissed for bad conduct."[65] The missionaries do not elaborate on what constituted "bad conduct" beyond inappropriate speech, actions, and insubordination, but they had little tolerance for girls whose behavior did not match their expectations and did not hesitate in expelling them.

Other girls were extracted from the Fowler Orphanage by family members. Many Egyptians were aware of the missionaries' agenda, or became aware once they saw the socialization of the children, and moved to extract a daughter before conversion could be accomplished. Smith noted in 1910 that three girls had been withdrawn, among them "a dear little ten-year-old Mohammedan . . . stolen by her father and married soon after because he feared she might become a Christian" and "a Jewess . . . taken away recently—being stolen by her mother, also on account of the religion of Jesus."[66] Others were concerned with their daughters' marriage prospects. One father wanted to withdraw his ten-year-old daughter to arrange her marriage, but Smith apparently "spoke to him so sternly that he put off the wedding for two years."[67] Under Islamic law, there was no minimum age for marriage; but the courts started setting a minimum age for the consummation of marriage (twelve) and the registration of marriage (sixteen) in the 1920s and 1930s.[68]

Roughly a quarter to a third of the girls admitted to the Fowler Orphanage left prematurely, expelled or pulled out by relatives, though it is not clear if these relatives were parents, aunts and uncles, or grandparents. Of the twenty-three girls admitted to the orphanage in its first year, six returned to their families, which left seventeen.[69] Six months later, after the home had admitted a total of thirty-nine girls, only twenty-three remained.[70] With the exception of vacation visits to relatives, the missionaries strove to keep the girls in the home until the end of their schooling in order to get a return on their investment—the costs of raising them—in the form of conversion and service to the mission.

Eye on the Prize: Counting Converts

"One of the Moslem girls is very eager to be baptized, and Miss Smith says that she feels that this girl is a real Christian, although when she entered she was one of the worst characters in the orphanage," one of the missionaries wrote in the annual report of 1907–8. Smith had spoken with the girl, who "after having committed sin, at different times," had approached her in earnest "and requested her to pray with her."[71] "Winning a soul for Christ," Smith celebrated a moment that had been long in the making in the new orphanage.

The minutes of the Egyptian Missionary Association and annual reports of the American Mission carefully note the religious backgrounds of the girls in the orphanage. The evangelicals kept precise statistics on the religious identities of the girls in order to document religious transformations and to laud their achievements. The twenty-three girls in the home in July 1907 included ten Orthodox Copts, four Muslims, three Roman Catholics, three Greek Catholics, and three Protestants.[72] In subsequent years, the reports mention Syrian Catholics, Orthodox Armenians, and Jews among the residents. The number of Muslim girls at the orphanage, while never a majority, grew over time. In 1923, fifteen of fifty-one girls or 29 percent were Muslim; by 1930, twenty of fifty-seven or 35 percent were Muslim.[73]

When enumerating those served by the broad range of mission institutions, American missionaries typically emphasized Muslims, as they were the most prized converts. Yet there were obstacles to converting them: in 1908, two years after the orphanage opened, Smith recorded, "There are now fourteen Church members besides two Moslem girls who were examined and would have been baptized if there were religious freedom; but as there is no such freedom they were asked to wait until they are older."[74] The next year, Smith announced that all six of the "Mohammedan girls" had asked for baptism, but reported that they required further instruction before they could be baptized. Of the more senior girls, all had joined the church, "except the two Mohammedans, who will wait until they are older as there is no religious freedom in this land."[75] Under Egyptian law, the girls had to wait at least until they were eighteen, the age of majority in civil law, to convert.

Freedom of religion meant different things to evangelicals and Egyptian Muslims. To missionaries, freedom of religion meant the freedom to choose and to change their religion. To Muslims, it meant freedom of religious minorities to practice their religion and of the majority to protect their own, particularly the young and vulnerable, from proselytizing. Evangelicals occasionally pointed to the threat of death under Islamic law as an impediment to conversion of Muslims, noting in one case that the friends of a Muslim girl "threatened to kill her if she became a Christian."[76] Yet the stiffest penalty—death for an apostate—was not applied in Egypt after the Tanzimat reforms of the mid-nineteenth century (at least not by authorities; a few deaths occurred under suspicious circumstances). Still, Islamic law did not permit apostasy at any age and did not accept conversion into the faith before puberty; children were seen to be unprepared to make such a weighty decision.[77]

The Egyptian Constitution of 1923 broadly protected freedom of religion without spelling out exactly what this meant. Missionaries, who construed religious freedom to mean the freedom to change religion, complained about a lack of it, including the lack of freedom to convert protégés who had not yet reached the age of majority. Egyptian Muslims, on the other hand, seeing religious freedom as the right to protect their religion, bemoaned the fact that they could not effectively block missionary inroads. The number of underage girls who converted seemed to rise in the late 1920s, as the missionaries became bolder in baptizing them. "Nine of our girls united with the church this year," reported the head of the Fowler Orphanage in 1926. "Five of our Muslim girls have confessed Christ before teachers and girls. Three of them are asking to be baptized. One is preparing to be a Bible woman."[78] In both 1928 and 1929, two girls were baptized,[79] and in 1930, three more were baptized, "and two others are asking for baptism."[80]

Before being baptized, girls who wanted to join the church had to prove the strength of their commitment and depth of spiritual knowledge. The report for 1927 observed that seven girls wanted to join the church, "but we feel they should give more evidence of being born again before presenting them."[81] Part of the hesitancy was a desire to ensure that the girls were converting out of faith and not just for the practical rewards, including higher status within the orphanage family, privileges of membership in the local church, and access to mission jobs. The last would have been quite important for many. Na'ima, for example, one of the first Muslim converts in the home, supported herself and her blind mother, with whom she had lived in a room on the orphanage roof, after becoming a successful Bible teacher.[82] Another convert, Wajida, became a mission school teacher after graduating from the Pressly Memorial Institute in Asyut in June 1933. Many others went on to work for the mission.[83]

The Egypt General Mission offered sanctuary to female Muslim converts to Christianity at a home for Muslim girls and women established near the Zaytun headquarters in 1918. Many converts, who came under pressure from locals, sought respite and community there. The home had various names over time, one of which was the Matariyya Home of Safety and Peace.[84] After her baptism, Faʻiza, a convert who had been at the Fowler Orphanage from the age of five, took refuge in the home, where she made the decision to attend the Tanta Bible School to become a Bible woman.[85]

The upsurge in conversions in the late 1920s and early 1930s reflected the coming of age of a cohort of girls for whom the orphanage was probably the home they knew best. It came at a time when the American Mission in Egypt had begun to scale back in size in the face of the Great Depression and had undergone a change in thinking about the goals of foreign mission. Due to the decrease in resources and support from the folks back home, American missionaries in the field seemed to have become more aggressive in their tactics, wanting to prove to donors that they were successfully saving souls.

Years of Service: Teachers, Nurses, and Bible Women

As the Presbyterian evangelical Ellen Barnes drew close to her retirement, she provided an accounting of the girls who had passed through the Fowler Orphanage during its first thirty years: "about two hundred girls have found a truly Christian home and a training which has resulted in many of these girls going out into various lines of Christian service."[86] The report details the professions, years of service, and marital status of sixty-nine of those who went through the home: forty-one teachers in Christian schools; twenty-six in home work; seventeen as Bible women; and sixteen maids or nurses in hospitals. (The numbers do not add up, as one board member who tried to verify the results found, for some of the graduates took on more than one profession.) Collectively, the girls gave over 440 years of mission service, which evangelicals added up and considered an excellent return on the initial investment in raising them.[87]

"I felt that I owed it to the memory of dear Miss Smith to show that the daughters of this home which she started in 1906 are showing a willingness to serve," Barnes wrote.[88] Graduates who took up teaching joined the staffs of the American Mission, the Church Mission Society, the Egyptian Mission Society, and the Holland Mission—American, British, and Dutch outfits. A few drifted toward "evangelical schools," such as the Swedish Salaam Mission in Port Said, where a graduate named Lily took up a post. Several alumnae served as nurses or in other capacities at American Mission strongholds in Tanta, Asyut, and al-Fayyum. Others found employment in Coptic schools and hospitals, and two left the country altogether: a girl named Adelle worked in the Beirut Mission Hospital and ended up in Palestine.[89]

Bible reading proved a popular profession for graduates of the orphanage, with seventeen of the Fowler Orphanage girls taking up Bible work, giving 119 years of total service.[90] They may have been steered toward this profession after a missionary policy paper in 1912 argued for expanding what was dubbed in evangelical circles "women's work for women." Entering the homes of Muslim women to evangelize was considered central to the mission's strategy for spreading Christianity in the Nile Valley. American women missionaries like Margaret Smith often oversaw teams of Bible women, each of which typically consisted of six full-timers and some older part-timers.[91] Possessing the requisite linguistic skills and cultural knowledge, converts were well suited to become Bible women. Na'ima, the first Muslim to convert in the Fowler Orphanage, entered the home at the age of ten, was baptized as Rose at the age of fifteen, and later took up teaching and Bible work in the Upper Egyptian town of Bani Suwayf.[92]

The work of Bible women took them into Muslim neighborhoods and villages, where in the late 1920s and early 1930s they often became early targets of anti-missionary resentment, as Muslim awareness of missionary agendas spread. Two members of Lucy Lightowler's team of Bible women had started a Sabbath school that drew from forty to fifty women and children weekly to a Muslim village across the Nile from the Delta town of Mansura. In the winter of 1932, the pair "had quite an experience" when on one particular Sabbath, "they were met with a group of children and men armed with sticks and handfuls of mud, and literally driven out of the village."[93] The women retreated, hit with mud but not injured, and Lightowler postponed their work there, though they hoped to renew it.

Most of the Bible women deployed by American missionaries remained faceless and nameless foot soldiers fighting on the frontlines of the evangelical campaign. They were mobilized throughout the country to carry the Bible into homes, hospitals, and clinics, and win the hearts and save the souls of the local inhabitants. Given the importance of Bible women, the American Mission opened up special training schools for them. Two graduates of the Fowler Orphanage—Saniya and Ratiba—took up teaching at the Bible School for a year each and also worked as Bible women for four and five years respectively.[94]

American missionaries prepared the girls in the orphanage for lives in service as teachers, Bible women, nurses, and domestic helpers. Raised by single women and encouraged in turn to serve the mission, only twenty-eight of the sixty-nine graduates had married at the time the mission report appeared in 1937. It is not surprising that of those who married, one took vows with a preacher and another with an evangelist. Although those who married no longer worked in salaried positions for the mission, they could be touted as a success, given their "Christian homes."[95]

Barnes believed the years of service legitimized the funding of the orphanage and the investment in the girls. She took pride in the professions the graduates had taken up. "I may say that we are often troubled by remarks made that we are trying to turn out ONLY teachers and Bible women," Barnes wrote confidentially to a board member. "There seems to be a feeling that orphans should all be servants. One does not wonder at that point of view on the part of Egyptians, but it hurts when it comes from fellow missionaries."[96] The missionaries had expanded the possibilities for orphans raised in the Fowler Orphanage. Still Barnes recognized the anxiety and conflict surrounding them, and asked readers of the report not to publish their names.[97]

The report does not provide information on the other girls, the approximately one hundred and thirty who went through the home but cut their ties, either upon graduating or earlier if they were forced to leave by relatives or orphanage authorities. Nor does the report reveal how their Christian socialization prepared them to live in a predominantly Muslim country outside of missionary circles.[98] Most of the girls disappeared back into the streets of Cairo from which they had come, so it was hard to know what became of them. But occasionally a former resident resurfaced: in early 1933, a girl in the street recognized Jane Smith, a missionary resident of the Fowler Orphanage and the director of a mother-child welfare clinic. "About a month ago we were walking in the street when a girl stopped and spoke," reported Jane Smith. "I recognized her face but had to ask her name." The girl, Safiyya, had spent several years in the orphanage and after graduating had gone back to living with her mother. Smith and her companion accepted Safiyya's invitation to visit her at home some days later. "I was so glad to find her willing and able to read her Bible which she did with us. She still is a Moslem by name but she knows much of the truth."[99]

Jane Smith viewed Safiyya's willingness to read from the Bible as confirmation that she recognized the gospel as a higher truth. For Smith and her fellow American missionaries, there only was one truth, a Protestant one. Having come to Cairo to bear witness to that truth, they counted girls such as Safiyya among their successes, even though she may have seen the Bible as part of a history accepted (and corrected) by Islam and called herself a Muslim. The chance meeting occurred just months before the Turkiyya Hasan affair would force American missionaries to rethink their strategies and the place of Muslim children within their institutions.

In 1922, failing eyesight, age, and exhaustion forced Margaret Smith to hand over the reins of the Fowler Orphanage to Ella Barnes. After stepping down as director, "Maggie" Smith resumed her daily rounds of Bible reading in Harat al-Saka'in. By then nearly blind, the seventy-five-year-old relied upon the guidance of one of the orphans to get around the quarter. In 1931, she celebrated the twenty-fifth anniversary of the orphanage, joining in the prayer, praise, and remembrance of the early years.[100] The next year, at the age of eighty-four, after sixty years in Egypt, Smith resigned active service. Not wanting to become a burden on the missionary community, she returned to the United States, where relatives cared for her in the short period before her death. In the semi-annual gathering of missionaries in Egypt that followed in the summer of 1932, Smith's colleagues recognized her as one who in "distress over and pity for poor neglected children created in her heart a great desire for a home where she could take them in and care for them." They acknowledged that it had taken her many years to realize the dream, but the orphanage remained as "a memorial to her great faith in God," and she left "the indelible impress of her godly life upon many of the girls who were her daughters in this home."[101]

Although the Presbyterian Board of Foreign Missions had initially balked at starting a refuge in Cairo, the Fowler Orphanage became an integral part of the American Mission in Egypt. It enjoyed a wide circle of support, including continuous donations from the Fowler Orphanage Association in Ohio in memory of the Quaker couple who seeded the project, and support from a network of missionaries as well as local Egyptian sources. Even though the number of its alumnae was small—some two hundred girls went through the home in its first thirty years—the orphanage proved to be one of the most successful American Mission institutions in reproducing the mission work force. Roughly a third of the girls who lived in the home provided crucial labor to American Presbyterians in the Nile Valley and to the larger community of Protestants there.

Many of those who walked through the doors of the Fowler Orphanage walked out as converts. Christian conversion came with certain benefits—

higher education and a steady job—but also came at a price—irreparable rifts with friends and relatives. Those who left the orphanage early, whether expelled or taken out, may have had a greater chance of being absorbed back into Egyptian society than those who stayed on longer, under the sway of the Presbyterians. But the days of American missionaries evangelizing and baptizing so freely were numbered, and the passing of Margaret Smith and her good friend Anna Thompson shortly thereafter marked the end of an era. The pair did not live to see a wave of anti-missionary activity crest in response to efforts to convert orphaned and abandoned Muslim children in missionary refuges such as the Fowler Orphanage.

3 SPEAKING IN TONGUES

Pentecostal Revival in Asyut

THE IMPACT OF THE TURKIYYA HASAN AFFAIR was felt almost immediately in Asyut, the capital of Upper Egypt, where by the summer of 1933 the orphanage for boys and girls started by the American missionary Lillian Hunt Trasher (1887–1961) contained over seven hundred children and widows. "I am very much in need of the prayers of all the Lord's children as there is a great stir among all of the Muslims against the missionaries here," Trasher confided to supporters back home. Relaying the version of the incident she had heard, she wrote: "a girl acted naughty and rude to one of the missionaries in the Swedish Orphanage in Port Said. The missionary spanked her; she ran away and went to the police station, saying she [had] been beaten because she refused to become a Christian."[1] Newspapers carrying accounts of the affair spurred investigations of missionary institutions throughout the country, including the Asyut Orphanage.

Unlike the members of the American Mission, who were dispatched by a Presbyterian board, Lillian Trasher had come out to Egypt in 1910 as an unaffiliated evangelical. Within months of her arrival, she launched the faith-based Asyut Orphanage, which she moved across the river to Abnub when it ran out of space. The enterprise eventually grew into a village with its own schools and dormitories, as well as a church, clinic, bakery, dairy, and even swimming pool; its scale far eclipsed the Fowler Orphanage and similar institutions. At its peak, the Asyut Orphanage sheltered 1,400 children and widows, with roughly eight thousand orphans passing through its doors in its first fifty years.

As a young woman, Lillian Trasher had been attracted to the nascent Pentecostal movement, whose practices included faith healing, speaking in tongues, and a vibrant, emotional style of worship. She was among the first Pentecostal evangelicals in Egypt, who, unfettered by a foreign mission board or home church and protected by the British occupation, had great freedom to improvise. In exercising this freedom they often acted impetuously, at least in the eyes of the Egyptian population and, often enough, in the eyes of British colonial officials and the more measured Presbyterian missionaries. Yet they also often impressed locals with the scope of their projects and won support. Trasher's Asyut Orphanage became the centerpiece of the Pentecostal mission in Egypt, producing many of its preachers, leaders, and converts. The enormous size of the undertaking gave Trasher a special status among Egyptians that helped her weather regime changes and ride out political storms.

The story of Trasher's success has made her, to this day, one of the most recognized Pentecostal missionaries worldwide and an iconic figure of the Assemblies of God Church, with which she became affiliated nearly a decade after starting the orphanage in Asyut. Her supporters followed the events of her life abroad and the growth of the home through letters, magazine features, biographies, and the movie *The Nile Mother*.[2] These depict her as a larger-than-life figure, one whose work testifies to the power of faith. Among other factors in her mission's success were the generous support of the local Coptic community, the work of widows in the orphanage, and the spirit of the children who found refuge there, some of whom became caught up in raucous revivals in the late 1920s and early 1930s.

A Calling and a Cause: Asyut's Orphans

Born in 1887 in Jacksonville, Florida, Lillian Trasher was raised in Georgia and reportedly did not see a Bible until age sixteen, when friends of the family sparked her interest in Christianity. She attended Bible school in South Carolina and then worked in a faith-based Pentecostal orphanage in Marion, North Carolina, where she learned to care for infants and children. After hearing the lecture of a female missionary who had worked in India, she felt called to Africa and broke off her marital engagement. In a chance meeting with G. S. Brelsford, one of the first Pentecostal missionaries in Egypt, she was invited to join him and his wife in their mission home in Asyut. Accompanied by her sister, Jennie Benton, Trasher set out at the age of twenty-two for Upper Egypt.

Within months of her arrival, an Egyptian knocked on the Pentecostal mission door calling Trasher to the side of a dying woman. It is quite likely that the locals hoped she would bring medicine to revive the young mother, something that the Presbyterians who had started a hospital in Asyut might have done. But faith-healing Pentecostals had only prayers to offer, and upon the woman's death, her family entrusted Trasher with the baby. Back in the mission house, Trasher's hosts soon lost patience with the infant's crying. Rather than return the baby to its family, as the Brelsfords suggested, Trasher decided to found a refuge for abandoned and orphaned children. To fund her home she relied upon the generosity of local Christians, whose conversions—or "accessions"—from Orthodoxy to Evangelism reflected half a century of Presbyterian evangelizing in the region.[3]

The American Mission had established a base in Asyut in the mid-nineteenth century in the hope of reforming religious practice and attracting local Copts, and the emerging landed elite proved receptive to its message. Hanna Wissa, a scion of a notable Coptic family, relates in his family memoir that his paternal grandfather, Hanna Buktur Wissa, left the Coptic Orthodox Church in 1865 after a confrontation with the Bishop of Asyut, and that his maternal grandfather, Akhtukh Fanus, converted to Protestantism while attending the Syrian Protestant College (which later became the American University of Beirut).[4] Whether out of a desire to reform the church, to challenge the Coptic Orthodox hierarchy, and/or to gain access to Western education and culture, a small but significant number of Asyut's elites became Protestants and in time members of the Evangelical Church (the name of the Egyptian Presbyterian church). The new Protestant converts helped finance missionary institutions that served the community: the Khayyats funded a girls' school and the Wissas supported a boys' school. The Wissas also financed the building of the first Evangelical church in Asyut, which was dedicated in 1870, and the building of a larger church when that one grew too small.[5]

Although Protestant missionaries tended to share family resemblances, there were important geographic and class distinctions as well as gendered ones. The Presbyterians hailed from Pennsylvania, Ohio, and the northern Midwest; the Pentecostals generally came from the American South or West. The better-educated Presbyterians sought out converts from wealthier backgrounds; the Pentecostals were populists who focused on the poor. The two groups also had differing notions of gender roles in church and society: Pentecostal women could preach, if they felt "chosen" to do so; Presbyterian women never preached. The proliferation of Protestant missionaries of different denominations inevitably generated some competition. "One of the weaknesses of the Protestant movement in Egypt," noted Hanna Wissa, "was that there were many different Protestant missions trying to do the same thing. They stepped on each other's toes and there were sometimes petty misunderstandings among themselves."[6]

By the time Trasher arrived on the scene in Asyut in 1910, a vibrant Protestant community was thriving. Local members of the community quickly became her main patrons, for she identified a need that was not being addressed in the region. Preachers and schools were plentiful, but no refuge for orphaned and abandoned children existed in the city or its environs. The Presbyterians, who relied on approvals and instructions from a board back home, generally established self-sustaining and money-making operations that could charge fees. Since orphans could not pay fees, they were wary of starting homes for them, as demonstrated by the many years it took to found the Fowler Orphanage. Pentecostals like Trasher, by contrast, came to Egypt "on faith," expecting to raise money from local and global Protestant networks alike.

Taking the first baby entrusted to her as a sign, Trasher rented a house in February 1911 for $12.50 a month and started a home for orphans, calling it the Malja' al-Aytam al-Khayri bi-Asyut (Charitable Refuge for Orphans in Asyut) or simply the Asyut Orphanage. To her surprise, the home did not fill quickly. She took in a few children, "but at first it was very hard to get them."[7] A missionary orphanage may have seemed a strange institution to Upper Egyptians, who were used to taking care of their own family members or arranging informal or secret adoptions. Trasher thought that another reason for the resistance to sending orphans to the Asyut home was the suspicion that she planned to enslave her charges and/or take them to America, a sentiment that could have stemmed from Asyut's historical role as a major depot in the slave trade—a destination for slave caravans on the "forty days road" from Darfur and Kordofan in the Sudan—as well as the American history of slavery.[8]

The Asyut Orphanage's first year was a rocky one, hitting its nadir when a child who entered the home was discovered to have bubonic plague. Authorities closed down the refuge, and Trasher, who had become ill, traveled to the United States to convalesce. There, once she had recovered, she took advantage of being back to become an ordained evangelist in North Carolina.[9] She returned to Egypt reinvigorated, and the orphanage population quickly grew. "Every week I have to turn away four or five little ignorant children from lack of space who might be taught and led to Christ," Trasher agonized to readers of the Pentecostal periodical *Word and Witness* in 1913.[10] By then she had fifty children under her care, and a staff that included Sarah Smith, an older missionary from Indianapolis, and a Turkish woman who taught rug-making.[11]

With space tight, Trasher moved the home out of the city in 1915, building a new structure across the Nile in Abnub on a half acre that Balsam Wissa, Hanna's grandmother, sold her at the generous price of $250. Balsam Wissa, who had been one of the first students in the girls' school of the American Mission, was enthusiastic about moving and expanding the orphanage and arranged for a title transfer within the family for the purpose of the sale.[12] With a base on the east side of the river, the orphanage had room to grow, and the orphans were removed from the center of town and the public eye.

Tumultuous Times: World War I and the 1919 Revolution

Trasher moved the orphanage in the midst of a war that changed Egypt's political status. In August 1914, the British severed Egypt's ties to the Ottoman Empire, which had allied with Germany, fearing Egyptians would rally to the side of their Ottoman co-religionists. They replaced Khedive 'Abbas Hilmi II, who was summering in Istanbul, with Husayn Kamil, naming him sultan. Fearing rebellion and needing material support, they sent dissident Egyptian notables to their country estates, pressed peasants into service in the military labor corps, and requisitioned farm animals and hay for transport and feed.

In the midst of a war pitting an occupying Christian power against a Muslim empire to which many Egyptians still felt loyal, anti-colonial sentiment escalated and missionaries became a target of protests. They seemed to provoke it as well. Florence Bush, an American Pentecostal missionary who had fled Ottoman Jerusalem, tried to continue her evangelical work in the Delta town of Tanta and encountered stiff resistance. "It was necessary for us to have a soldier in all of our meetings as the Moslems stone us and try to break the windows while the services are being held and also through the day," she reported in April 1915.[13] That the British deployed soldiers in wartime for the protection of Pentecostals suggests that this show of force was critical to the larger imperial project.

Pentecostal missionaries in the capital aroused similar hostility. "We were stoned out of our Mission and had to move to another place," wrote C. W. Doney, the head of Pentecostal operations in Cairo. "Stones larger than a man's head were thrown with great violence from high buildings and came crashing through our roof."[14] Yet the missionaries continued preaching, trying to spread their gospel message. They simply did not understand or care to understand the depth of the antagonism that many locals felt toward the British for the occupation and the military campaigns against the Ottomans as well as toward foreign missionaries for their brazen efforts to proselytize. Pentecostals seemed especially vulnerable when their evangelical activities were not offset by medical, educational, or social welfare services. Almost all of the American Pentecostals were eventually evacuated from Egypt during the war, leaving the nine or ten stations they had built in the hands of local converts.[15]

Trasher's work with orphans away from the public eye kept her under the radar. Of the loosely knit American Pentecostals, only Trasher remained in Egypt for the duration of the war, running the Asyut Orphanage with a staff that included the matron, Shakir Jad Allah, and two other Egyptian women. Feeding a growing group of children at a time when prices were spiking challenged Trasher's resourcefulness. After the May wheat harvest, when peasants still had funds and food, she rode out to villages on a donkey, staying in police stations and soliciting donations for the children.[16] Trasher gained the peasants' trust, along with donations, showing a willingness on the part of locals to give to the poorest of the poor. Her meanderings in the Egyptian countryside made her a familiar figure—the "lady on a donkey"—and village mayors who met her later sent orphans to her.

The war created dislocations and deaths that doubled the numbers in the orphanage from roughly fifty to one hundred children. To accommodate the new residents, the older boys in the home built additional rooms, baking and laying bricks in a process that was repeated regularly over the years. At the end of the war, an influenza epidemic that created more orphans further increased the numbers in the home. "We are glad to be able to accept the most needy cases," Trasher reported in early 1919 in the *Latter Rain Evangel*, "and have had to enlarge our house, adding four new rooms which are about filled."[17]

As the war wound down, Egyptian nationalists sought a place at the table in the Paris peace talks. Having remained quiet during the hostilities in spite of resentment at forced contributions to the British war effort, they thought that they had earned the right to independence. But the British turned down the request by a *wafd* (delegation) of nationalist leaders to attend the international talks, preferring to discuss Egypt's fate with a hand-picked government in bilateral negotiations. The nationalist leaders mobilized support with speeches and petitions, and the British responded by arresting the delegation's leaders, which in turn provoked massive demonstrations in Cairo. Some of Trasher's most loyal supporters—women such as Esther Fahmi Wissa—were among those who rushed to the capital to protest British colonial actions.[18]

The revolution quickly spread to Asyut, where students, workers, lawyers, and others staged peaceful protests. Fearing the worst, foreigners in the provincial capital took refuge in a Presbyterian mission school. However, Trasher refused to leave Abnub and her charges to join them. With communication to Cairo severed and banks limiting access to funds, Trasher and the head matron, "Auntie" Zakiyya, sent children with family in Asyut and nearby villages to their relatives. Those who had no place to go remained at the orphanage, which came under attack by Bedouin looters. In describing events, Trasher saw a divine hand protecting her and the children, but also acknowledged the importance of the intervention by Egyptian neighbors, who dissuaded the attackers from hurting the orphans and the lady who took care of them.[19]

Meanwhile, events in town turned violent when protesters set fire to the massive piles of hay that the British had requisitioned from the countryside. Demonstrators next attacked the police station, confiscating arms and engaging British troops in pitched battles. The British rushed reinforcements up the Nile and used their air advantage to bomb and destroy pockets of resistance, including the little village of Waladiyya, which sat on the western edge of the river between the orphanage and Asyut.[20] After British reinforcements reached the orphanage, they moved the boys into an American Mission school in town and the girls and babies into the American Mission hospital. Trasher was forced to leave the evacuated children in Zakiyya's charge and join the stream of foreigners sent to Cairo. She was therefore not on hand to see the British charging the commissioner of Asyut, Muhammad Kamil Muhammad, with inciting attacks and supplying the rebels with arms. Although he asserted in his defense that he had been told by the head of the police not to resist when a crowd of demonstrators attacked the district office, the military tribunal sentenced him to death by firing squad.[21] The revolt in Asyut had been suppressed, punishments meted out, and imperial order restored.

Faced with a forced separation from the orphanage, Trasher decided to visit the United States. During her first leave in seven years, she registered as an evangelist of the Assemblies of God Church, which had not existed when she first set off for Egypt, and she set up a partnership with its Division of Foreign Missions. She also went on a speaking tour to raise funds, telling her audiences about the perils the orphanage had faced during the revolution.[22]

Building (a) Trust: Communal Support for the Home

In the wake of the 1919 Revolution, Egyptians argued that they needed to establish their own national institutions to care for orphans and abandoned children rather than leave this to foreigners. Leading by example, social reformers such as Labiba Ahmad launched new homes in Cairo and Alexandria.[23] But Asyut remained underserved, and when Trasher returned there in February 1920, she found little competition in the region from social reformers or other missionaries. Rather than continue to refuse children entry, she decided to expand the home once again. A gift in 1921 of $1,500 from Sultan (later King) Fu'ad (r. 1917–36) after a visit to the orphanage helped make this enlargement possible.[24] His visit to the orphanage was one in a series of visits by Egyptian and foreign royals and notables, who sought to demonstrate their benevolence and enhance their prestige through charitable giving; few looked at the social and economic problems that fueled the need for the orphanage or were involved with the quotidian operation of the enterprise.

The local elite took a more active role in funding, fixing, and expanding the orphanage, reassured that they were giving to an institution that would serve Upper Egypt for the long term. Their enthusiasm for the enterprise sprang from the good will Trasher had earned and the way she established the legal basis of the refuge. Balsam Wissa's brothers—Zaki and George—teamed up in 1922 with Amin Khayyat and Bushra Hanna to buy over two acres for the equivalent of $2,625 for the orphanage, and equipped the land with water and electricity at the added cost of about $1,000.[25] Four years later, in 1926, Trasher went to the Shari'a Court of Asyut to establish a *waqf* (trust) for the lands and buildings of the Asyut Orphanage. "All those who have helped buy the land are absolutely satisfied, now that the land is made over 'Wafk' [sic]," she explained, "as I myself can never sell it."[26] Her strategy contrasted with the practice of the American Mission, which had the power to dispose of property accumulated in its own name, and in this way Trasher encouraged further donations. In 1928, two years after she set up the trust, Amin's older sister, Amina Khayyat, donated $3,100 to cover the sale of two and a half additional acres. Trasher, who remained head of the trust as long as she lived, appointed a committee of interrelated Wissas, Khayyats, and Alexans, along with her sister Jennie, to administer the trust after her death.[27]

The Asyut Orphanage was located next to the Nile Sporting Club, the playground of the local elite. Members of the same families who sold or donated land to Trasher for the orphanage had built the club, where they played tennis and golf, and they regularly left donations for the orphanage in a box that Trasher periodically emptied.[28] Their support took other forms, too: women such as Lily (Alexan) Khayyat and Esther Wissa took out subscriptions, started sewing circles, and sent gifts of wheat, beef, cooked meals, cotton, and cloth to the home. In addition, they celebrated major life events such as births and weddings with donations to the orphanage.

Elite Coptic women took care of Lillian Trasher, too, making sure that she had whatever she needed, along with some extras. Adopting her as one of their own, they invited her to meals, took her on outings, and sent her new dresses. "They feel they have a real personal interest in the work," Trasher told supporters, for "they realize that I have given my life for their children and show their appreciation in many ways."[29] By the late 1920s, her days of riding out to villages on a donkey to collect donations were over. She had become an iconic fixture in Upper Egypt, remembered in the Coptic community as a "remarkable lady," in the words of Hanna Wissa, who visited his grandparents in Asyut each summer.[30]

Support for feeding a constantly growing brood of children and funding expansions extended beyond the Coptic elite. It also came from middle strata merchants, poor workers, and rugged peasants, who gave sums of money and gifts in kind to the orphanage. Such gifts ranged from free taxi rides for the children to stocks of soap or food staples. Trasher's letters abound with stories of local generosity, often from people of modest appearance and humble origins, whose bills may have been wrinkled but whose donations came from the heart. Indeed, she was often most grateful for these gifts, which she wrote were delivered at just the right moment and matched a particular need, affirming the power of faith for her and her supporters. The community valued Trasher's commitment to caring for orphaned and abandoned children and supported the home, for it provided a service that locals had been unable or unwilling to provide.

"Mama" Trasher: Taking in Those in Need

Trasher's institution welcomed all children, regardless of their backgrounds. "You cannot imagine how I feel when I have to refuse some. I just know that no one else will take them or ever give them a chance," she lamented. "There are no other orphanages within hundreds of miles from here and the other orphanages in Cairo and Alexandria will not take in new ones until some of the older ones leave."[31] Residents of Upper Egypt turned to the orphanage to raise those for whom family and communal safety nets had failed. The orphanage accepted boys under ten and girls under twelve, charging no admission fees. Trasher explained that the home required relatives "to sign a paper that they give the children to us until they are eighteen years old," which granted the orphanage legal custody of the children and at the same time discouraged relatives from retrieving them before the work of the missionaries had been completed.[32] Trasher wanted the children for as long as possible—at least six years with girls and eight with boys—in order to be able to complete the transformations of body and soul she envisioned, making of them Pentecostals.

Fathers brought in babies after their wives had died in childbirth or from complications afterward. Many of the infants deposited at the orphanage were thus not legally orphaned but rather the offspring of men who had insufficient knowledge, will, or means to raise children on their own. "I received a new baby girl last night three months old, whose mother is dead and she is nothing but skin and bones," wrote Trasher in 1925.[33] "We got three newborn babies this month; their mothers died when they were born," Trasher reported a few years later.[34] "Yesterday we got nothing at all in the way of money," Trasher noted in 1931, "but the Lord sent us a darling little baby boy three days old. His mother died when he was born."[35] Maternal mortality rates were high at a time when women married young (often as girls) and went through multiple pregnancies, giving birth at home and attended by midwives whose training was often limited to rudimentary pre- and post-natal care. Complications may have arisen during or after delivery from preexisting medical conditions, loss of blood, infections, perforation of the uterus, or issues related to their own earlier circumcisions. Sometimes multiple gestations led to special difficulties, as they increased the risks during pregnancy and in childbirth. "Someone brought us tiny twin babies this morning," Trasher recorded in March 1933. "Poor little things—their mother died when they were born. They look very weak; I am afraid they will not live, but we will do our best."[36]

Infants found abandoned in various locations were also deposited at the Asyut Orphanage, left on the doorsteps, or handed to Trasher. "About two weeks ago I had some one knock at my door about midnight and hand me a wee tiny baby, just a few hours old which they had found in the street," Trasher wrote in 1921. "We had one like this one a little while ago, but its head had been injured when it had been thrown away and it went quite blind and then it died."[37] Due to the circumstances surrounding the abandonment of such infants, the haste with which they were left, and the time that elapsed until they were found, they often arrived at the orphanage in precarious health. "Lageah [Laqiyya], the baby we found on the bridge, died last night," Trasher noted in a diary entry in 1927.[38]

The following year, she described the condition in which an infant found near the railroad track arrived: "They brought me the baby, a little boy, with not even a cloth over him, he was on a saddle pad and an old bran sack, covered with sand and dirt." It was the middle of the winter, and the baby "had been out in that awful cold wind for hours, quite naked, and only a few hours old."[39] Trasher took him in, bathed him repeatedly in pans of hot water, and he survived.

The abandoned infants that ended up in Trasher's orphanage were found by assorted people—one by a carpenter who worked at the American College— who came across them in different locations: in a field, on a bridge, near a railroad track, by the Nile, or on a doorstep. Egyptians often assumed that the act of throwing away an infant was meant to hide an illicit origin, but Trasher never seemed to condemn the mothers. It is, in any case, hard to know exactly why any particular individual newborn was abandoned. In some cases a family may just not have had the resources to feed another mouth. By whatever path foundlings came into her care, Trasher could claim guardianship through the "finders-keepers" clause enacted in a 1912 law.[40]

One of the first things Trasher did when she received abandoned infants was to name them, for they generally came without identification or indication of place of origin or religion. Of the three-month-old who was skin and bones and whose mother had died, "We named her Sophie [Safiyya]."[41] The baby found on the bridge (presumably the one spanning the Nile that linked Abnub to Asyut) was named Laqiyya.[42] The boy found on the railroad track and covered in sand and dirt was named Fahim 'Abd Allah; his surname, "servant of God," was a common one for those whose father was unknown.[43] Other children came with names, such as the three infants—Amina, Ubjy, and Maryam— whose mothers had died in childbirth or shortly thereafter.[44]

Trasher sent the weakest babies to the American Mission hospital in Asyut for immediate care and kept the healthier ones close by, housing them in her own home, where she often became quite attached to them. She supervised the older girls who assisted her in caring for the babies, including those sent back from the hospital in town. When the number of the infants in her home became too high, a separate house was built for them. Rather than rely on wet nurses for breast-feeding the foundlings, Trasher turned to bottle feeding, which was made easier after the American Mission donated Jersey cattle to supply cow's milk for the children.

Some children at the refuge whose fathers had died came to live at the home with their mothers. Trasher explained that "it quite often happens that a child is received with its widowed mother, who earns her support by working in the orphanage," while "the child receives full training along with the others."[45] Roughly ten percent of the population of the orphanage at any given moment consisted of widows who lacked the financial resources or willing relatives to help them raise their offspring. They worked for food and shelter, performing menial tasks such as baking, cleaning, cooking, and doing laundry, and, later, milking the cows. Replacing the servants hired in the orphanage's first years, the widows became an indispensable part of the labor force.

The orphanage provided an alternative to poverty and hunger for widows and their children. This came at a price: the widows were not permitted to care for their own children once they had stopped breast-feeding them. The American Pentecostal missionaries believed, as Florence Christie put it, that the widows "were still too much like the village they had left. The widows brought with them habits of uncleanness, cursing and ignorance," and the missionaries did not want them to socialize their children in peasant ways. Weaned children were separated from their mothers and placed in dormitories, where the older girls, who were "clean and cultured" and had been remade into Americanized Protestants, cared for them.[46] While widows were separated and socially distanced from their children, they at least maintained some physical proximity to them. Single mothers who felt forced by social circumstances to abandon their children at birth (or married ones forced to do so by economic exigencies) lost all connection. As Trasher became "Mama Lillian" to these children and the other missionaries or local workers became "aunts," their birth mothers (if they were still alive) no doubt experienced a profound sense of loss.

A few unwed mothers who would not or could not abandon their newborn infants also found refuge in the orphanage along with their offspring. British officials in Cairo asked Trasher to give safe haven to one such "fallen girl" (and her child) who had lived through harrowing circumstances. The girl's father and brother had killed her boyfriend, for which they had been tried and executed, and now her mother and younger brother threatened to kill her in order to save the family's "honor," according to what Trasher had been told. "We should be very grateful if you could see your way to admitting this girl to your home," the authorities had written Trasher, hoping "to give her a chance to lead a decent life and avoid the risk of assassination by her family." At a time when it was nearly impossible for an unwed mother to raise her child in Egypt, Trasher accepted the young woman and infant into the home, pointing out that they were not the first such pair to take refuge there: "Others have come like this and have been wonderfully saved."[47] By "saved," of course, she meant both physically and spiritually. Some women came with their children when their husbands became disabled: the husband of one mother of three became mentally ill and was placed in the asylum. Several Coptic women came when their husbands converted to Islam and were readily accepted because the missionaries shared their concern that the children would be brought up as Muslims.[48]

Those with physical disabilities, whether from birth, accidents, or illnesses, also found refuge in the orphanage. This group included a relatively large number of blind girls (but not boys, for whom there were other facilities in Egypt) and a much smaller circle of children of lepers, whose pariah status made it close to impossible to raise their own children.[49] Some of these children, like those of unwed mothers, would have had few options for integration into Egyptian society outside the orphanage. Whatever their origin or condition, the residents seemed to find common bonds with others in the home and created their own extended family. This was crucially important in a society that stressed family ties and genealogies above all else.

Trasher presided as head of this large family, maintaining strict gender segregation. Boys and girls lived in separate dormitories, attended different schools, and sat apart in church and the dining halls. Only siblings were allowed to socialize across gender boundaries. All the children in the home worked, with the orphanage reinforcing a gendered division of labor. Boys were taught artisan skills such as carpentry and chair-making, and girls were trained in domestic arts such as infant care and sewing. Both had farming tasks, with girls feeding chickens and collecting eggs and boys working with barn animals. The boys attended primary and secondary schools at the orphanage; if they were thought to have aptitude, they could continue on to college. They took up the trades into which they had been apprenticed or became teachers, clerks, and pastors. The girls attended a general school in preparation for marriage. Even if they excelled in their studies, they were not offered the option of higher education or the option was made so difficult as to be nearly impossible. In this Trasher diverged from women's advocates in Egypt who supported legal, medical, and educational careers for women. Trasher also made it clear (as Ellen Barnes had as head of the Fowler Orphanage) that her girls were not hired out as domestic servants, which would have hurt their chances of marrying.

Most girls from the orphanage ended up marrying one of the boys from the home, with Trasher being the final arbiter on the suitability of the pair. An older boy would approach Trasher as he prepared to leave the orphanage to ask permission to wed one of the girls. He could not date or court the girl but they could meet in Trasher's presence. At a time when Egyptian women's rights advocates were challenging such conventions, the rules may have seemed overly harsh and may have been broken. Unlike the Fowler Orphanage, which raised female orphans to become Bible readers, teachers, nurses, and the like, the Asyut Orphanage churned out married women, sending them back into Egyptian society. All of their training was geared in this direction. Girls who did not marry stayed on at the orphanage as workers. And the blind girls, whom Trasher blocked from marrying, stayed on too. The only exception were a rare few who felt "called" and were allowed to join female American missionaries in their work outside the orphanage.[50]

"Baptized in the Holy Spirit": Revival on the Nile

Trasher opened the doors of the orphanage wide: "I take into my orphanage Mohammedans, Syrians, Catholics—anyone. My work is not denominational, although I myself am Pentecostal," she explained in 1919.[51] Under the terms of the charitable trust that was executed in 1926, the orphanage was established "as a home for the training and education of poor orphans, of any religion and of any denomination." As a Christian missionary she saw religion not as an inheritance but as a matter of faith that could be cultivated and changed. She was in Egypt for exactly this purpose: to instill her faith, which she experienced daily, in others. The trust stipulated that Christian children were to be "instructed in the teachings of the Assemblies of God," the church with which Lillian had become affiliated in 1919, and that Muslim children were to be trained in Islam.[52] The children learned English and listened to hymns on the gramophone such as "Onward, Christian Soldiers!," "We Are Going Down the Valley," and "Joy to the World."[53] But there is no mention in Trasher's letters that the roughly ten percent of Muslim children who were in the home ever went to a mosque or that an imam ever came to the home to instruct them.

Trasher propagated a fundamentalist version of Christianity, stressing American values and culture. In 1926, a decade and a half after its opening, the Asyut Orphanage experienced its first revival, which Trasher described to supporters back home: "After crying and praying like the sound of many waters, they [the children] began to testify." She pointed in particular to the involvement of Muslim children, attuned as she was to the importance of their testimonies of Christian belief. "One little Mohammedan boy got up on top of the bench and testified saying, 'In my village I was a sinner but now

God has saved me and if I was cut in little pieces I would not serve idols.'"[54] The boy had clearly absorbed Pentecostal forms of practice as well as a Protestant critique of icons.

Conversion in the Asyut Orphanage bore little resemblance to that in the American Mission's Fowler Orphanage. Presbyterians examined those seeking baptism closely, impressing upon them the need for further instruction; the girls had to demonstrate their piety, commitment, and knowledge over time before being admitted into the church. The Pentecostals, on the other hand, stressed religious experience—speaking in tongues, faith healing, and prophesying—and baptism came as part of a religious experience that was a much more spontaneous and raucous affair than that in the Presbyterian home. "Souls are being saved and others baptized in the Holy Spirit," a thrilled Trasher wrote.[55]

The movement grew, and a year later, after seventeen "dry" years, Trasher began to "harvest" the fruits of her work. "Today I witnessed the greatest revival I have ever seen in my life," she wrote on April 7, 1927. Three days earlier the missionaries started a revival meeting among the children. "The Spirit was with us from the very first meeting, dozens getting saved and dozens seeking the baptism of the Holy Spirit," Trasher enthused, noting, "the most wonderful sight I ever saw in my life was when I followed the noise up to the housetop. There were dozens and dozens of little girls shouting, crying, talking in tongues, rejoicing, preaching, singing—well, just everything you can think of—praising God!" Yet there was more: "Several of the children saw visions," Trasher reported.[56]

"The power of God is just sweeping the Orphanage like a mighty flood," Trasher wrote two days later. "Hundreds of the children are on their faces screaming out to God for mercy, some shouting for joy and rejoicing in the marvelous, new found blessing, others talking in tongues, others standing on top of the tables, preaching, still others seeking the baptism." Trasher pointed to her first real "harvest" with great pride, noting that it had even included the Muslims in the orphanage: "Just now a little Mohammedan girl is downstairs preaching to a little cripple girl; no one is tired though they have prayed and prayed for hours."[57]

The revival spread from the girls, to the widows, to the boys, and to the older boys in town who came back to the home to participate. When word about the revival got out, H. E. Randall, a Pentecostal pastor visiting Egypt, traveled to the Asyut Orphanage to authenticate and sustain it. The revival was still reverberating in the home, with children in trances and ecstasies, having completely stepped outside of quotidian routines and time. According to Randall, there was no count of how many had been "born again," though he observed that fifty had received "the Baptism with the Holy Spirit with the sign of speaking in other tongues."[58]

If a Pentecostal revival on the outskirts of Asyut in the 1920s sounds strange, to Trasher it was perfectly natural, a validation of her mission in Egypt and her years of labor. Preparatory work at the orphanage—Bible instruction, singing, praying, modeling piety, and instilling lessons about Pentecostalism—had set the stage. By the 1920s, the children and adults in the home knew what a revival entailed, and once it had started, they joined in. The timing of the revival coincided with a spike in aggressive proselytizing by missionaries elsewhere in Egypt. By the late 1920s, many evangelicals faced cutbacks in resources due to waning interest in foreign mission on the part of mainline Protestants and the looming worldwide depression, which led to bold improvisation and a push to produce greater results. For Trasher, the first harvests proved fruitful: the spirit of revival spread as her graduates carried the spark to villages and towns around Asyut, evangelizing and assisting in Assemblies of God missions, and these students later started schools and churches, and staffed missions around the country.

Lillian Trasher chose the most marginal of people for her mission—orphaned, abandoned, and disabled boys and girls—those who lacked close kin in a society that favored familial bonds above all others.[59] Children arrived at the orphanage through different paths: some came after the death of one or both parents, others after being found abandoned, and a few came with special needs. The children in the home worked hard, building new rooms, sewing clothes, cleaning dishes, collecting eggs, and performing innumerable chores to sustain the institution. They also raised one another, with the first generation of girls and boys in turn caring for the next, creating a family. This was crucial for their lives within the orphanage and later in the larger society outside of it.

Local Egyptians of all classes supported Trasher's venture of helping an underserved population, allowing her to carve out a niche in Asyut. She cultivated the support of a Coptic elite that preferred to subcontract the care of orphaned, abandoned, and disabled children, and appealed, too, to supporters in the

United States and elsewhere who saw the mission as an affirmation of Christian faith. Her initial independence from a board or church provided her with broad scope for working with local inhabitants and foreign donors in launching, running, and expanding the home. But ultimately the Asyut Orphanage thrived because people in the region nourished it—wealthy Egyptians provided the land and means to establish a base across the river from Asyut, villagers sent donations, neighbors protected the home, and widows provided labor—and in the process, they reshaped it.

Trasher's orphanage sat at the intersection of imperial and national projects, a busy and sometimes dangerous intersection. British colonial officers protected American Pentecostal missionaries, lending them security, material aid, and assistance. At the same time, the colonial presence generated resentment on the part of the indigenous population, which saw missionary and colonial projects as intimately linked. Trasher, however, had an uncanny ability to navigate the political cross-currents, thus insuring the longevity of her mission. The marginality of orphaned, abandoned, and disabled children, as well as Lillian Trasher's location in Asyut as a Pentecostal woman, served to shelter her undertaking, allowing the orphanage to flourish in unimagined ways.

The home Trasher created provided a haven for large numbers of children who had few alternatives. Yet it was often overcrowded and mixed disciplining measures (e.g., rules about segregation) with undisciplined practices (e.g., revivals). While Trasher sought to "civilize" the offspring of Upper Egyptian peasants and workers, her modernizing agenda had real limits. She propagated a fundamentalist version of Christianity that included speaking in tongues, being baptized in the Holy Spirit, and prophesying. Her vision of gender relations also contradicted the models of modernizing Egyptians. She discouraged secondary or advanced education for the girls in her care and maintained strict gender segregation, policies that contrasted with those of Egyptian social reformers, who pushed for higher education and the integration of men and women.

The force behind the orphanage, Trasher evoked both admiration and fear. One of the missionaries who worked with her confessed: "She possessed a loving, but strong personality, which people sometimes found hard to follow." In addition, she was known to be demanding and difficult to work for, and could be jealous of "her children" giving their attention to others. But she also impressed people with her simple faith.[60] That faith inspired the revivals that continued from the late 1920s into the early 1930s, with Trasher reporting on one in

February 1933.[61] The glow from that revival would be short-lived, however, for in June of that year news of the beating of a Muslim girl in the Swedish Salaam Mission in Port Said reached Asyut. We turn now to the story of that mission and its Home for Destitutes, famous—or infamous—as the site of the Turkiyya Hasan affair.

4 NOTHING LESS THAN A MIRACLE

The Swedish Salaam Mission of Port Said

AMERICAN PROTESTANTS dominated the mission field in Egypt, but they did not monopolize it. Protestants from Europe joined the call to carry Christianity to the Nile Valley, and the Swedish Mission to Mohammedans of Port Said founded by Maria Ericsson in 1911 stands out as one of the most intriguing of these smaller foreign missions.[1] Unlike the American Presbyterian Mission, which targeted Copts in the hope that they would carry the gospel to Muslims, the Swedish Mission specifically sought out Muslims. In spite of Islamic injunctions against apostasy, the Swedes opted for an aggressive approach to winning Muslim adherents. They could do so under the protective umbrella of the British occupation, whose military headquarters in nearby Isma'iliyya provided security. This gave them the liberty to preach and enabled the "miracle" of teaching the Bible in a Muslim city.[2]

The story of the Port Said orphan scandal starts with the religious awakening of Maria Ericsson, the founder of the Swedish Mission. In choosing to respond to a calling, Ericsson, like Margaret Smith and Lillian Trasher, lived out her faith on a daily basis. Ericsson found a partner for this venture in Anna Eklund, a Swedish-speaking Finnish native ten years her junior. Eklund stepped in to run the mission in Ericsson's absences and shouldered a good deal of the work throughout the years. The faith of the two missionaries, and of the other Europeans and Americans who joined them, sustained the pair. At the same time, it blinded them from seeing how their evangelizing unsettled some of the people in whose midst they worked.

Egyptians initially supported the mission, with local Muslims in the Mediterranean port city approaching the two European women to start a school. Parents were desperate to educate their daughters and provide them with opportunities for training and advancement. Girls flocked to the Swedish Mission School, hungry for the tools to live in a modernizing Egypt. Some, like Turkiyya Hasan, stayed because they had no homes of their own to return to, becoming residents at what became the mission's Home for Destitutes.

Maria Ericsson had arrived in Port Said with Anna Eklund with an eye to establishing a faith mission at this crossroads of the world. Port Said gave the Scandinavian missionaries fertile grounds to recruit students and supporters. Benefiting from the benevolence of passengers traveling through the Suez Canal and others, they built a network of social welfare institutions. These included orphanages and schools in several towns and cities, which were staffed by an international band of Protestant evangelicals. Yet they were set in the midst of a mostly Muslim population (proportionally larger than in Upper Egypt, where Lillian Trasher lived). The work of the Swedish Salaam Mission eventually galvanized Islamic activists, who attempted to stop the conversion of children and to dismantle the missionaries' network.

Born Again: Maria Ericsson's Early Years

Born in 1864 into an affluent family at a manor in a province west of Stockholm, Maria Ericsson was a sickly child who found solace in the religious atmosphere at home. In the fall of 1886 at the age of twenty-two, under the influence of the Holiness revival, which sought to renew churches and spread scriptural holiness across borders around the world, she was born again: "One day when the hunger after light and peace had become so intense that it consumed me, I locked myself into my room, determined to wait before God the Father, in Whom I believed, until He would reveal the truth to my thirsty soul." Her quest was answered, "and I had that day a wonderful meeting with the glorified Son of God, and received Him as my Saviour, Healer, Bridegroom and King." A few weeks later, in the midst of singing in the dining room at her home, "I had a most sacred experience and a heavenly vision. The windows of heaven opened unexpectedly and a deluge of God's love and power came over and in me, filling me with heaven's glory and joy so that my body could hardly bear it. . . . from that time I went to all I could reach and spoke to them about my wonderful Saviour."[3]

Maria Ericsson went out two years later, in 1888, to proselytize among Muslims in 'Annaba, Algeria, under the auspices of the North African Mission to Women. That mission was sponsored by the Swedish pioneer of modern pedagogy and social work, Elsa Borg (1826–1909). Having experienced physical healing through prayer, Borg had become active in the Holiness revival movement. Through her influential periodical *Trons Hvila* (Faith's Rest), Borg helped fund and publicize the work of Bible women in Lappland, children's homes, and foreign missionaries, among other projects. The theological underpinnings of the missions she supported were holiness and healing, with social values centering on poor relief, social justice, and women's rights. In 1898 (ten years after Ericsson went out), Borg's North African Mission to Women became part of the Kvinnliga Misjonsarbetare (Female Mission Workers). Headquartered in Sweden, it soon had branches in Norway and Denmark. Its middle- and upper-class members, many of whom were teachers and nurses, emphasized prayer and female community.[4]

Full of faith and eager to carry the gospel to other lands, Ericsson joined a wave of Swedish missionaries who went abroad to Africa and Asia, to countries such as Iran and China (where her two sisters served).[5] Like others, she faced daunting challenges in the field. The fellow missionary with whom she lived suffered from mental instability, which was unknown to the board at home. On top of that, hostility from the local population and harassment from French colonial officials who had little sympathy for Protestant missionaries exacerbated an already difficult situation. Ericsson experienced loneliness and frustration, later recounting, "Only by God's grace was I kept from losing my reason."[6] After three years, she returned home on leave completely worn out; she took a year reprieve and then was sent out again, this time to Bizerta, Tunisia. There she joined a small group of female missionaries whose work included setting up schools, supervising Bible women, and distributing Arabic Bibles, standard fare for a single Protestant woman missionary in the late nineteenth century.[7]

Still, Ericsson seemed to find little satisfaction, recording that "a state of chaos still existed and I had a lurking conviction in my heart that I was not fully in the will of God."[8] Frustrated by the lack of progress in her work and a lack of autonomy, she rebelled against the hierarchical and authoritarian board structure and resigned from the mission when on a furlough in Sweden in 1908. The board, taking Ericsson's separation as a blow, asked her "not to appear in their midst any more," which pained her after twenty years of service: "Leaving the Mission meant leaving everything. I had no support, no friend, no human source from which to expect any comfort or help. I was cut off from my homeland, having no more connection there, nor any in other lands."[9] Ericsson's resolve to strike out independently, to see where God would lead her, was extraordinary amongst the Swedish missionaries, who emphasized female community.[10] But she would not go out completely alone: she would be accompanied by Anna Eklund, a younger missionary who had been with her in Tunisia.[11]

Born in Helsinki, Finland, in 1874, Anna Eklund grew up in the Swedish-speaking southwest part of the country. Like Ericsson, she had experienced sickness as a child that had strengthened her Christian faith. As a young woman, she graduated from a girls' school in Turku, taught Sunday school, and entered a four-year teacher seminary. In response to an appeal for help working among North African Muslims, Eklund set out to join Ericsson in Bizerta, Tunisia, in 1905, sponsored by the Finnish Young Women's Christian Association. On her way out, she attended a Bible course in Freienwald, Germany, base of the German mission's women workers, and in Tunisia, she worked closely with Ericsson. Three years later, she received a letter from Ericsson, who had resigned from the Mission, telling Eklund that God had asked her to start new work. Eklund knew she had to follow her friend.[12]

The pair initially set their sights on Arabia, a far outpost of the Ottoman Empire that was home to Islam's holiest sites. They met up in Vienna, made their way to Istanbul, boarded a boat to Beirut, and then traveled overland to Damascus. But without authorization to work in the highly restricted Arabian peninsula—the few missionaries who gained access to the region generally had medical training—they could go no further. The two evangelists began to rethink their plan and concluded that it might be better to be in a larger community, "where the roads of the world meet up," and where they would find "like-minded people, which will benefit us spiritually and materially."[13] After backtracking to Beirut, they took a ship to Alexandria, arriving only months after another intrepid Protestant woman missionary, Lillian Trasher. Like her, they had set off on faith alone, without the support of a church or board. While Trasher and her sister, Jennie Benton, had headed south, along the Nile, to Asyut, Ericsson and Eklund headed east, along the coast, to Port Said, arriving there in March 1911.[14]

Gateway to the World: Port Said

Ericsson and Eklund landed in a harbor city with a unique maritime character. With the Suez Canal to its east, the Mediterranean Sea to the north, and Lake

Manzala to the south and west, the city was almost an island. Founded as the base of the Suez Canal Company operations in 1859 when digging on the canal had commenced, it was named for the then ruling viceroy, Saʻid. After a decade of digging that took a high toll in lives of Egyptian and foreign laborers, the canal was inaugurated in 1869 with great fanfare under Khedive Ismaʻil. Linking the Mediterranean and Red Seas, the canal significantly shortened travel time between Europe and Asia by eliminating the need to circumnavigate Africa or take an overland route.[15]

The constant flow of international traffic gave Port Said a rich cosmopolitan character and provided the missionaries with plenty of potential donors and visitors, including evangelicals in transit to India. The traffic also fueled an underside to the city, which developed an international reputation for debauchery. The canal was an important link in what was euphemistically called "white slavery": the traffic of women and children from Europe to the East—Egypt, India, and elsewhere—for the sex trade. Some of the girls and women caught up in the trade disembarked in Port Said, taking up residence on streets such as Rue Babel. Egyptian women and girls as young as fifteen (and possibly younger) also took up the trade, working as prostitutes in the native quarter. Foreign and local prostitutes were visited by a range of clientele, including British soldiers stationed nearby to defend the canal.[16]

Ericsson and Eklund found the entrenched British occupation force, which was cognizant of Protestant interest groups back home, preferable to the hostile French colonial authorities they had encountered in Tunisia and Algeria. The British-French imperial rivalry played out in Egypt: Great Britain had long tried to block French schemes for building a canal linking the Red and Mediterranean Seas in Egypt; but once it was built, the British had a vital interest in protecting the main artery to India, their most important imperial possession. Buying canal shares from Khedive Ismaʻil, who was short of capital, the British gained a major presence on the Suez Canal Company Board. They occupied Egypt in 1882 in large part to safeguard the investment and the empire's transit route, landing troops for the conquest in Port Said.

The Swedish missionaries encountered a divided metropolis: an Arab quarter, where mostly Muslim locals lived, and a foreign sector, where mostly European canal administrators, merchants, and religious minorities resided. The architecture around the international sector grew to rival that of Cairo and Alexandria, with public squares filled with busy restaurants and cafes, and department stores, hotels, and villas set among broad boulevards and well-lit streets. In contrast, the Arab quarter contained homes made of shoddy wood construction that had few amenities.[17] Since the missionaries were there to evangelize among the locals, they settled in the vicinity of "Arab town," in a home near the red light district.[18]

Ericsson and Eklund followed in the footsteps of earlier evangelicals who had chosen the global crossroad of Port Said, a "city of sin," as an ideal spot to redeem souls. The Suez Canal Company made establishing missionary institutions easy by ceding free land to religious groups who promised to build orphanages, schools, hospitals, and places of prayer. The company relied on such groups to provide needed social welfare services to local and foreign workers.[19] Catholic orders were the first to take up the offer: Franciscans arrived in 1862, building a chapel, a home for the aged, and a school for boys. The Sisters of Bon-Pasteur d'Angers arrived next, in 1863, and over the course of two decades built a hospital, a home for female repentants, an orphanage, a boarding school, and a day school for girls.[20] Protestant evangelicals followed the inroads of Catholic orders, with an Anglo-American orphanage. Ericsson and Eklund arrived in Port Said a couple of years after an orphan scandal involving the Anglo-American mission had riveted the attention of the residents of Port Said.

Precursor: The Orphan Scandal of 1908

In fall 1908 an Anglican missionary affiliated with the British Church Missionary Society in Palestine spirited an orphan named 'Aisha out of Ottoman Jerusalem to sanctuary in British-occupied Port Said, placing her in the Anglo-American Orphanage there. The missionaries claimed they had moved her to protect her from the wrath of family members who had ill-treated her after she had converted from Islam to Christianity. According to the Austrian head of the orphanage, 'Aisha would be murdered if handed back to her kin.[21]

'Aisha's brothers traveled to Port Said to bring her back, claiming that she was "not yet of age" and not free to leave home on her own, and furthermore, that she had been promised in marriage to a man who had already paid a dowry for her. This case, like similar ones, hung on the question of the age of the girl/woman, which was difficult to determine in the absence of a birth certificate, and was confused by competing conceptions of the age of majority. Under Islamic law a girl/woman was considered a minor until she married or reached menopause, whereas civil law fixed the age of majority at eighteen.[22] After examining 'Aisha, two European physicians employed by the Port Said governorate certified that she was only seventeen, confirming the brothers' claim about her status as a minor. But the head of the Anglo-American Orphanage, an Austrian protected subject, assisted by the Austrian consul, countered with certification from two other physicians. They set 'Aisha's age at twenty-two or twenty-three, making her well past the age of majority, at least in civil law.[23]

As the case was being reviewed by officials in Cairo, a struggle ensued over 'Aisha's lodging. To remove her from the orbit of the missionaries, the girl had been placed in the home of a local Muslim family; after pressure from the head of the orphanage, she was moved again, this time to the domicile of a servant of the commander of the Suez Canal police. Meanwhile, 'Aisha's brothers pressed ahead with their case, bypassing state officials and secular justice, and presented testimony to the Shari'a Court of Port Said. The judge there decided that 'Aisha was a minor and had to be returned to the custody of her brothers. The head of the orphanage and several Protestant clerics then urged the consul general to block the court's decision, but Eldon Gorst chose not to intervene in "a question of so delicate a nature, which had been de-cided by the competent Tribunal."[24] Trying to calm those opposed to the out-come, he promised to communicate their concerns about 'Aisha's future safety to British colleagues in Jerusalem, and they assured him that she would be treated properly upon her return.

The affair touched a chord among Port Said's residents, who followed the proceedings closely. Locals collected funds to pay for 'Aisha's return voyage by steamer to Jaffa and then overland to Jerusalem. What 'Aisha herself wanted is not at all clear from the evidence. At one point she signed a document that she was ready to revert to Islam, but in court she apparently protested that she did not want to go back to her family. What happened to her once she returned, too, is not clear: Ottoman apostates from the mid-nineteenth century had es-caped death at the hands of the court, though they could face it at the hands of vigilantes and family members. Whether 'Aisha was quickly married off (as her brothers promised) or killed (as the missionaries feared) is unknown, for her trail is lost soon after her return to Jerusalem.[25]

The 1908 orphan episode pointed to a paradox of British colonial rule in Egypt. Colonial officials protected the right of Christian missionaries to pros-elytize, but they did not go out of their way to protect converts and allowed Islamic courts to decide cases of personal status. Faced with the launching of political parties and a growing nationalist movement, the British carefully picked the cases in which they were willing to intercede on behalf of foreign missionaries and their protégés, and this was not one of them.

The plot line of missionaries harboring a young Muslim orphan of modest means whose family sought her return would be repeated in a series of affairs in the early 1930s in Port Said and elsewhere in Egypt. Many of these incidents involved girls or young women whose fathers were deceased and whose relatives had handed them over to orphanages to be raised. At critical moments, often involving an imminent conversion or a proposed marriage, the missionaries and Muslim relatives battled over the custody and religious identity of the orphan. The tug of war, in which a young woman was caught in the middle of contending forces, represented more than the fate of one girl. It came to represent the frontline in the war between missionaries and Islamist groups such as the Muslim Brotherhood. And it showed contestations over legal jurisdiction between the state, religious authorities, and foreign representatives, as well as the limits to the sanctity of religious boundaries. Most of these cases were adjudicated in shari'a courts under the personal status laws rather than in mixed courts, for in spite of foreign interest in the outcome, the missionaries were not actual parties to the dispute.

Educating Girls: The Swedish Mission School

Maria Ericsson and Anna Eklund arrived in Port Said in 1911 without a clear plan but knew that, unlike missionaries who focused on reforming or converting Orthodox Christians or Jews to Protestantism, they wanted to save Muslims. "Islam is not an invention of man; it is an invention of Satan himself against the Son of God and against human souls. It is one of the real antichristian religions of earth." Concerned for the two hundred and fifty million people "who have been caught in this terrible snare," Ericsson argued that Christians had a great responsibility to bring them the word. "As I plead on my knees for those millions of Mohammedans and think of how few have heard the Gospel, there comes a fear over my heart as I think of the day of reckoning for the Christian church when we stand at the judgment seat of Christ."[26] Against skeptics who doubted Muslims could be saved, Ericsson countered, "Praise the Lord that He saves the Mohammedans the same way He saves us."[27] Yet the Swedish missionaries faced resistance.

If saving Muslims could be done, it would not be easy, as Ericsson admitted: "No people are more difficult to win for the truth of the Gospel, than the Moslems, because they are so deluded by the lying spirit of the false prophet."[28] She had to rely on her faith: "When we came to Port Said in 1911 we knew that no human power could open the doors and give us an entrance into the homes, and that no human power could bring Mohammedans to us, but we got on our knees before the Lord and prayed," recounted Ericsson. The Swedish missionaries hoped to be led to "prepared works" and looked for signs through prayer. "After about two weeks of continuous prayer, things began to move. The Holy Spirit was moving, and a wonderful thing happened: The Mohammedans came to us. The fathers brought their daughters to us and asked us to teach them."[29] Apparently a number of curious women had visited them, asking about when they would open a school, and their landlord had launched the operation by spreading word that a school was going to open.[30] Ericsson saw the hand of God in leading them to Port Said and in leading the locals, who wanted to educate their daughters, to them.

The locals had a decidedly different perspective: at a time when missionaries had come to be equated with a certain quality education, the arrival of the two Swedish missionaries signaled an opportunity. The women of Port Said who knocked on the door of the Swedish missionaries asking them to educate their daughters simply had few alternatives. State investment in public education had stagnated under the British, who depended upon the private sector, including missionaries, to handle the growing demand for schooling. The state investment in schools for girls, the specialty of single women missionaries, proved particularly skimpy. The locals did not distinguish, and could not afford to, between the missionaries of different nationalities or sects who landed on Egypt's shores. Seeing missionaries as conveyers of literacy and morality, they would not have found the two Swedish women missionaries any more threatening or militant than other missionaries. And evangelicals were not as forthright with the locals about their goals as they were with the folks back home (although admittedly they were not always forthright with the folks back home either, often proselytizing less than they claimed[31]).

The multiplication of girls' missionary schools in early twentieth-century Egypt unleashed a debate in Muslim circles, as some Egyptians viewed the spread of missionary institutions with alarm. In a speech on "The Danger of Foreign Schools" printed in 1908 in the journal *Tarqiyat al-Mar'a*, the activist Najiya Rashid warned that foreign schools aimed "to mislead the minds of youth" and "to nurture their souls with Christian learning." She asked parents how they could send their daughters to such schools once they learned of their aims.[32] Aware of the danger of such schools, Muslim reformers started schools to counter missionary endeavors, often locating them in proximity to evangelical enterprises to pull students away. American evangelical Margaret Smith noted in

1910 that a Muslim school was opened "in opposition to us" in another section of the same building as the Fum al-Khalij mission school.[33] But with their focus on recitation of religious texts, the mosque schools springing up did not offer the sort of domestic education that parents increasingly sought for their daughters. Nor did they offer the advantage of learning a foreign language, which had a certain prestige and practicality at a time when the foreign presence was so pronounced. Muslim parents wanted schools for girls that would strengthen morality and literacy, as well as give them skills, and those who chose to send their children to missionary schools felt that they could offset the religious instruction in missionary schools with Islamic instruction or practice at home.

Given that few options existed for girls' education in Port Said, Ericsson and Eklund found a ready market. A town crier combed the streets, announcing the opening of the new Swedish school, and students recruited from the Muslim lower classes quickly filled the rooms to capacity.[34] The reception by Port Said residents far exceeded Ericsson's expectations: "It seemed I was in a dream and that it could not be true to have that crowd of Mohammedan girls and the liberty we had to tell of the Gospel from the first and read to them the Bible, because that was why we were there."[35] Having worked with frustration for many years in Algeria and Tunisia under French colonial rule, Ericsson appreciated the freedom she had to proselytize in Egypt. "It is nothing less than a miracle to have such liberty in a Moslem city," she admitted.[36] The miracle was made possible, of course, by the British occupation and presence of imperial soldiers nearby. Within three years, the enrollment in the Swedish school had climbed to 125, and the missionaries sought larger quarters. Having launched the school on faith, Ericsson and Eklund welcomed donations from native teachers, local inhabitants, foreign residents, and Christian travelers as well as items such as clothes and blankets from churchgoers in Finland, Norway, Sweden, Switzerland, Canada, and the United States.[37]

The early years of growth were followed by the uncertainty of war: British soldiers and war refugees poured into the city during World War I, contributing to rampant disease, high prices, and overcrowding. German and Turkish forces twice mounted ground attacks on the Suez Canal, and sent multiple air forays over Port Said. Bombs hit locations close to the Swedish school, destroying much of the Arab quarter. The end of hostilities did not bring tranquility either. The missionaries purchased their own home in 1918, but in the revolutionary fervor that rocked Egypt the next year, angry mobs stoned the mission house more than once as anti-imperial and anti-missionary sentiments converged.[38] Protests died down, and local support picked up again. The house was expanded, renovated, and furnished, and by the early 1920s, the school had roughly 250 pupils in ten classrooms.[39]

Even though many parents objected to Bible readings and forbade their daughters from bringing their Bibles home, they continued to send their daughters to the Swedish school. Demand for education simply outstripped anxieties about proselytizing, and parents thought they could avoid the perils of a missionary education and minimize the pressures on their children to convert. Yet not all children in the school had parents to protect them or present a counterweight to the religious pressures coming from the school.

Disciplining Unruly Girls: The Home for Destitutes

The Swedish school began to take in boarders almost by accident, as impoverished and homeless students, many orphaned or abandoned, took up residence in the mission house. By the mid-1920s, the number of boarders passed fifty, with forty-eight girls and four little boys. The Home for Destitutes, as the missionaries called the new institution, joined a circle of orphanages in Port Said that included the Sisters of Bon-Pasteur d'Angers and Couvreux orphanages, the latter of which had been built by the widow of the chief engineer at the Suez Canal Company. The demography of Port Said was such that it could support another home, particularly a Protestant one attached to a school, especially since the Anglo-American Orphanage had been transformed into an Evangelical church sometime after the 1908 orphan scandal.[40]

Children ended up in the Home for Destitutes by various routes. Some were the daughters of prostitutes: one such girl became the object of dispute when her foster mother died; the police returned the girl to her birth mother, who in turn brought her to the home shortly thereafter.[41] Other prostitutes, seeking a life for their daughters that would be better than their own rough existence, handed their offspring over to the missionaries for safekeeping early on. Some of the girls in the home were possibly the offspring of unions with British soldiers. During the war, upwards of thirty thousand British troops— among them Australians, New Zealanders, and Indians—were stationed along the Suez Canal, and the hospitals of Port Said catered to those wounded in action at the Dardanelles. Other abandoned or orphaned children came to the home from families whose fortunes had turned or whose finances were otherwise in distress. One of the teachers brought in a girl whose parents had died during the war and who, along with her brother, had been given shelter for a few years by a local Muslim family that had found the pair of children begging in the streets.[42]

Like Margaret Smith and Lillian Trasher, Maria Ericsson wanted to have the girls in the Home for Destitutes in her care for an extended period to be able to enact the spiritual transformation that she envisioned. She signed a formal agreement with a child's guardian setting out the conditions of her care: the girl (initially almost all were girls; only later was an orphanage for boys started) would stay in the home until the age of eighteen; would spend vacations with relatives; and could not be removed for a lengthy amount of time before the age of eighteen without relatives paying the annual cost of care for the time the child had spent there.[43] Having the girls reside in the refuge until the age of eighteen and controlling their movements meant that they could be converted away from the prying eyes of relatives.

Yet the missionaries first had to discipline the girls, for many who came were considered unruly and difficult to manage. Writing in the 1920s, Ericsson characterized one as "such a clever little thief and liar"; another, though "gifted," had "an ungovernable temper"; and a third was "a most bigoted Moslem," who tried to convince the girls not to listen to the staff and "caused a strong spirit of opposition and hatred to prevail in the school, which gave us much suffering."[44] Turkiyya Hasan, the girl at the center of the orphan scandal of 1933, would similarly be labeled by the mission historian a "difficult-to-educate bad-mannered girl," who had always been "a source of grief and sorrow at the Mission."[45]

The missionaries strove to wear down the resistance of those girls whose "unruly" behavior challenged the disciplinary regime, but breaking their spirits and remaking them was not necessarily easy. Consider the case of E., who according to Ericsson had "inherited much evil from her parents" and for years was "tormented by evil spirits." The missionaries considered her possessed by a "spirit" or "wicked host," who stopped her from eating, confined her to bed, and made her curse or act "wild and violent, or crying and moaning and depressed." The missionaries could not accept that her behavior may have expressed her own desire to reject their regime and theology. As a result, they force-fed E. and used physical punishment to break her.[46] "Finally when she became broken and humbled, and confessed her sins," Ericsson wrote, the missionaries at last "got the victory in the Name of Jesus. It was a great deliverance, and oh what a joy it was to us!" The girl later became a housekeeper at one of the missionaries' outstations.[47] But behavior that the missionaries classified as caused by "evil spirits" may have reflected the will of a youth who had few tools at her disposable to gain autonomy and resist missionary authority.

The missionaries kept the girls busy, sensing that temptations lurked everywhere. Their location near the red light district of the Arab quarter, with cafes flanking the house on both sides, meant that visitors to that district passed by the refuge and that inhabitants of the district walked nearby. The area was lively at all hours in spite of police patrols meant to keep prostitutes indoors and visitors away late at night, with fights constantly breaking out. Ericsson tried hard to insulate the girls from contacts with rougher elements, hoping to raise workers for Christ, not streetwalkers; but just as several girls in the Home for Destitutes came from the streets, several were lost to them as well.[48]

The missionaries used a busy schedule of prayer, Bible reading, study, and work to transform the residents in the refuge and the day students into pious Protestants. The school day began at eight in the morning with prayer and learning Bible verses and ran until four in the afternoon, after which the girls met with their peers for more prayer, singing, and testimony. Outside of school hours, the girls performed household chores, such as mending clothes, cleaning and peeling vegetables, washing dishes, and selling candies to tourists to raise funds. They had some recreation as well, with trips to the Mediterranean shore.[49]

Like Lillian Trasher in her early years, Maria Ericsson turned to faith healing to combat disease. This was a risky tactic, for a port city such as Port Said proved particularly prone to outbreaks of small pox, cholera, and typhoid fever, and had a strict quarantine regime. When one girl became particularly sick, Ericsson prayed with a group of her friends, using illness and disease to show the power of religion, and she happily reported that the girl got better. "This does not mean that they were all saved, but it *does* mean that the Holy Spirit is working in the hearts of these precious girls," wrote Ericsson, who took a larger lesson from this, too, reflecting on the epic battle she saw pitting Christianity against Islam: "Surely the powers of Islam are shaking!"[50] She fought off her own illnesses in this way. During a small pox epidemic, she and the other missionaries spent weeks visiting the sick and dying "but were kept from infection by the power of God." After visiting a woman dying from cholera, Ericsson was attacked "by evil spirits, who would by force put cholera on me," but after hours of conflict, she was completely delivered.[51]

In a similar way, many of the girls in the home were "delivered" and "saved" as "the love of Christ prevailed," and they became "sweet helpers" and teachers.[52] Among the first girls in the refuge who embraced Protestantism were Egyptian

Copts and Syrian Eastern Orthodox Christians; later the missionaries converted Muslims. Outings to the Mediterranean seashore, Lake Manzala, or Zaytun— site of the Egypt General Mission home for female converts—were opportunities to baptize those who were "saved" and celebrate their conversions.[53]

Beyond Port Said: Expanding the Swedish Mission, Forging Transnational Ties

Having built a strong center in Port Said, the Swedish Mission looked to expand beyond the borders of the city to other Suez Canal and Delta towns. In the early 1920s, the evangelicals started an outstation in Dikirnis, a town near Mansura. Ericsson noted that it took a long time to "obtain a footing" among the Muslims of Dikirnis due to the "many Copts there who claimed our mission as divinely sent specially for themselves." When the mission replaced a beloved teacher, the Copts organized a strike and convinced the Muslims to join in.[54] Egyptian Copts had come to see foreign missions as catering specifically to them, since the strategy of the largest mission—the American Misson—had been to focus on reforming or converting Orthodox Christians so that they would carry the message to Muslims.

In selecting sites for expansion, the evangelicals from the Swedish Mission had initially avoided al-Manzala, a Muslim town of over twenty thousand residents midway between Dikirnis and Port Said. "Many had warned us not to go there, it was such a fanatical town," Ericsson explained, with fanatical being shorthand for Muslims who objected to Protestant proselytizing. During the missionaries' first week in the town, local notables interested in educating their daughters came to examine them, asking "pointed and difficult questions." The missionaries passed the test and opened a girls' school that got off to a good start. Soon, however, local Muslims opposed to missionary education built a large modern school that siphoned off nearly all the students. The two schools competed for a time, according to Ericsson, but in the end many of the girls returned to the missionary school.[55] The story was not over, though. A decade later, al-Manzala proved to be the site of the Swedish Mission's undoing when word leaked of the imminent conversion of a Muslim student there, leading to the close watch of Swedish Mission institutions in other locations by Islamists.

The staff of the Swedish Mission grew, until by the mid-1920s it included fourteen native Egyptian teachers, among them seven converted girls who had grown up in the Home for Destitutes. The number of foreign missionaries affiliated with the Swedish Mission also grew to fourteen, with five each from Finland

and Sweden (including the teacher Erika Lindstrom, whose manuscript became the basis of Helmi Pekkola's history of the mission, *On God's Path in the Desert of Islam*), and two each from England (including Alice Marshall, acting principal of the mission during the Turkiyya Hasan affair) and Switzerland (including Alzire Richoz, the matron who beat Turkiyya). "Our sisters have given up everything to come and suffer in the Moslem field," Ericsson wrote, "to win these hard, but precious souls, for the Saviour."[56] With missionaries from multiple countries, the Swedish Mission had outgrown its name and took a new one: the Salaam (Peace) Mission to Mohammedans. The mission retained firm ties with Finland and some links with Sweden, notably the protection offered by its legation, and at the same time welcomed Americans as missionaries and donors.

Maria Ericsson found one of her most important allies in the American Reverend Samuel Zwemer, a native of Michigan from a Dutch immigrant family. Zwemer had begun his evangelical career with the Arabian Mission of Basra and the Gulf sponsored by the Board of the Reformed Church in America. Proficient in multiple languages, including Dutch, German, and Arabic, he traveled the globe, seeking to unify far-ranging Protestant missionary efforts. A prodigious speaker and writer, he churned out scores of books, among them *Islam: A Challenge to Faith* (1907), *Our Moslem Sisters* (1907), and *Mohammed or Christ* (1915), many of which were co-authored. In 1906 he participated in a conference in Cairo for mission work among Muslims and came to see Egypt as a more central stage to advance his evangelical agenda. In 1911—the year Ericsson and Eklund arrived—he set up his base there, becoming affiliated with the American Mission and drawing support from a variety of churches, organizations, and individuals.[57]

Zwemer's aggressive approach to proselytizing irritated some of his compatriots and eventually got him into trouble with the Egyptian authorities. But Ericsson and Zwemer agreed on the imperative of directly proselytizing amongst Muslims and mutually assisted one another: he had included a photograph of the Swedish Mission School and discussed it in his book *Childhood in the Moslem World* (1915), and she listed him as the Salaam Mission's field referee in her brochure *Salaam Mission to Mohammedans* (1924).[58] Both were members of the Conferences of Christian Workers among Moslems convened in Helwan in 1924. The conference concluded that "direct Moslem evangelization is possible only when the various societies already in the field, and any new societies that may enter Egypt in the future, set their faces resolutely to occupy unoccupied territory, i.e. villages and towns predominantly Moslem."[59]

Ericsson had long since broken ranks with the Scandinavian missionary society with which she had been affiliated when working in North Africa and had few family ties in Sweden. She looked toward North America for support, and with contacts provided to her by Zwemer, she traveled there after the Helwan conference aboard the transatlantic steamer the *Olympic*. Using Flint and Grand Rapids, Michigan, and Chicago, Illinois, as bases, she fundraised amongst the Swedish diaspora and other circles.[60] She cast her net wide and spoke in a variety of Midwestern venues, listing them as: "Scandinavian churches, Baptist, Lutheran, and Mission churches, Free churches, Salvation Army and Pentecostal Missions."[61] In a brief book and brochure produced at the time, she outlined the history of the mission she had founded, mailing out a thousand copies of promotional materials to supporters and potential donors. The tour proved a success, as Americans sent money: with $8,000 donated from Philadelphia, the mission opened an orphanage for boys.[62]

The renamed Salaam Mission to Mohammedans had become firmly entrenched in the Canal Zone and transnational mission circles. It now had an income of 1,500 pounds, a sizeable staff, properties in Port Said and elsewhere, and its own boat. To keep supporters informed, the mission published its own periodical, *Egypt Salaam Mission Bulletin*.[63] Ericsson's American connections provided missionaries as well as money: two Americans took up residence in the mission house in 1931, and two more—John Afman and his wife—moved in the following year.[64]

In 1931 at the age of sixty-seven, Ericsson sailed again to North America, targeting Canada and making stops in Montreal, Toronto, and Vancouver. She visited with groups that regularly prayed for the Salaam Mission, publicized its activities, and donated funds. Her ultimate destination was Colorado, which she, by then a U.S. citizen or soon to become one, had made the Swedish Salaam Mission's headquarters. She left the mission in the capable hands of the British missionary Alice Marshall and her old friend Anna Eklund.[65] Ericsson left behind a city that had been transformed over the course of the twenty years she had resided there. Sectors of Port Said that had been destroyed in the war were rebuilt, and at the same time, a new colony for European canal employees and wealthy Egyptians—the upscale Port Fuad—had been established. The port city was no longer the provincial town it had once been: it had its own radio station, rail service to Cairo, and wide boulevards.[66]

Port Said also had an Egyptian elite that was increasingly suspicious of Christian missionary activity. Although Muslim residents had initially em-

braced the Swedish Salaam Mission, approaching its missionaries and asking
them to teach their daughters, the militancy of the mission put it on a crash
course with locals, who were increasingly disturbed by its aggressive proselytizing. By 1933 they had begun organizing under the auspices of Islamist organizations such as the Muslim Brotherhood to push back missionaries and take
back social welfare services. The Port Said branch of the Muslim Brotherhood
closely watched the Swedish Salaam Mission, anticipating, or perhaps provok-
ing, the orphan scandal that rocked Egypt in the summer of that year.

What exactly occurred on the morning of June 7 at the Swedish Salaam Mission
between the fifteen-year-old Turkiyya Hasan and Alzire Richoz, the Swiss missionary who had been left in charge, was a matter of dispute. The reports suggest a certain sequence of events: Turkiyya did not rise out of respect for foreign
visitor(s), which Richoz thought she ought to have done; Turkiyya and Richoz
exchanged heated words and then the matron beat the girl; the police became
involved; the Department of Prosecution of the Ministry of Justice, or Parquet
as it was known, investigated; and the press got wind of the affair. But beyond
this basic account, there are questions: Was the beating of Turkiyya meant to
force a conversion to Christianity or merely compliance with school regulations? Was it precipitated by a person or group outside the orphanage or was it
spontaneous? And why were Muslim girls in a Christian orphanage anyway?

The conflicting answers to these questions reveal a wide gulf in the ways
in which Christian missionaries, Islamic activists, and others understood the
affair. It is clear that there were more than two sides to the story. Indeed, there
were almost as many perspectives as there were participants, as views were
not necessarily shared across national, generational, religious, or gender lines.
Among Egyptians, for example, the orphaned teenager Turkiyya Hasan saw
her missionary guardians as brutes; Dr. Muhammad Sulayman saw them as
a threat to Islam; the governor of Port Said, Hasan Fahmi Rifaʻt, did not really care much about the religious aspects of the affair; and the interior minister, Mahmud Fahmi al-Qaysi, cared mostly about keeping the British at bay.
Among the British, the acting principal, Alice Marshall, and the head of the
Inter-Mission Council, George Swan, saw the missionaries as the victims
in this story, while the director of the European Department, Sir Alexander
Keown-Boyd, had little patience for their brand of "muscular Christianity." The

American Mission scholar Charles Adams showed great sympathy for the missionaries, whose cause he supported; the American consul in Port Said, Horace Remillard, while very close to the action, felt little sympathy for any of the actors. And the Finnish historian Helmi Pekkola had sources that could put her inside the mission, yet wrote from a great physical distance, a continent away. While each of these participant-observers viewed events through their own prisms and experiences, the woman most responsible for setting off the scandal—Alzire Richoz—left no known account, having been quickly spirited out of the country.

Protestant evangelicals pushed for an interpretation of events that emphasized Turkiyya's unruly behavior, not their own. In the space of a couple of weeks, Miss Marshall told the Parquet that Turkiyya was "ill-mannered and rude," reported to Keown-Boyd that she was "rude and aggressive," and confided to Remillard that she was "violent, abusive and blasphemous."[67] Although Marshall had not actually witnessed the incident, the girl's behavior grew progressively worse with each telling. It is worth noting that the issue was less about whether missionaries in general tried to convert Muslims—this they did not deny—than about whether they used force to do so, which they vehemently denied.

The missionaries maintained the line that they never, under any circumstances, forced children to convert. Admitting that forced conversions occurred even occasionally would have undermined the entire edifice of the Protestant mission in Egypt. Missionaries thus differentiated between legitimate discipline and illegitimate attempts to forcibly convert. Throughout this episode, they were keen to distinguish between required school activities, which included prayer and Bible study, and compulsion in religion. A student was required to follow the outer forms of Christian practice and discipline but was not obligated to accept the tenets. The missionaries maintained that they provided students a choice in religion, exposing them to the gospel through prayer and study, without forcing them to accept it. Turkiyya and her supporters would disagree.

The orphan scandal played out under the watchful eyes of British officials; not wanting it to escalate, they manipulated meetings and attempted to orchestrate outcomes, revealing the workings of semi-colonialism in practice. Although Egypt was technically independent, and had been for a decade, the British still cast a long shadow over internal affairs, particularly when it came to episodes that involved Europeans or foreign interests. They permitted missionaries to proselytize as long as they did not cross any red lines. In beating a child severely enough to leave marks on her body, or in pressuring her through fear tactics in writing, the missionaries had clearly crossed a line. The caning in the Swedish Salaam Mission reverberated, setting in motion a sequence of events that resounded far beyond Port Said and the set of actors originally involved in the scandal. Watching events unravel from the frontlines, the Muslim Brotherhood became the vanguard of the anti-missionary movement.

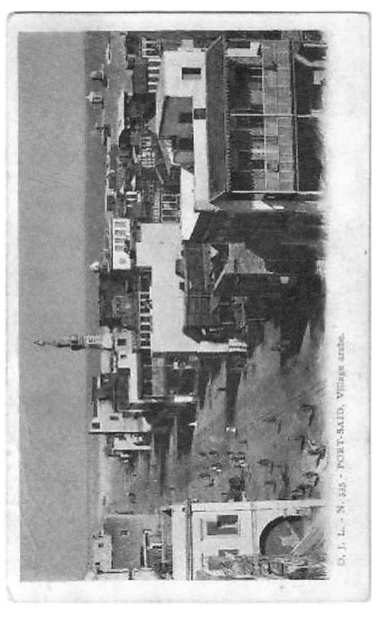

Arab village, Port Said. Postcard, one of 33, cardboard, maker unknown, used by Frederick Boddington, 1915. National Library of Australia.

Turkiyya Hasan. *Al-Lata'if al-Musawwara*, 19 June 1933, 1.

Turkiyya Hasan at the office of *al-Balagh*. ʿAbd al-Qadir al-Hamza is on Turkiyya's right; Dr. Muhammad Sulayman is on her left; standing from the right, Muhammad Sarhan, al-Ustadh al-Ghamrawi, and Muhammad Sharubi. *Al-Lataʾif al-Musawwara*, 2 July 1933, 1.

Girls in the Fowler Orphanage, Cairo, 1907. *Annual Report of the American United Presbyterian Mission in Egypt, 1907–1908*, Presbyterian Historical Society, Presbyterian Church (U.S.A.), Philadelphia. Reproduced by permission.

Lillian Trasher with young children at the Asyut Orphanage, c. 1920. Courtesy of Flower Pentecostal Heritage Center.

Lillian Trasher in a Model T with children from the orphanage, 1928. Courtesy of Flower Pentecostal Heritage Center.

Swedish Salaam Mission headquarters, Port Said, c. 1920s. Maria Ericsson, *The Egypt Salaam Mission Story* (Port Said: Egypt Salaam Mission, 1930), 17.

Maria Ericsson with another missionary and children on the roof of the Swedish Salaam Mission, c. 1920s. Maria Ericsson, *The Egypt Salaam Mission Story* (Port Said: Egypt Salaam Mission, 1930), 11.

Teachers and pupils in the Swedish Salaam Mission Girls' School, c. 1910s. Maria Ericsson, *The Egypt Salaam Mission Story* (Port Said: Egypt Salaam Mission, 1930), 10.

The school in Port Said, c. 1920s. Maria Ericsson, *The Egypt Salaam Mission Story* (Port Said: Egypt Salaam Mission, 1930), 20.

Swedish Salaam Mission workers with candy seller. Seated from left to right: Anna Eklund, Maria Ericsson, Alice Marshall, c. 1920s. Maria Ericsson, *The Egypt Salaam Mission Story* (Port Said: Egypt Salaam Mission, 1930), 38.

Swedish Salaam Mission workers, c. 1930s. Maria Ericsson, *The Egypt Salaam Mission Story* (Port Said: Egypt Salaam Mission, 1930), 2.

A young Hasan al-Banna, c. 1920s. www.dunyabizim.com

Journalists on the battlefield of the press from *al-Balagh*, *al-Jihad*, *al-Siyasa*, and *al-Kawkab al-Sharq* challenge missionaries protected by the Capitulations. "Every one of the knights is a chivalrous hero . . . fighting those who are hidden in the fortress of colonialism." *Al-Lata'if al-Musawwara*, 3 July 1933, 28.

Al-Shaykh al-Maraghi defends Islam. "His esteemed honor is boxing . . . and his adversary is the symbolic figure of evangelization. . . . What's wrong with him, he's curved like a bow!!" *Al-Lata'if al-Musawwara*, 24 July 1933.

The beating of al-Shaykh al-Maraghi. The group: "What is the defense of Islam and combating missionaries that you are talking about now?" Al-Shaykh al-Maraghi: "I'm closing my mouth and what happened, happened. By your honor, be merciful." Cartoon by Fawzi, *al-Kashkul*, July 1933.

"The Means of Missionaries." The head of the gang: "Kidnapping of children, hypnotism, drunkenness, and licentiousness . . . love and passion . . . all this and are we not righteous servants of God?" Cartoon by Fawzi, *al-Kashkul*, July 1933.

"Combating Missionary Activity." Al-Qaysi Pasha: "The government will not permit Egypt to become a field for evangelization. This declaration was not serious till yesterday, but now it is serious . . . just leave." Cartoon by Fawzi, *al-Kashkul*, 14 July 1933, 1.

II UNINTENDED CONSEQUENCES

Islamists and the State

5 FIGHT THEM WITH THEIR OWN WEAPONS

The Origins of the Muslim Brotherhood

WHEN MEMBERS OF THE SWEDISH SALAAM MISSION in Port Said reported that Turkiyya Hasan's actions had been instigated from outside the school, they focused on "Dr. S"—Dr. Muhammad Sulayman—a local notable. They were familiar with Dr. Sulayman, but had little understanding of his political affiliations, particularly his connection to the Muslim Brotherhood. The Port Said branch of the Brotherhood had been tracking local Muslim girls in the Swedish Salaam Schools for months, awaiting an opportunity to strike a blow at the Protestant mission. With the caning of Turkiyya, the Brotherhood found the perfect cause and stepped in at the critical moment to publicize the girl's story. The national press picked up the compelling drama of a young "tortured" girl who had stood up to foreign missionaries, and the Muslim Brotherhood then took credit for exposing the orphan scandal.[1]

Founded as part of the Islamic reform movement in the Suez Canal city of Isma'iliyya in 1928 by Hasan al-Banna, the Muslim Brotherhood rose on the anti-missionary tide, using it to recruit and rally members. As a grassroots organization with close links to communities that felt beleaguered, the Muslim Brotherhood saw Christian missionaries as a serious threat to Islamic society: they undermined the faith of Muslims, going after orphaned, abandoned, and poor children, whose care was mandated by Islam. The prevalence of female evangelicals roaming the countryside freely and targeting young girls as well as occasionally "seducing" young men, according to critics, presented a cultural challenge to Islamists and the gender order they envisioned. While the number of Muslims who converted to Christianity was never very substantial, conversion tore at the social fabric, breaking family ties and rupturing Muslim unity. The Muslim Brotherhood helped to organize opponents to missionaries under the banner of Islam and stood at the vanguard of the fight against proselytization.

It is no accident that the decade in which anti-Western Islamist organizations emerged, the 1920s, was also the decade in which Protestant evangelicals hit their apex in the Nile Valley. Evangelical enthusiasm gave rise to numerous incidents, often involving children, which provoked a strong anti-missionary response. Although American and other Protestant evangelicals failed at mass conversion, they helped to transform Egyptian society in ways they could not foresee.

Hasan al-Banna: Remembering Missionaries

Hasan al-Banna (1906–49) was born in al-Mahmudiyya, a small town forty miles from the Mediterranean coast on the Rosetta (Rashid) branch of the Nile. He learned the precepts of Islam from his father, Shaykh Ahmad al-Banna, a man noted for his piety and religious learning who often gave the call to prayer, led mosque services, and penned Islamic scholarship. Religion was the family vocation, though not its only means of livelihood: his father supported the family with income from his religious offices, rents on landed property, and watch repairing, a skill he taught his eldest son. As a young man Hasan al-Banna became a disciple in the Hasafiyya Sufi order, immersing himself in its rituals and ceremonies. He also got caught up in the marches and protests of the 1919 Revolution, which had a big impact on him like many of his generation. After finishing schooling in al-Mahmudiyya, al-Banna enrolled in the government Primary Teachers' Training School in Damanhur, choosing a life as an activist rather than as a scholar or mystic.[2]

As a student commuting between al-Mahmudiyya and Damanhur, al-Banna encountered missionaries in both locations. Opposing evangelicals became a central goal of the reform organization that he and his friends started in al-Mahmudiyya, the Jam'iyyat al-Hasafiyya al-Khayriyya (Hasafiyya Welfare Society), a spin-off of the Sufi order. The society worked on two tracks: first, encouraging people to do what was permitted and refrain from what was forbidden (drinking alcohol, gambling, and taking up innovations connected to the West) and, second, "fighting the evangelical mission that descended upon the town and became firmly settled in it."[3] With al-Banna as secretary and his lifelong companion Ahmad al-Sukkari as president, the organization served as a rehearsal for the Muslim Brotherhood, which would continue the struggle against missionaries.

The missionaries al-Banna encountered in his small Delta town were single women who preached Christianity, as he wrote, "under the guise of practicing medicine, teaching embroidery, and sheltering boys and girls."[4] In his memoirs, he mentions there were three missionaries working in the town and refers to a "Miss White." She was part of an "English mission" that had sent members to settle in that "upright town."[5] The particular mission that al-Banna and his friends fought in al-Mahmudiyya had been established by the Egypt General Mission (EGM).

The Egypt General Mission was started by an interdenominational band of seven single Protestant laymen from England and Northern Ireland who arrived in Egypt in 1898, setting up headquarters in Alexandria. Originally called the Egypt Mission Band, the group believed that because Muslims were the majority of the population and "more particularly in need of pioneer work," they ought to be its main concern.[6] After an experiment in the village of Abnub in Upper Egypt, the missionaries realized that "a village which had a large percentage of Coptic Christians was not the easiest in which to preach the Gospel to Mohammedans."[7] They shifted their attention to Lower Egypt, where the American Mission had established stations in the provincial capitals of the Muslim-dominated Delta region but had left scores of towns open to "occupation." From their field headquarters in Alexandria, the EGM moved inland, launching stations in the early 1900s in Bilbis, Shibin al-Qanatir, and Suez; in 1907, they transferred their headquarters to Zaytun, a town near Cairo, where they built their home for female converts and a Bible distribution center.[8]

"As a Mission we are keen upon aggressive evangelism," wrote George Swan, head of the EGM, in 1923, "and during the past year have taken a very large part in a scheme for the rapid evangelisation of the Nile Valley."[9] As part of this scheme, the EGM set up a station in al-Mahmudiyya that year. The evangelicals found the conditions in al-Banna's hometown "most primitive" and had a hard time finding premises in the face of local hostility. As an evangelical noted, "From the outset determined and constant opposition has been encountered."[10] Al-Banna's Hasafiyya Welfare Society evidently made the lives of these missionaries so miserable that al-Mahmudiyya stood out in missionary annals: "Perhaps in no other station has the fight been so stiff," an evangelical admitted, "but constant prevailing prayer and persistent effort in assailing the enemy has brought a measure of victory."[11]

In spite of the opposition, two British evangelicals—Miss Webb and Miss Langford—initiated work among women, starting a dispensary, a school, and industrial work, and visiting homes.[12] The third missionary counted by al-Banna was probably a local Bible woman, who may even have knocked on the door of Hasan al-Banna's household to read the Bible to the women within. In any event, Webb was possibly al-Banna's "Miss White," with the difference in Arabic between Webb and White being only one letter (a printer's error or an honest mistake in memoirs set down nearly a quarter century after the period). That al-Banna attempted to give her a name and a nationality suggests that Miss W. left an indelible impression. To most Egyptians, the exact names and provenance of missionaries and fine (or not so fine) lines between Christian denominations ultimately did not matter. What mattered was that missionaries seemed to be everywhere, not only in Cairo and port cities, or even in provincial capitals, but in small Delta towns. These included al-Mahmudiyya and Damanhur, the provincial capital, where EGM evangelicals later set up a station as part of a general expansion of their work. They used it as a base to reach women in surrounding villages where they set up dispensaries, "with the hope of establishing friendly contacts and breaking down prejudice by their ministry of healing."[13]

After getting his high school diploma, Hasan al-Banna moved in the fall of 1923 to Cairo, enrolling at the state teacher training school, Dar al-'Ulum. He preferred its curriculum to that of al-Azhar, the centuries-old bastion of Islamic learning, for he wanted to acquire practical tools to rejuvenate Islam. During his time in the capital, al-Banna capitalized on his father's ties to meet Islamic reformers such as Muhibb al-Din al-Khatib and Muhammad Farid Wajdi. Al-Banna frequented al-Khatib's bookstore, the Maktabat al-Salafiyya, and took up his offer to publish articles in a journal he edited, *Majallat al-Fath*. Al-Banna also had contacts with the Islamic activist Labiba Ahmad, whose journal *al-Nahda al-Nisa'iyya* reported on some of his early speeches and activities.[14]

Al-Banna used his father's contacts to meet Muhammad Rashid Rida, who edited the Islamic reform journal *al-Manar*. Rida had arrived in Cairo in 1897 from his home in Tripoli, Syria, where he had become familiar with the methods of American missionaries. According to the American missionary Charles Adams, who wrote about Islamic reform in Egypt, Rida discussed the necessity of Muslim's responding to Christian propaganda by similar activities. He founded Jam'iyyat al-Da'wa wa-l-Irshad (Society of Preaching and Guidance) in 1912 to counteract the endeavors of Christian evangelicals in Muslim lands and to provide instruction on the doctrines and responsibilities of Islam. The society sponsored a school for preachers and missionaries to non-Muslims, before it was disbanded due to the outbreak of World War I.[15]

In Ismaʿiliyya: The Muslim Brotherhood Meets the Egypt General Mission

After al-Banna graduated from Dar al-ʿUlum in 1927, the Ministry of Education assigned him to teach Arabic in a primary school in Ismaʿiliyya, a city ninety miles northeast of Cairo on the Suez Canal and midway between Port Said (to the north) and Suez (to the south). The young teacher found a divided city, with a wealthy section for upper-class Egyptians and European Suez Canal Company employees and a poorer section for native Egyptian workers. He saw, too, the impact of the nearby British military base, which served as a glaring symbol of the British occupation. After teaching hours, al-Banna preached and lectured in mosques and coffee shops in addition to writing articles for Islamic journals such as *al-Fath*. He followed developments in Cairo closely, having joined the Jamʿiyyat al-Shubban al-Muslimin (often translated as the Young Men's Muslim Association, YMMA) in 1927, right after it was launched by leaders of the Islamic reform movement to bring together Muslim youth in response to the YMCA and other foreign groups.[16]

Less than a year after his arrival, in March 1928, he launched the Muslim Brotherhood. As he tells the story in his memoir, he had been approached by six laborers from the British army camp who had heard him speak; they told him that they were "tired of this life, a life of submissiveness and shackles" and noted the lack of dignity and honor of Arabs and Muslims, who were forced to work for foreigners. They put their trust in al-Banna and wanted him to take responsibility before God for guiding them.[17] The new "brothers" swore allegiance to al-Banna, who became the general guide of the organization, which strove for Islamic revival. Al-Banna recruited members from the working classes as well as from the middle classes, particularly professionals. The group set as its first project the building of a mosque and registered as an Islamic welfare society.[18]

In Ismaʿiliyya, al-Banna found an active Protestant mission that was run by the Egypt General Mission, the same outfit that he had encountered in al-Mahmudiyya. By the late 1920s, this British mission had grown to become the second largest in Egypt, after the American Mission, with over fifty missionaries in the field, the overwhelming majority of whom—roughly 70 percent—were women. The EGM had started a hospital in Shibin al-Qanatir and developed a large network of dispensaries, schools, publications, and distribution centers throughout the Delta and Canal Zone. The faith-based mission drew support from a home council headquartered in London (having moved from Belfast) and donors from as far afield as Australia and the United States. The EGM also relied upon Egyptian donors and workers, who served as principals, teachers, Bible women, nurses, and staff in its institutions.[19]

The EGM's first foray in Isma'iliyya had been a book depot that distributed Bible translations and was run from Suez; the British evangelicals then established a base in Isma'iliyya itself. Having identified education as central to winning Muslim converts, they opened schools for boys and girls.[20] The Kings, a missionary couple, initially ran the boys' school as a day school, sheltering one or two of the boys in their home. They opened a boarding school in 1917 after the mission purchased a new building near Lake Timsah. "Our aim was to get Moslem boys," wrote Ashley King's wife, who ran the "Christian house," and they succeeded, with eight of the first ten boys being Muslims.[21]

"The change we have been privileged to see in the lives of these boys, even during the few short months that they have spent here, is truly blessed," reported Ashley King, British superintendent of the school, in 1918, noting that "when one looks at the surroundings from which they have come, and thinks of the evil to which they have listened from their earliest years, one just rejoices at the privilege of being allowed to attempt to rescue even a few of these young lives."[22] The number of boarders in the EGM boys' school grew in the 1920s to twenty-five, as the number of day students at the school rose to two hundred, more than three-quarters of whom were Muslim. The Egyptian staff grew as well, with an Egyptian headmaster overseeing seven "native" teachers. The mission in Isma'iliyya, of which the boys' school was a part, was among the EGM's largest; only the field headquarters at Zaytun and the hospital at Shibin al-Qanatir had bigger staffs. And while the EGM closed other boys' schools, focusing their attention elsewhere, they kept the boys' school in Isma'iliyya open.[23]

Its students' high success rate in passing the government primary certificate exam partially explained the popularity of the Isma'iliyya boys' school. The British missionaries also counted it a success that all the boys who went through the school had been "taught the message of the Gospel" and given a knowledge of Christianity. Mrs. King noted that many left school believing in that message but "had no liberty to be baptized" since they were not "of age," though "a few have had courage to confess Christ openly in baptism." She mentioned one boarder in particular who in a ceremony in the chapel one Sunday in 1930 "had chosen Christ as his Master." Since he was an orphan who had spent nine years at the school without contact with any of his relatives, "there was perfect freedom for him to be baptized."[24]

The presence of a Christian boys' school in Isma'iliyya that actively converted boys was a huge affront to al-Banna and his associates. The Muslim Brothers protested that the missionaries used schools in ways that their Egyptian hosts had not intended. Contrary to the claims of evangelicals about rescuing children, the Brothers insisted that missionaries had induced some "gullible" boys and girls to convert, preying on their "simple intelligence."[25] Al-Banna was keenly aware of the missionaries' methods. Having seen them up close in his youth, he now read reports from their congresses and quoted missionary leaders.[26]

Al-Banna saw the education of youth along Islamic lines as his main mission and the key to Islamic reform and revival, and felt the YMMA and other societies were not taking the mission of bringing youth back to Islam seriously enough. One of the reasons he had launched his own society, in spite of being involved in the YMMA, was that he did not think the group spent enough energy on education. To combat missionary activities in Isma'iliyya, the Brotherhood built an institute and school for roughly two hundred boys above its new mosque as one of its first projects. Completed in 1931, the Ma'had Hurriyya al-Islami (Islamic Freedom Institute) had enough space to serve all the boys enrolled in the EGM boys' school. In addition to their studies, the boys at the new institute prayed regularly with the community in the mosque.[27] The Brothers were quite straightforward about their reasoning for launching the institute: they had seen the activities of missionaries, "and we founded the Islamic Freedom Institute to give refuge to those the society rescued from them."[28]

The Muslim Brotherhood next turned its attention to the situation of Muslim girls and women in Isma'iliyya, recognizing their vulnerability to missionary "propaganda" as well.[29] The five female evangelicals of the Egypt General Mission visited the homes of Christian and Muslim women and ran a Sunday school and a school for girls. The day school for girls (there was no EGM girls' boarding school) was close to the native quarter, and had an average attendance of 130 pupils. In their pamphlets and newsletters, evangelicals pointed to students who had proven receptive to Christianity.[30] The Brothers would have learned about these conversions, imminent conversions, and near conversions when tensions erupted over them within families in the community.

To woo girls attracted to Christianity back to Islam, and prevent others in Isma'iliyya from straying, the Muslim Brotherhood rented quarters and started its own school for girls in September 1932, calling it the Madrasat Ummahat al-Mu'minin (School for Mothers of the Believers). Again, the Brothers were explicit about their motives for launching the enterprise: "We founded the School for Mothers of the Believers to provide refuge for those girls enrolled in the mission school for girls."[31] The school was a great success, serving as the launching pad for the first Muslim Brotherhood affiliated branch of al-Akhawat al-Muslimat (Muslim Sisters) in April 1933.[32] One of the Brothers explained: "A branch of Muslim Sisters was founded to obliterate the influence of female missionaries by going to homes to warn the residents against getting trapped in their snare."[33] The Muslim Sisters thus aimed to counter activities of EGM evangelicals and Bible women, such as Sitt Sa'da, whose job at the time was to "faithfully visit the homes of the people bearing the Good Tidings."[34]

The Muslim Brotherhood also sought to counteract the activities of itinerant male preachers and teachers. EGM missionaries proselytized in Isma'iliyya as well as nearby towns and villages such as Abu Suwayr, trying to re-create the atmosphere of outdoor revival meetings that had been used so effectively to move crowds in Great Britain. Since these were banned in Egypt, they modified the format and preached in village and town halls opening on to main streets on market days.[35] The Brothers adopted similar tactics, setting up a mobile unit that preached and provided guidance, and visiting village markets to discourage people from listening to the missionaries or accepting their pamphlets and books. Learning from the missionaries, al-Banna and Brothers preached in clubs and cafes; traveled to towns and villages to spread the call (da'wa); and set up weekly lectures designed to counter the influence of missionary talks.[36]

The Brotherhood also learned from missionaries' publication projects, which were pivotal in disseminating the evangelical call to Christianity. EGM's book depot in Isma'iliyya served as a distribution center for Bibles and biblical tracts, making the gospel accessible in Arabic translations that could be read aloud and broadly circulated. EGM missionaries also produced a monthly magazine for Muslim men, *Bashir al-Salam* (Preaching Peace), and launched one for Muslim women in 1927. The goal of these magazines was, according to George Swan, "to put the Gospel in a way which will arrest the Mohammedan."[37] Given the example of Arabic evangelical literature flooding Egyptian towns and villages, and the prominence of the Arabic press, the Muslim Brotherhood realized that it had to develop its own publications to reach the general population. Expanding its literary output beyond an occasional pamphlet or article, the Brotherhood launched its own weekly newspaper, *Jaridat al-Ikhwan al-Muslimin*, in June 1933, just in time to chronicle the organization's response to the Turkiyya Hasan affair.[38]

In the fall of 1932, al-Banna moved to Cairo to teach at a primary school there, having been transferred at his own request by the Ministry of Education. The headquarters of the Muslim Brotherhood moved with him. The year before, the Brotherhood had opened a branch in Cairo, combining forces with an association founded by 'Abd al-Rahman al-Banna, one of Hasan al-Banna's younger brothers, and some of his associates. After the move, a rebellion broke out in the Isma'iliyya branch, which Hasan al-Banna quickly quashed, successfully solidifying his control over the growing organization. But in 1932 and 1933 his attention remained focused on the area around the Canal Zone, the organization's flashpoint with the missionaries. As al-Banna noted in his memoirs, "the campaign that was launched against missionary activities and missionaries in 1932 had its first real sparks in al-Manzala. Then it ignited in Port Said."[39]

Sparks and Ignition: The al-Manzala–Port Said Connection

The Muslim Brotherhood founded some of its earliest branches in towns around Isma'iliyya and along the Suez Canal, where missionaries had been aggressively proselytizing. A young man who had worked in Isma'iliyya and become active in the Muslim Brotherhood there started a branch in Port Said when he returned home. Members were thrilled when Hasan al-Banna came by train to speak at the opening of a new center.[40] Brotherhood activities in Port Said, home of the Swedish Salaam Mission headquarters, soon sparked interest in the Bahr al-Saghir (Little Lake) region, including nearby al-Manzala, where a Salaam school existed and a new Brotherhood branch was founded. Other early branches were established in Abu Suwayr and Suez, as well as the Delta town of al-Mahmudiyya, where the Hasafiyya Welfare Society had become a Muslim Brotherhood branch. Planting its earliest branches in the neighborhood of missionary stations could have been "good luck or bad luck," according to a member, who noted that the groups soon clashed: "It was natural that friction would occur between the two organizations," he explained, "for one of them defended Islam and the second attacked it."[41]

Brothers in al-Manzala carefully watched the local Salaam Mission girls' school. In January 1933, a member alerted the head of the branch, the 'alim Shaykh Mustafa Muhammad al-Tayr, of the intention of the Salaam Mission to convert a girl from a poor family. The branch head then called members to an urgent meeting, at which it was decided to intercede with the girl's family to extract her from the school. The girl, or woman, subsequently identified as Wafiqa, had worked from the beginning of that year as a teacher. A Brotherhood delegation sent to her home reached an agreement with her father to withdraw her from the school, and one of the Brothers went with Wafiqa's father to inform the head of the school of the decision. The Brothers then gathered funds to help the family, who had depended on Wafiqa's salary.[42]

Recognizing the real financial constraints facing this family and others, the Muslim Brotherhood branch in al-Manzala decided to open a training school for poor girls as an alternative to the missionary school. A little over two weeks after having been alerted to Wafiqa's impending conversion, the Brothers launched the workshop, with a curriculum that included lessons in the principles of Islam, child-raising, and housekeeping for a Muslim wife. Those in need could receive tuition assistance; the numbers of those enrolled climbed from seventy-one girls at the school's opening to over one hundred. When Wafiqa, who worked as a teacher there, and the other teachers began to pray five times a day, observers termed the enterprise a great success.[43]

One of those girls "rescued" by the al-Manzala Muslim Brotherhood branch—diverted from the Salaam Mission School to the new workshop—reported that another Muslim girl (Afkar Mansur) in the Salaam School in al-Manzala was on the verge of being converted. According to the young informant, the girl had been smuggled from the Salaam Mission in Port Said to the school in al-Manzala under the guise of going on an excursion in order to hide her conversion from her family. The secretary of the branch in al-Manzala sent an urgent letter to the Muslim Brothers in Port Said in late January 1933, noting the "vehement movements against Islam" of missionary societies in Egypt in recent years. In spite of the integrity of Muslims in spreading Islamic instruction and morals, missions had lately "become emboldened," the secretary asserted. He alerted the Brothers in Port Said of the imminent danger facing a daughter from the Arab quarter in their city. The letter called upon the Brotherhood in Port Said to launch an effort to remove the "helpless" girl from the "pit of iniquity."[44]

The Brotherhood in al-Manzala followed this letter with one to Hasan al-Banna in early February 1933 identifying five Muslim girls (including Afkar) who had been surreptitiously sent to the al-Manzala Salaam School from Port Said. Ranging in age from seven to twenty-three, four were orphaned or had been abandoned and one had an ill father who could not support her. The Muslim Brothers of al-Manzala pleaded that the Brothers had to come together to attack the "site of malady" so that the school in their town would meet its "inescapable fate." The letter challenged the Muslim Brothers of Port Said and in other towns to do all in their power to rescue Muslim girls from such schools. And the Brothers from al-Manzala specifically requested that Hasan al-Banna intercede with the Brothers in Port Said to encourage them to exert "the greatest possible effort" to extract the girls from the Salaam School in al-Manzala.[45]

While the Brothers of al-Manzala wanted to rescue the Muslim girls in the missionary school in their town, they were limited in what they could do, for they had no claim on the girls and no connections to their families. They thus called upon the Brothers in Port Said to take action, which meant contacting the girls' families where they existed. In such cases, the impoverished parents of the girl or the girl's guardian had often signed her over to missionaries, and family members, or state officials in the case of an abandoned child, had to be persuaded to consent to retrieve the girl. This was very difficult when families and officials had few resources for her support and housing, or they depended upon the girl's stipend for their own support. Without the cooperation of parents, guardians, and state officials, as well as of the girls themselves (some of whom willingly chose conversion), the Muslim Brothers were powerless to "rescue" girls and close down missionary schools.

Hasan al-Banna responded to the call from al-Manzala by drafting a letter to Port Said and other branches of the society. He then dispatched several delegations to Port Said to see what could be done about the Muslim girls in its evangelical schools and orphanages.[46] In the winter and spring of 1933, the Muslim Brotherhood had the Salaam Mission in its radar. It was in this context that on June 7, Alzire Richoz beat Turkiyya Hasan when she refused to rise for foreign missionary visitor(s). The branch office of the Brotherhood learned about the beating—whether through medical, legal, police, or personal contacts—"and with their determination lifted the curtain on the dreadful events that newspapers discuss every day."[47] Dr. Sulayman took Turkiyya under his protection, and soon the press carried photographs of her, published letters evangelicals had sent to encourage her to convert, and ran interviews she gave. The Muslim Brotherhood's own newspaper, *Jaridat al-Ikhwan al-Muslimin*, faithfully reported on the story, which sparked outrage among the Egyptian public.[48]

The caning of Turkiyya Hasan and intervention by the Muslim Brotherhood changed the equation of how missionaries were seen in Egyptian society.

Opponents of evangelical activities now had incontrovertible proof—a medical report, letters, and the testimony of a "tortured" girl—that missionaries had crossed the line between persuasion and force, and used illegal means to pressure their wards to convert. If they did this with one girl, they were doing it with others; if they did this in Port Said, they were doing it elsewhere. Having watched the mission for months and broken the story, the Muslim Brotherhood served as the vanguard of the anti-missionary movement, lobbying public opinion against foreign missionaries and urging state officials to take action.

A Hundred Turkiyyas: Rescuing Endangered Muslim Orphans

In mid-June 1933, at the height of the storm over the attempt to forcibly convert Turkiyya Hasan, the Muslim Brotherhood held its first general conference in Isma'iliyya, which was dedicated to a discussion of the problem of missionary proselytizing in Egypt and how to combat it. Representatives of the then fifteen branches in the Canal Zone (five), Cairo (one), and the Delta (nine) gathered together, with al-Banna's good friend Ahmad al-Sukkari leading the group from al-Mahmudiyya. The conference reception was held in the courtyard of the School for Mothers of the Believers.[49] After the conference, the Majlis al-Shura al-'Amm (General Advisory Council) announced the formation of a Maktab al-Irshad al-'Amm (General Guidance Bureau) and sent a petition to the king, which became a model for the anti-missionary movement. It also announced that special subcommittees would be formed in every branch "to warn the people through peaceful, lawful means of falling into the snares of the missionaries."[50]

The story of the caning of the teenage orphan Turkiyya Hasan took on a life of its own, finding a national audience and echoes in dozens of local variations. In the wake of the scandal at the Swedish Salaam School in Port Said, heightened public vigilance led Egyptians to investigate missionary institutions throughout the country. Numerous cases of Muslim girls and boys converted or nearly converted by Protestant missionaries came to light. The Muslim Brothers already had a deep familiarity with missionaries when the story broke, and it spurred the battle they waged to save children. Responding to the call of the General Advisory Council, they formed local committees that launched new initiatives to oppose evangelicals. These initiatives often bore a deep resemblance to evangelical enterprises, showing the clear imprint that missionaries had in shaping the activities and institutions of the early Muslim Brotherhood.

In Isma'iliyya, the directive of the General Advisory Council and the occasion of the conversion of a local camel driver spurred members of the branch to step up their campaign against missionaries and organize a special committee to fight proselytizing. Headed by the 'alim and imam of the Muslim Brotherhood mosque, with the principal of the Islamic Freedom Institute as secretary, the newly formed committee of teachers and other branch members devised a multipronged plan for fighting evangelicals of the Egypt General Mission and other missions. The first step was to issue a general call to the Egyptian public about the danger of missionaries, "warning them against falling into their traps." Second, the committee encouraged the School for Mothers of the Believers in its duty of extracting Muslim girls from missionary schools and giving them shelter, and likewise encouraged the Islamic Freedom Institute to do the same for boys. In a third initiative, the committee formed a special unit of educated Muslim Sisters to be in contact with women in their homes to inform them of the danger of proselytizing and "roving female missionaries," including Bible women.[51] In a fourth initiative, the Muslim Brotherhood subcommittee in Isma'iliyya discussed founding an orphanage to shelter poor girls and boys, which would prevent them from "being thrown into the arms of missionaries who take advantage of their destitution and indigence in stealing their consciences and ruining their beliefs."[52]

The Muslim Brotherhood in Isma'iliyya had a long history of fighting missionaries and had launched some of its earliest initiatives in response to evangelical inroads: the group, in the words of an Isma'iliyya Brother, "fought them with their own weapons." The members became particularly concerned when they realized after launching the special committee that missionaries were trying to use their city as they had used al-Manzala, turning it into a retreat for girls smuggled from other places who were on the verge of conversion. Showing "no less zeal for Islam" than activists in other locales, the Isma'iliyya branch of the Muslim Brotherhood "rose up" to counter missionary plans to turn their city into a haven for converts.[53]

When in the summer of 1933 the Egypt General Mission evangelicals tried to "extend their tentacles" into nearby Abu Suwayr and open a branch of the Isma'iliyya English primary school there, depicting it as an educational and scientific service, the local Muslim Brotherhood branch took action. The Brothers uncovered the missionaries' "ruse" and announced their own determination to open a primary school in Abu Suwayr. A committee drafted and implemented a plan, which it pushed forward quickly so that the school would be ready for the start of the academic year. This forced the missionaries to shelve their own plan, to the delight of the Brothers.[54]

In Suez, the local branch of the Muslim Brotherhood remained on high alert. Male missionaries had opened one of the first EGM bases there in 1901, considering it a strategic spot given the number of Muslim pilgrims passing through. Shortly thereafter women missionaries had taken over the base, visiting homes, running a "ragged Sunday School," and starting a girls' school. As EGM head George Swan remarked of the boarding and day school, "one can never estimate the value of such in taking the children right out of their Moslem surroundings."[55] The school was considered by evangelicals to be a great success: "From the very first there was definite spiritual blessing in the school, the close and intimate contact resulting in a number of conversions and in a few open confessions of Christ in baptism."[56] By 1933, roughly ninety girls attended the EGM Suez girls' day school and eighteen girls boarded, fifteen of whom were Muslim. Several of these, according to one of the missionaries, "had made definite decisions to love and serve the Lord."[57]

Among those who had converted was Kawkab Kamil (Hayat Ibrahim), who was at the center of Suez's own conversion scandal in 1933. Kawkab worked as a teacher in the EGM Suez girls' school, where she had boarded on and off since she was a child. According to a missionary pamphlet, Kawkab's elderly father, who had divorced her Sudanese mother, put her in the school in Suez as a boarder in 1915 at about the age of six, not knowing what else to do with such a rambunctious child. He withdrew her three and a half years later but permitted her to return after a couple of years. When she was about thirteen, she told the missionaries that she "longed to serve and follow the Lord Jesus."[58]

In December 1926, at about the age of seventeen, Kawkab (Hayat) attended the Conference for Women Converts at Zaytun, and the following year, at eighteen, she was baptized, at which time she took the name Kawkab. In May 1933, her mother turned up on the scene, along with a cousin who sought her hand in marriage, and her uncle demanded that she be turned over to him as his ward, arguing that under Islamic law, as an unmarried (virgin) woman, she needed a male guardian. The dispute came up in the Islamic legal courts at exactly the moment that "were heard even at Suez rumblings of the storm that had broken at Port Said, and was soon to sweep over the whole of Egypt, threatening the very existence of Mission work in that land."[59] Much to the chagrin of British and missionary officials, the court awarded custody of Kawkab, who was then about twenty-three or twenty-four years old, to her uncle.[60]

In the face of conversions such as Kawkab's, Islamic activists in Suez went on the offensive. They sent a town crier into the streets to denounce those who enrolled their children in the English (Egypt General Mission) school; delivered sermons in mosques to warn residents about the missionaries to which they invited women in particular; circulated papers and wrote graffiti on walls; and sent a letter of protest to the missionaries, which was signed "the Black Hand."[61] Having "uncovered a nest of proselytizing" in the Suez neighborhood of Hayy al-Arbaʿin, where missionaries were based, the Muslim Brothers rescued a boy and a girl from the "trap" that the missionaries had set for them. Through their vigilance, the Brothers claimed that many incidences of near conversion had come to light. They now planned to found a school in Hayy al-Arbaʿin for those who had sought refuge in the missionary school and safeguard their beliefs.[62]

In Hasan al-Banna's hometown of al-Mahmudiyya, which by 1933 contained a large pumping station that supplied Alexandria with water and was also the pivotal point of a power scheme to drain large areas of the northern Delta, the EGM had expanded its mission. The female evangelicals now offered schools, a dispensary, and training in industrial work. The Brotherhood in al-Mahmudiyya warned people of the danger of sending their children to the missionary women, "beseeching by all legitimate means."[63] The three evangelicals al-Banna had noted in his youth had grown to nine, counting foreign missionaries and their local assistants. The latter included such women as Sitt Latifa, who taught upper classes in the school; Sitt Kawkab, a kindergarten teacher; and Sitt Victoria, a convert who was one of the first dispensary patients and ran the rug-making and sewing section of the industrial school, which attracted a regular attendance of twenty-five to thirty girls.[64] "And for the older fellaheen [peasant] girls who have never been to school we have classes for needlework, rug-making and other handicrafts," noted George Swan of this sort of EGM activity, pointing to its purpose, "so that they too may come regularly under the sound of the Gospel, and also learn some trade by which they may earn their own living and so become more independent of the marriage market."[65] The missionaries had a very negative image of Muslim marriages, and constantly critiqued the status of women within those marriages.

In order to show residents the danger of the missionary enterprise in their town, the Muslim Brothers in al-Mahmudiyya pointed to the story of a girl whose mother had died and whose father had been "tricked" by women missionaries into leaving her at the mission so that they could raise her. They "taught her the principles of their faith, maligned the religion of Islam, and tried to baptize her and send her away." When the Brothers learned of this, they rushed to rescue the girl and after great effort succeeded in extracting her from the mission. When the report was lodged with the Brotherhood's General Guidance Bureau in Cairo, the girl who had set off the maelstrom in al-Mahmudiyya was still staying in the home of Ahmad al-Sukkari, who headed the Brotherhood branch in al-Mahmudiyya and sat on the General Guidance Bureau.[66] The struggle to "save" Egypt's children from the missionaries, who themselves were trying to "save" these children from Islam, became a very personal one for many Islamist leaders. The care of orphans and the poor were central tenets of the religion they were attempting to revive.

This incident caused the Muslim Brotherhood in al-Mahmudiyya "to focus attention on the serious efforts that those missionaries spent in realizing their ambition."[67] In short, the Brothers studied their methods in order to learn from them. The local Muslim Brotherhood branch decided to start a factory for textiles and rugs, "to accommodate those girls who fell into the trap of the missionaries" and give them a way out. In this way, they "rescued" thirty girls and thirty-five boys from "apostasy."[68] The number of girls in the new factory nearly matched the number of those who had sought training in the missionary workshop, which had clearly responded to a practical need. The missionaries had recognized this, and in turn the Brothers in al-Mahmudiyya were forced to recognize it as well. The Brothers launched a project that matched that of the missionaries, fighting fire with fire, or, in this case, factory with factory.

Stories of orphans such as Turkiyya Hasan who faced "forced" conversions echoed across the Canal Zone and Delta region. Some of the children had multiple names, such as Hayat/Kawkab of Suez; others, such as the girl in al-Mahmudiyya, remained unnamed. Their plight sparked the local branches to take action, often through the courts, to "rescue" these youth, though often what the young woman wanted was unclear. Some may have found spiritual comfort in conversion, economic relief in missionary training and jobs, and alternatives to unwanted marriages. Others may have found themselves trapped in missionary institutions, eager to get out. Yet it was not enough for Islamists to remove Muslim children from missionary schools, homes, and workshops; they had to be offered alternatives. Thus the pattern of Muslim Brotherhood branches countering specific missionary projects with similar institutions repeated itself throughout the Delta and Canal Zone.

✳

The origin and spread of the first Brotherhood branches, institutions, and activities in the Canal Zone and nearby Delta were intimately connected to the trajectories of missionaries in Egypt and their evangelical activities. The presence of Christian missionaries in Hasan al-Banna's hometown of al-Mahmudiyya and in nearby Damanhur had been formative in shaping his worldview and that of his close friend and collaborator Ahmad al-Sukkari. The organization they started, the Hasafiyya Welfare Society, battled missionaries and metamorphosed into a Muslim Brotherhood branch after al-Banna launched that organization in Isma'iliyya. There the Muslim Brotherhood founded its earliest institutions—boys' and girls' schools, the Islamic Freedom Institute, the School for Mothers of the Believers, a branch of the Muslim Sisters, and roving preacher-guides—in direct response to missionary inroads. The first Brotherhood branches in the Canal Zone carefully watched missionary activity, trying to remove children at risk of conversion, with Brothers in al-Manzala alerting members in the branch in Port Said to the danger of Swedish Salaam Mission schools. Port Said Brothers and supporters subsequently helped publicize Turkiyya Hasan's story in the press. Foreign missionaries thus helped to give rise to the Muslim Brotherhood and to galvanize its membership, which stood on the frontlines in the battle with missionaries for the bodies and souls of Egyptian youth.

Using the discontent fostered by aggressive Christian proselytizing, the Brotherhood rallied support, mobilized members, and started new branches, with al-Banna touring the Canal Zone and Delta countryside in the summer of 1933 for that purpose. Yet the missionaries served as more than a rallying point for the Muslim Brotherhood and other Islamists: they also provided an excellent model for organizing and a template for action. Islamist organizations such as the Brotherhood developed, in part, in response to missionary enterprises as well as in their image, mimicking their ways and borrowing their tactics. Taking a page from the missionaries' script, the Brothers rewrote it for their own purposes. The copying and adapting was local and specific: a school answered a school, a factory challenged an industrial workshop, a branch of Muslim Sisters responded to Bible women. In this way, striving to take back the terrain ceded to missionaries and protected by British colonial officials, the Muslim Brotherhood established the foundation of their own network of social welfare institutions. The Brothers learned from their first adversaries that providing social welfare was an excellent way of recruiting supporters and spreading their message.

Members of the Brotherhood recognized that they were using the missionaries as a model at the time. As one Brother wrote, their strategy regarding missionaries was first to inform people of the danger arising from exposure to them, and second to adopt "the active means of the missionaries."[69] In contesting the presence of evangelicals and co-opting their ways, the Brotherhood had a very effective mold for producing its own missionaries, who could spread its ideas and the call (*da'wa*) to Islam throughout Egypt and beyond its borders. Christian missionaries helped to give the Brotherhood its shape, as the Brotherhood's activities and itineraries bore a striking resemblance to those of Protestant missionaries. When faced with inroads by evangelicals from the Egypt General Mission and others, the Brotherhood consciously learned from them and adapted their tools to fight them, in the process transforming these tools and techniques.

Hasan al-Banna noted in his memoirs that the anti-missionary campaign that started in al-Manzala and took off in Port Said "spread after that to many regions in Egypt," resulting in "the founding of a number of institutions, refuges, and foundations."[70] The Muslim Brotherhood inspired Muslims throughout the country to launch new social welfare projects. If al-Manzala provided the sparks and Port Said the ignition, then Turkiyya Hasan was the engine that drove the anti-missionary movement. The Muslim Brotherhood capitalized on her beating, elevating it from a local incident to a national scandal with international repercussions.

6 COMBATING CONVERSION
The Expansion of the Anti-Missionary Movement

TURKIYYA HASAN GOT A GREAT SEND-OFF at the Port Said train station on June 22, 1933, a week after addressing a gathering of more than fifty local citizens in an attempt to galvanize the anti-missionary movement and to raise money for a new orphanage. Supporters presented her with flowers to express "the admiration of the Muslim people of Port Said for her heroism and stead-fastness in withstanding the threats and cruelties of the missionaries who tried to force her to abandon the faith of Islam."[1] The fifteen-year-old symbol and spokeswoman of the anti-missionary movement boarded the train for Cairo at a quarter past noon. Escorted by a delegation that included Port Said Islamists Dr. Muhammad Sulayman, Muhammad Sarhan, and Muhammad Shirdi, she arrived four hours later at the Cairo Station, where again she received flowers, this time from the girls on the reception committee.[2]

After resting at a hotel, Turkiyya proceeded to the offices of the newspaper *al-Siyasa* for a ceremony in her honor and to thank the staff of the paper for the interest they had taken in her case. Muhammad Husayn Haykal, a well-known writer at the paper and a member of the Liberal Constitutionalist Party, and Hifni Bey Mahmud, the editor, welcomed her with refreshments. Her hosts asked her questions about evangelical methods used to convert Muslim students to Christianity and wondered why she had not consented under torture to accept Christianity. In reply, she expressed discomfort with the idea of a trinity, explaining that she could not believe that if God is One, as the Qur'an said, that he could be three, or that Jesus could have been a son of God, and she affirmed that she was ready to die for her beliefs. Her remarks impressed her hosts, who found them sincere and thoughtful.[3]

Keeping Turkiyya in the news antagonized Egyptian state officials, British colonial officers, Americans consuls, and foreign missionaries, who had all hoped to put the affair quickly behind them. The teenager played her part well, coming to Cairo expressly for the purpose of energizing the anti-missionary movement. After the reception at *al-Siyasa*, Turkiyya rode in a car with Haykal and Dr. Sulayman to the headquarters of the Jam'iyyat al-Shubban al-Muslimin (YMMA). The orphan from Port Said must have been duly impressed when she arrived at the hall, packed by activists who had gathered to launch the Jama'at al-Difa' 'an al-Islam (League for the Defense of Islam). Turkiyya watched as a coalition to fight proselytizing and combat conversion came together, inspired by her actions.[4]

The intensification of Protestant proselytizing had helped to spur the growth and spread of Islamic associations. Members of these associations sought to strengthen Islam and Muslim faith at a time when the community faced threats from within—secularists who looked to the West for models—and from without—foreign missionaries and occupiers who undermined Muslim religious practice and belief. The protests of Islamic activists reflected outrage over the impotence of Egyptians to rein in or oust missionaries under the British occupation and system of Capitulations inherited from the Ottoman Empire, which protected foreign nationals and gave foreign missionaries in Egypt a relatively free hand to proselytize.

In Cairo, the Muslim Brothers teamed up with a wide array of forces under the umbrella of the League for the Defense of Islam, a coalition of activists and intellectuals eager to cooperate in the struggle to contain the advances of missionaries and take back the terrain ceded to them. Drawing on the experiences of the Muslim Brotherhood in the Canal Zone and parts of the Delta, it came up with a national strategy to take on missionaries. Through petitions and appeals in the press, it advocated peaceful means to contain evangelical activity, including fundraising to start alternative institutions. Yet the league threatened more than the missionaries: it directly challenged the traditional standard bearers of Islam, throwing down the gauntlet to the leadership of al-Azhar, and spurring older social welfare associations, such as the Islamic Benevolent Society, to respond.

A Prescient Voice: Labiba Ahmad's Advocacy

The headquarters of the YMMA was the logical location for a group of Muslim activists to launch an organization to combat conversion. Founded in November 1927, the YMMA was consciously modeled after the Young Men's Christian Association, which had started a branch in Cairo in 1923.[5] Under the presidency of Dr. 'Abd al-Hamid Sa'id, the YMMA fought the Westernizing influence of foreigners and gave young men a place to congregate. It quickly became one of the largest Islamic associations in Egypt, drawing heavily from loyalists of the Watani Party.[6] Although she may not have been in the hall of the organization that evening, Labiba Ahmad had called for the establishment of such an association on the pages of her journal, *al-Nahda al-Nisa'iyya*, and had been advocating a stricter posture toward missionaries for years. She could find solace in the fact that others had finally seen the danger of evangelicals.

"It was our idea from the first appearance of the missionaries' movement . . . to ward off their attacks, end their movement, and close the doors through which they were accustomed to entering," wrote Labiba Ahmad in the summer of 1933.[7] She recognized the gendered dimension of the missionary threat. Most evangelicals were single women, who were cheaper to send abroad and in greater supply than their male counterparts, and they targeted young women by starting girls' schools, mother-child welfare clinics, and orphanages. They did this at a time when the Egyptian state and private associations were particularly slow in responding to the need for social welfare services for women and girls.

Labiba Ahmad followed the Turkiyya Hasan affair and the ensuing political storm it unleashed closely, taking to the airwaves in the summer of 1933. Like many of the stories of attempted conversion that surfaced that year, the Port Said orphan scandal centered on a young Muslim woman, a member of a demographic Labiba Ahmad had sworn to protect. "Their schools spread, their orphanages increased in number, and their hospitals multiplied," for the missionaries had found these paths effective to achieving their goal. The way to combat missionaries, Ahmad suggested, was to fight them on their own terms. "We said that day that it was a necessary duty for all of us to stand together as one unit . . . and gather funds and build orphanages for the poor and refuges for the elderly and hospitals for the wretched in order to block the path of the missionaries."[8] Ahmad had done precisely that, founding an orphanage for girls in the wake of World War I.

Although Labiba Ahmad had implemented her own orphanage project and acknowledged the hard work of others who started similar institutions, she recognized that Egyptians in general were slow to counter missionary enterprises. "Our call was not heard that day because many thought that the evangelical movement had weakened in intensity and folded." But, she wrote, missionaries took their work seriously, and "a frightening specter appeared, a large demon came out." As a consequence of the beating of Turkiyya, "the whole country rose up, informing the unaware and awaking the sleeping. We all sensed the danger to the people, and we learned that the danger would in the end cause the loss of religion."[9]

Labiba Ahmad served as patron of several associations, including the Society for Protecting the Holy Qur'an, which had been formed to promote knowledge of the Qur'an among the poor in response to inroads by missionaries and Bible women.[10] And she assumed the presidency of the Muslim Sisters branches of the Brotherhood at the behest of Hasan al-Banna, who had the highest regard for "the pious lady al-Hajja Labiba Ahmad" (she had made the pilgrimage to Mecca many times).[11] She, in turn, recognized his youthful talent and ability to organize. The first branch of the Muslim Sisters in Isma'iliyya had been followed by a second in Cairo and a third in Port Said, all as a direct response to proselytizing by foreign female missionaries and local Bible women. The Muslim Sisters worked to counter the effects of proselytizing.[12]

On the National Stage: The Muslim Brotherhood's Petition Campaign

Organizing from the ground up, the Muslim Brotherhood had set up its first branches in the provinces, coming into direct contact with evangelicals and gaining expertise in fighting them. After the move of the general headquarters from Isma'iliyya to Cairo, the Muslim Brothers could draw on that experience and combine a strategy of working locally to uproot missionaries with attempts to draw national attention to the problem of proselytizing. Al-Banna's years of fighting missionaries would help shape the strategy adopted by the League for the Defense of Islam. He was on hand for the planning and launching of the league, having just returned from the Muslim Brotherhood's first conference to address the problem of missionaries in Isma'iliyya. There the Brotherhood's General Advisory Council planned a petition campaign, setting out a plan of action against missionaries.[13]

The Muslim Brotherhood addressed its first petition to King Fu'ad, appealing to the "protector of Islam" to use his authority to help curtail evangelical activity. After a prelude singing the king's praises and pointing out the danger of missionaries, the petition gave concrete suggestions for containing proselytizing. It called for the imposition of strong controls on missionary schools, institutes, and centers as well as the students within them if it was shown they were proselytizing; demanded the withdrawal of the permit from any hospital or school where it was established that proselytizing occurred; and urged the government to deport all those who were proven to have "corrupted the faith" or hidden boys and girls. It also asked the government to block financial aid and grants of land to missionary societies, and called upon foreign representatives to help the government implement this "prudent course" for guarding security and improving relations. Hasan al-Banna, as the general guide, signed the petition first, followed by, among others, branch representatives from Isma'iliyya, al-Manzala, and Port Said.[14]

A second Muslim Brotherhood petition targeted the prime minister and the ministers of interior, education, and endowments as well as the heads of the Majlis al-Nuwwab (Chamber of Deputies) and Majlis al-Shuyukh (Senate). It opened by articulating the injury missionaries had inflicted: "The damage of missionaries to Islam and Muslims has increased, they have even invaded al-Azhar, and they have made hospitals, schools, and orphanages tools of aggression to Islam and the sons of Islam." A number of known events provided the best evidence of "this crude, recurring aggression."[15] The suggestions for actions to be taken were similar to those presented to the king but tailored for the ministers. The petition specifically called upon the Ministry of Education to investigate schools more closely, and it asked the minister of interior to distribute the money that had been earmarked for new girls' orphanages to Islamic societies, so that they could increase the number of orphanages and hospitals.[16]

Al-Banna sent a copy of the petitions to Shaykh Muhammad al-Ahmadi al-Zawahiri, the rector of al-Azhar, to enlist his support in the struggle against the missionaries.[17] But it would be al-Zawahiri's nemesis, Shaykh Muhammad Mustafa al-Maraghi, who was asked to serve as the president of the League for the Defense of Islam. The Brotherhood and other Islamic activists recognized that al-Azhar was simply too closely tied to the king, who controlled the pay scales of the rank and file 'ulama' (Muslim clerics) as well as the upkeep of mosques throughout Egypt through the Ministry of Religious Endowments. The history of the two competing clerics—al-Zawahiri and al-Maraghi—went back some time. Al-Maraghi had been selected rector of al-Azhar in 1928 with the backing of the prime minister, who wrangled with the king over the right to make the appointment. When al-Maraghi's reform agenda failed, he was forced to resign, and King Fu'ad named al-Zawahiri to the post. Al-Zawahiri still held the position in the summer of 1933, having worked with Fu'ad to make the university a royal stronghold.[18]

The Muslim Brotherhood received praise in Parliament and acknowledgment in the press—particularly in *al-Jihad* and *al-Fath*—for its role in disseminating news of the beating of Turkiyya Hasan and exposing missionary excesses. But there were limits to what the young organization with its twenty-something leader could do on its own. Combating missionaries would take a larger army than al-Banna marshaled, and he looked for allies, joining forces with others to form a coalition opposed to proselytizing.

Fighting Proselytizing: The League for the Defense of Islam

The day before the gathering at the YMMA, Dr. ʿAbd al-Hamid Bey Saʿid, president of the association and a Watani Party deputy, took the floor in the Chamber of Deputies to confront the interior minister, Mahmud Fahmi al-Qaysi, who had appeared to discuss legislation earmarking 20,000 pounds for establishing homes for orphans and destitute children. Arguing that the "amount of this authorization is not enough," Dr. ʿAbd al-Hamid Saʿid urged the government to take decisive action to curb missionaries and asked it to set aside a more reasonable amount to stop a movement the likes of which they had not seen "since the Middle Ages." He reminded his fellow parliamentarians, "The prime minister [Sidqi, who was then abroad] declared last year in your presence that Egypt would not become a field for evangelizing," but, he said, missionaries continued "their excesses, terrorization, and crimes." The YMMA president noted that foreign missionaries were clearly not frightened by the government and "worked at destroying the Islamic religion, as happened recently in the city of Port Said." To a Parliament packed with Sidqi supporters, he called upon the government to limit aid to the American University in Cairo and other missionary schools, to sponsor a law to control nongovernment schools, and to prosecute missionary crimes against the innocent.[19]

In Parliament, Dr. ʿAbd al-Hamid Saʿid rehearsed the demands of the League for the Defense of Islam. The preceding Sunday, the organizing committee had met to draft proposals for the launch of the league. Representing the YMMA, he was joined by Dr. Ahmad Yahya al-Dardiri (editor of the group's review), Shaykh Muhammad ʿAbd al-Latif Diraz (another YMMA activist), ʿAbd al-Qadir Hamza (editor of *al-Balagh*), and Shaykh ʿAbd al-Wahhab al-Hajjar, among others. The organizers cast a large net for the gathering planned for Thursday evening, trying to assemble a broad coalition of political activists, social leaders, religious scholars, intellectuals, and energetic youth for the launch of the league.[20]

On the one hand, there were young activists such as Hasan al-Banna. On the other, there were intellectuals such as Haykal. Turkiyya's tale had captured the attention of Haykal, who as a journalist at *al-Siyasa* and a fiction writer had shown an interest in the lives of women. His first novel, *Zaynab* (considered by many to be the first Arabic novel), took up the story of a romance between an illiterate peasant woman and an educated urban man. In the 1930s, he shifted his focus from secular to Islamic subjects. At the time of the orphan scandal, he was working on a biography of the Prophet Muhammad, chapters of which were published regularly in the weekly edition of *al-Siyasa*. When *Hayat Muhammad* subsequently came out as a book, Haykal explained that he had been motivated to write it by the combination of "the activity of Christian missionaries in Islamic nations and the support of Western policy for the spokesmen of Islamic stagnation."[21]

Haykal arrived at the YMMA the evening of the launch of the League for the Defense of Islam with Turkiyya Hasan. Over four hundred prominent Muslim men of various classes, from effendis to pashas, and various party affiliations, from Liberal Constitutionalists to Watanists, had gathered. After a reading from the Qur'an, Shaykh al-Maraghi delivered a lengthy oratory on the plan to combat conversion and coordinate the attack against missionary proselytizing. A representative of the organizing group then read proposals to the crowded hall, reiterating many of the points articulated by the Muslim Brotherhood. The proposals called for publicizing the League for the Defense of Islam's positions through letters, petitions, and press releases; raising funds to establish Muslim institutions to replace those of missionaries; and urging government ministries to shore up Islamic education and open more hospitals. Additionally, the planning group proposed establishing a higher committee and subcommittees in Cairo and throughout the country. It called for the mobilization of imams and 'ulama' to counter missionary activities and the formation of a committee of 'ulama' and writers to edit a book on the preaching of Islam.[22]

The League for the Defense of Islam drew upon the Muslim Brotherhood's hands-on experience in fighting missionaries to formulate its strategic plan. This was not surprising given the involvement of Hasan al-Banna and other members of the Brotherhood in the league. Like the Brotherhood, the League for the Defense of Islam sought to fight fire with fire, using methods similar to those of the missionaries to counter them. An important component of this was developing alternative social welfare institutions to those of the missionaries. Al-Maraghi would tell Sir Alexander Keown-Boyd that the government could not do this on its own, so the league hoped that it could sway public opinion and raise funds to place orphaned and poor children in better situations.[23]

The assembly voted to accept the proposals and elected a higher committee of former cabinet ministers, parliamentarians, political activists, and prominent writers to carry them through. The higher committee, like the league itself, represented a broad coalition. Those elected included Dr. ʿAbd al-Hamid Saʿid, ʿAbd al-Rahman al-Rafiʿ (a Watani Party deputy and public historian), Bahaʾ al-Din Barakat (a former cabinet minister), and Haykal. The Muslim Brotherhood was represented on the committee by Hasan "Effendi" al-Banna and Muhibb al-Din al-Khatib, a YMMA founder and director of the Muslim Brotherhood newspaper *Jaridat al-Ikhwan al-Muslimin*. Dr. Muhammad Sulayman was also elected to the higher committee.[24]

After the organization's launch, the higher committee of the League for the Defense of Islam met and prepared a series of petitions similar to those penned by the Muslim Brotherhood. This, of course, was not a coincidence, as the Brotherhood members on the committee not only brought their expertise from encounters with missionaries to the table but no doubt brought drafts of the petitions they had penned.[25] Al-Maraghi, in the company of a delegation, took the league's first petition to the palace, hand delivering it to the vice chief of the royal cabinet. In the petition, the League for the Defense of Islam pointed out that Egypt had been "invaded" by missionaries, who initially had tried to work honestly, but when they did not succeed had turned to "base methods," arousing public anger. The nation, as a result, appealed to the Egyptian monarch to direct his government "to repulse the repeated transgressions on the religion of Islam by missionaries." The petition warned that things could escalate if the government did not rein in the missionaries.[26]

A few days later Shaykh al-Maraghi and two deputies from Parliament presented a petition to Acting Prime Minister Muhammad Shafiq Pasha. This second petition noted assaults on Orthodox Christians as well as on Muslims and urged the government to take definitive action to "put a stop to all subversive activities of the missionaries." Explaining that it was not enough to send away one missionary who had been cruel to a girl who had refused to accept Christianity—acknowledging the treatment of Turkiyya Hasan—the petition pressed the government to discontinue assistance to missionaries, withdraw land grants, enact and enforce criminal legislation, and prevent missionaries from working with the young.[27]

A third petition in French and Arabic targeted representatives of foreign powers in Egypt, including the head of the American legation. It affirmed Egypt's commitment to good relations with foreign guests: "This country has warmly welcomed foreign societies and missions, persuaded that they intended only to spread instruction and to serve humanity." Some had "noble aims," but others had used their schools to proselytize, and the petition pointed to the symbol of the movement: "This year they have not hesitated to employ violence against a young girl of fifteen years, Turkiyya Hasan of Port Said." The petitioners mentioned that missionaries used sweets in other localities to attract children, "invaded" villages to distribute circulars attacking Islam to peasants, and utilized other "offensive means." Noting that criminal acts aroused hatred and anger, and threatened public order and cordial relations between Egyptians and their guests, the petition appealed to foreign representatives to end the "offensive actions" of missionaries.[28]

While making appeals to the king, ministers, and foreign powers, the higher committee of the League for the Defense of Islam turned its attention to the Egyptian population, circulating a series of proclamations to "the nation" pointing out the danger of missionary institutions, whose evangelizing was strictly forbidden by Islamic law. "You know that the missionaries in this country have been converting children by cruel and abominable measures and you know that they have taken an evil attitude toward your religion," one proclamation stated.[29] The public call advocated boycotts, urging Muslims to remove their children from missionary schools and to refrain from sending them to missionary orphanages.[30]

The League for the Defense of Islam recognized that boycotts would not be effective in the absence of orphanages and schools for Muslim children. It appealed to the population for funds, noting that the league's "programme cannot be executed without the financial assistance of the Nation," and that it was time to send money to "defend your honour and ward off this disgraceful attack," an attack of those who appear "in a civilized guise, but have in fact, the qualities of wolves."[31] Directing attention to "the missionary invasion of Egypt," the league argued that the only way possible to fight "the harm of their orphanages, hospitals, and schools, was through charitable works," and called for all who were capable to "sacrifice a piaster to defend Islam."[32] This initiative mimicked the successful Piaster Plan inaugurated in 1931 by a circle of nationalist students trying to promote Egyptian industry. The group had collected enough money in a year to start a fez factory, gaining credibility and transforming itself into the Young Egypt Society, a popular patriotic youth group with its own para-military organization.[33]

When asked later, Shaykh al-Maraghi told Keown-Boyd that he had accepted the presidency of the League for the Defense of Islam for a variety of reasons, among them his "strong personal feelings and convictions" regarding missionary activities in the country. Al-Maraghi had sent his own daughter, 'Azza, to a Church Missionary Society girls' school in Khartoum when he was grand qadi of the Sudan. From "his own knowledge and experience," Keown-Boyd wrote, he knew that missionaries "got hold of young Moslem boys and girls and persons of weak intelligence" and converted them as well as others motivated by personal (rather than spiritual) objectives (e.g., jobs and marriage). "This was an evil to which an end must be put."[34]

When Keown-Boyd pointed to the health and education benefits of missionary enterprises, Shaykh al-Maraghi suggested that "it was high time for the country to supply its own needs in this matter and render itself independent of outside help." Yet he stopped short of wanting to expel missionaries altogether, for he realized that this would make it impossible to send Muslim missionaries to China or other Eastern countries in the future "or if need be in years to come to England."[35] Al-Maraghi also had practical reasons for taking on the post of president of the League for the Defense of Islam, for he thought that he could use his contacts to help the cause and steer the group away from extremist action.

Catch-Up: Al-Azhar Enters the Fray

The would-be protectors of Islam at the center of Islamic learning could no longer afford to sit on the sidelines as spectators in the struggle between missionaries and Islamic activists and let the ex-rector of al-Azhar take the lead. They had to answer the actions of competitors and respond to accusations that they were passive in confronting Christian proselytizing. While the Brotherhood had appealed to the rector of al-Azhar to join the fight against missionaries, the press was less gentle, lampooning the Shaykh al-Azhar for inaction in articles and cartoons. A cartoon in *Ruz al-Yusuf*, in particular, showed him in a highly negative light.[36]

Al-Azhar had been the sight of a painful missionary-Muslim encounter only a few years earlier. On the morning of April 10, 1928, Dr. Samuel Zwemer entered the hallowed halls of al-Azhar with a small group of visitors, including a couple of women, to engage students in conversation and distribute missionary tracts. The outing was not unusual for the affiliate of the American Mission and field referee of the Swedish Salaam Mission to Muslims: Zwemer had been a regular visitor to al-Azhar for a dozen years and held a license issued by the Ministry of Religious Endowments to enter mosques, museums, and monuments as a scholar for free.[37]

"It is always my custom to offer a printed tract as a Christian message to those who are interested and willing to read," Zwemer explained to the American chargé d'affaires investigating the incident that occurred that day. "I did so that morning to three or four individuals who asked for it," he said, indicating that he responded to a request for literature rather than pressured people to take it, which would have been illegal (though such hair-splitting meant little to the guardians of al-Azhar). The pamphlet he distributed, *Return to the Old Qibla*, called upon Muslims to return to their former direction of prayer, in short, to Christianity. One of the shaykhs at al-Azhar confronted him for his audacity and "bad taste" in distributing Christian tracts to Muslim students and tore up the tract. A student from the shaykh's entourage then yelled, "Down with evangelism," creating a stir. News of the confrontation spread, leading to a strike by three thousand Azhari students and to protests in the Egyptian Parliament.[38]

In the aftermath of the incident, Zwemer turned in his visitor's pass to the authorities, apologized, and decided to leave the country for the summer to allow the storm to die down. Once the aftershocks of this episode had subsided, senior scholars at al-Azhar retreated to their scholarship. Over a year later, in the summer of 1929, however, the American maverick nearly sparked a "second Zwemer incident," though this time not in the sanctified halls of al-Azhar. After rumors surfaced that he was distributing missionary literature in cafes in Alexandria, the American chargé d'affaires again questioned him. Zwemer acknowledged that he had become a "marked man" after the first incident at al-Azhar and assured the official that he had not distributed unsolicited Christian tracts, but he admitted that he still handed literature out when asked and had done so recently on a train. Shortly thereafter, Zwemer left Egypt to become a professor of the history of religion and Christian missions at the Princeton Theological Seminary.[39]

Zwemer's aggressive proselytizing amongst Muslims during his tenure overseas left a lasting impression at al-Azhar. But in June 1933, in the midst of the orphan scandal, the 'ulama' of al-Azhar stood on the sidelines, preferring not to lead the charge against evangelicals. Still, quiescence in the face of growing popular protests would not do, especially when competitors—and the former rector of al-Azhar at that—took the initiative. On Monday evening, June 26, 1933, three days after the launch of the League for the Defense of Islam, al-Zawahiri convened a meeting of the Body of Grand 'Ulama' to discuss the missionary conversion scandal. The group issued a manifesto, calling upon the government to enact legislation protecting Egyptians from proselytizing, "to tear this iniquity out by the roots," and to find a cure for this "epidemic disease."[40]

The statement was "not as bad as it might have been, but it is not very calming," Keown-Boyd wrote to the British acting high commissioner Ronald Campbell. "It seems the Sheikh-el-Azhar was kept quiet for some time, but, bullied by the Alema ['Ulama'], spurred by the press who made cartoons of him and accused him of 'trading in religion' and galled by Sheikh El-Maraghi stepping into the place where he felt he should be, threatened that he and his dean and others would resign if not allowed to make some public sign of activity."[41] The leadership of al-Azhar had its response to the League for the Defense of Islam vetted in three days of discussions with Egyptian government officials, who toned down the statement released. The original version, according to the acting prime minister, had been "extremely violent."[42]

Joining the war of words would not by itself win the clerics control of the anti-missionary movement. The Body of Grand 'Ulama' therefore issued a strong appeal for donations to combat missionary work: "O Muslims! The saving of Islam and Muslim children is in building hospitals, schools, and orphanages like those [of the missionaries] and paying for this is the duty of the Muslim community—the government and the people of different classes, led by the 'ulama.'"[43] To set an example, the rector of the university and the grand mufti, among others, publicized the amounts of their donations.[44]

At the meeting of the Body of Grand 'Ulama', al-Zawahiri, acting "under instructions," had overseen the production of the draft of a sermon that was meant to be delivered in all mosques throughout the country the next Friday. Before it could be delivered, however, it had to be submitted to the Ministry of Interior for approval, and "if necessary, correction," Keown-Boyd told the acting high commissioner.[45] The text was supposed to focus on the opposition to violence in religious matters, but when it was received by the Ministry of Interior for review, it was discovered that the "Sheikh must have misunderstood the prescription, as some of the ingredients on analysis were found to be irritant rather than sedative," wrote Keown-Boyd. "The compound is being re-distilled here by a tame and cunning Alem ['Alim]."[46] The toned-down sermon was then sent around the country by the Ministry of Religious Endowments in the hope of keeping the message unified and quieting the anti-missionary movement.

After an attack on priests at Jirja in Upper Egypt in early July 1933, the grand mufti strongly endorsed nonviolence in an interview with *al-Ahram*: "I consider it my duty to declare that any person who attacks or attempts to attack any of our brethren, the Christians or others, cannot be but one who wishes to obstruct our attempt and to stand as a stumbling block in our way," al-Zawahiri said. "We have made this point clear in the appeal we addressed to the nation as well as it was made clear in the sermon distributed by the Ministry of Wakfs [Religious Endowments] for the Imams to read in all the Mosques." Theirs was a "peaceful struggle," raising funds for refuges, homes, schools, and hospitals: "Let every Moslem understand this fact and let him use the same weapons and let him give money as much as he can for this purpose."[47]

Al-Azhar strove to regain its reputation as the public protector of Islam, playing catch-up with the League for the Defense of Islam. Over a week after their rivals had presented a petition to the acting prime minister, al-Zawahiri carried a petition from the Body of Grand 'Ulama' to Shafiq.[48] But it was not the only group trying to play catch up in order to assume the leadership of the anti-missionary movement.

Into the Breach: The Islamic Benevolent Society

Two days after the convening of the Body of Grand 'Ulama', and nearly a week after the launching of the League for the Defense of Islam, members of the central committee of al-Jam'iyya al-Khayriyya al-Islamiyya (Islamic Benevolent Society) gathered in a special session. They assembled at the home of Muhammad Mahmud Pasha, president, one-time prime minister, and head of the Liberal Constitutionalist Party, to lobby for a chunk of the state funds that had been earmarked for orphanages for Muslim children. Hoping to assert its position as the pre-eminent Muslim social welfare association in Egypt, its officers wanted a slice of the pie and access to the funds of private donors.[49]

A circle of prominent Egyptians—among them the Islamic reformer Muhammad 'Abduh and nationalist leaders Mustafa Kamil, Tal'at Harb, and Sa'd Zaghlul—had launched the society in the early 1890s. The society drew support from the upper echelons of Egyptian society, from pashas and beys, ministers, and parliamentary deputies who made up the membership and gained prestige through their public contributions to social welfare projects. Breaking from older forms of Islamic charity, in which an individual set up a private endowment to fund a soup kitchen, fountain, school, or hospital, it adopted a collective model and developed a reputation for its institutions.[50]

Meeting Wednesday, June 28, the central committee of the Islamic Benevolent Society passed several resolutions. It allocated funds for the rapid expansion of schools in six locations, including Port Said; new wings to five schools to operate as refuges for poor children taken out of missionary orphanages; and an addition on a refuge for boys already in existence, the Malja' al-'Abbasiyya, to accommodate girls. The committee also planned to accelerate the building of two large orphanages—one for boys and one for girls—next to the hospital it had under construction in 'Aguza, Giza.[51] That project had been launched in response to regular reports of conversion in foreign mission hospitals, the largest of which was the British Church Missionary Society Hospital, known as al-Harmil, in Old Cairo. Even as construction commenced on the new hospital, a man complained to the Ministry of Interior that his sister Zaynab had been converted in al-Harmil and had taken the name Maryam 'Abd al-Masih.[52]

The Islamic Benevolent Society called for a unified effort with the Body of Grand 'Ulama' and the League for the Defense of Islam, hoping those organizations would cooperate and share funds collected for building orphanages. The society also requested access to public funds set aside by the state for this purpose. And it delegated members such as Dr. 'Abd al-Hamid Sa'id to approach the government, the league, and the Body of Grand 'Ulama' to convey its decisions and desires.[53]

Yet the society was not without its critics. Just as Islamists condemned the clerics of al-Azhar for their passivity in the face of missionary inroads, they challenged the curriculum in the schools of the Islamic Benevolent Society. The goal of the society was to provide social welfare to poor Muslims rather than to revive Islam as such. Some of its schools did not have compulsory prayer and, according to critics, emphasized the teaching of English or physical education over instruction in Islam. While abhorring the proselytizing of Christian missionaries, Islamists admired their commitment to teaching religion and saw an alternative model to the secularized fare of the Egyptian state, which the Islamic Benevolent Society essentially replicated. Rather than following secular models, Islamic activists called for copying Christian schools, especially Catholic ones such as those of the Frères and the Jesuits, which inculcated the principles and practices of Christianity and taught the literature and history of the church and Christian nations. And rather than simply churn out government bureaucrats, these schools prepared graduates, as one writer argued, to work in "the battleground of life"—in financial, economic, or trade markets—and as such did not become a "burden on the nation."[54]

❋

Activists such as Labiba Ahmad had railed against missionaries for years, and Islamists working on the ground, such as the Muslim Brothers and Muslim Sisters, were well aware of the inroads missionaries had made (or were threatening to make) in converting orphans and abandoned children. But it took a case like the Turkiyya Hasan affair to catalyze the movement against missionaries, marking a turning point in the encounter between missionaries and Muslims. A coalition, including individuals as well as groups such as the Muslim Brotherhood, the YMMA, and the Society for Protecting the Holy Qur'an, came together under the umbrella of the League for the Defense of Islam to rally against missionary institutions and to develop Islamic ones in their stead.

The formation of the League for the Defense of Islam set off a heated competition for leadership of the Muslim community. By calling for greater action in curbing the activities of missionaries in the wake of the beating of Turkiyya, Islamists challenged the traditional authority of al-Azhar as the protector of Islam. Most Islamists saw Azharis as uninterested or unable to lead a revival of Islam, due in part to their close ties to the government. The leadership of al-Azhar tried to regain the high ground and to restore its rightful role as public defender of Islam and leader of the Egyptian Muslim community by convening the Body of Grand 'Ulama'. While the Muslim Brotherhood cooperated with the League for the Defense of Islam, the league and the Body of Grand 'Ulama' competed for leadership of the anti-missionary movement.

The Islamic Benevolent Society stepped into the fray, seeking to preserve its dominance as the premier Muslim social welfare provider and control funds raised or set aside for the building of orphanages. The society sought to lead the effort, capitalizing on the momentum from the Turkiyya Hasan affair to expand its institutions and to launch new schools and refuges. Yet the group was not exempt from criticism, as Islamists, who were both inspired and repulsed by missionary institutions, considered the Islamic Benevolent Society schools too secular in orientation. Islamists wanted institutions that mirrored those of Protestant and Catholic missionaries in their rigor in inculcating religion, replacing Christian indoctrination with Islamic learning. In short, missionary institutions provided Egyptians with a new model of religious education, helping to derail a movement in the direction of secularized education that had been underway in Egypt for years.

Some of the intensity of the anti-missionary movement in the summer of 1933 may have been triggered by an opposition ready to exploit weakness on the part of the government and a press eager to capitalize on controversy. Yet the struggle went much deeper. The orphan scandal politicized Islam in new ways, as formerly liberal-minded thinkers such as Muhammad Husayn Haykal shifted from a secular to Islamic outlook, and those predisposed to Islamic politics found a compelling cause. The scandal fueled competition to lead the Muslim community, calling into question the ability of al-Azhar to spearhead an Islamic revival and opening the doors to laymen to take the initiative and interpret Islamic ideas and practices. This was not merely a return to Islam but a turning of Islam in a new direction, with new foot soldiers and leaders, and new agendas, marking a seismic shift in the place of Islam in Egyptian society and politics.

Christian missionaries had unwittingly launched a war in Egypt, leading to a volatile situation in the summer of 1933. Protests against missionaries grew louder, with echoes reverberating in Europe and the United States. If the semi-colonial Egyptian state could not control the anti-missionary movement through its religious proxy—al-Azhar—it had to crush it, starting with the League for the Defense of Islam.

7 CRACKDOWN

Suppressing the League for the Defense of Islam

IN THE DAYS AFTER attending the launch of the League for the Defense of Islam, Turkiyya made the rounds of newspapers to give interviews and promote the battle against Christian proselytizing and conversion. At each stop she answered questions from editors and writers about her experiences at the Swedish Salaam Mission, giving the most exhaustive account of her ordeal in *al-Jihad*. Between interviews, she had lunches at the Pressman's Club in the company of such writers as 'Abd al-Qadir Hamza, editor of *al-Balagh*. These meals must have been quite a treat for a fifteen-year-old who a couple of weeks earlier had been dining on the institutional fare served up in the orphanage. Turkiyya made some fundraising stops as well, visiting the home of a donor her escorts were cultivating to contribute to the building of an orphanage for Muslim children in Port Said. And she got a chance to visit such sites as the Zoological Gardens and enjoy a feature at the cinema.[1]

After an eventful visit in Cairo, Turkiyya Hasan and her party boarded the train back to Port Said. On the journey home, the train stopped in the Benha and Zaqaziq stations, where delegations greeted the returning party and congratulated its members on the anti-missionary movement that they had been pivotal in promoting. Upon her return from Cairo, Turkiyya began working in the Ophthalmology Hospital in Port Said where Dr. Sulayman practiced. Her patrons launched a campaign to raise funds to help her live independently of the missionaries, with one of her supporters stipulating that the proceeds of the sale of five hundred copies of an Islamic book he had sent to the city should go to Turkiyya.[2]

The Egyptian state had moved quickly to contain the Turkiyya Hasan affair, with the acting prime minister extracting Muslim girls from the Swedish Salaam School in Port Said, expelling the matron who had beaten Turkiyya from the country, and designating seventy thousand pounds for new orphanages. Yet after the minister of interior, Mahmud Fahmi al-Qaysi Pasha, appeared in the Chamber of Deputies on June 21, 1933, to discuss the government's plan, the representative from Alexandria, 'Ali Bey Hasan, asked some pointed questions. A Muslim Brotherhood sympathizer, he wondered if all the Muslim girls had been handed over to the government and what it had resolved to do regarding the upbringing of these girls. Did they have a permanent plan or only a temporary one? Was the government content with its presence in Port Said in the wake of the missionary incident? Had it decided to assert itself in other places in the country in which missionary stations were even more dangerous than in Port Said? He pointed to al-Mahmudiyya (Hasan al-Banna's hometown), where residents had turned to the Muslim Brotherhood to save their children from women missionaries, and al-Manzala, where one of the girls fleeing the missionaries had sought protection with the Muslim Brotherhood. His list went on—what about Suez, Dikirnis, Shibin al-Kawm?—a list that included places where the Salaam and Egypt General Missions had established bases and where the Muslim Brotherhood branches had mobilized in response.[3]

Many Egyptians saw the government measures as incomplete: the Turkiyya Hasan affair was only the latest in a series of episodes involving missionaries that Egyptian officials seemed unable or unwilling to manage. As public anger against missionary attempts to convert Muslim orphans to Christianity mounted and support for the League for the Defense of Islam grew, the state had to take action. Yet rather than move decisively to control the missionaries, which was impossible given the constraints of the British occupation and the Capitulatory regime put in place under the Ottomans, it focused on containing, then crushing, the anti-missionary movement.

The Semi-Colonial State Strikes Back

The Egyptian government operated under the fiction of independence, which Great Britain had declared unilaterally in 1922, giving up the formality of the protectorate established at the outset of World War I. The British retained indirect control of the country, overseeing the promulgation of the Constitution of 1923, the crowning of a king, and the formation of a multiparty parliamentary system. The Egyptian officials at the helm of what was effectively a semi-colonial government continued to face restrictions from the British, who retained a large occupation force near the Suez Canal ready for redeployment. The imperial power continued to assert its authority over realms that involved its interests, such as Egypt's relationship to the Sudan, foreign affairs, minority rights, and the matter of the Suez Canal, which were left for future negotiations.

The Egyptian state in the interwar period thus looked more like the mandatory regimes in Iraq or Jordan than the independent monarchy that it was declared to be. Although Egyptian politicians faced elections, they proved more responsive to advisement from British officials than to Egyptian voters, who were limited in number in any case. Some of these officials, such as Sir Alexander Keown-Boyd, were embedded in the government with special appointments. As director general of the European Department in the Ministry of Interior, Keown-Boyd's job was to act as an intermediary between the government and European citizens, whom he was meant to protect. Others acted as advisers whose recommendations to Egyptian ministers were to be respected. British and Egyptian officials, most of whom came from the landed elite, generally shared an interest in working issues out together.

In the summer of 1933, Egyptian officials faced multiple challenges. To start, Isma'il Sidqi, a strongman prime minister who had abrogated the Constitution of 1923, was out of the country convalescing in Europe. He left in place a Parliament packed with supporters (the opposition had boycotted the elections) along with an acting prime minister, Muhammad Shafiq Pasha, who lacked his political acumen. Wiring his delegates from abroad when the orphan scandal broke, Sidqi recommended "vigilance in the protection of minorities," for he feared that failure to protect local Christians would impede future Anglo-Egyptian negotiations.[4] The acting prime minister and acting high commissioner (Ronald Campbell had replaced Sir Percy Lorraine, who had stepped down that summer) faced a king—Fu'ad—with a decade of experience in making and breaking governments, and ambitions for a larger role in the Muslim world, even after his bid for the caliphate had failed. Egyptians governing the country in the summer of 1933 had to negotiate some rough currents if they wanted to retain their jobs.

The missionary orphan scandal placed Egyptian government officials in an awkward situation. Not only were missionaries protected by the Capitulations and the occupation, but they provided a range of greatly needed social services on the cheap. Ultimately, Egyptian officials saw the anti-missionary movement as a greater threat than the missionaries. Pressured by British officials, the

Egyptian government used a multipronged strategy to shut down this threat, targeting the League for the Defense of Islam as the embodiment of the movement. Shifting its focus from missionary excess to excessive anti-missionary activity, it squashed press coverage, public meetings, and fundraising, with little respect for civil liberties. Most of the missionaries themselves emerged that summer relatively unscathed from attempts by the state to control their activities or censure them, but the tide had begun to turn against them.

Stifling Dissent: The Suppression of the Press

Journalists saw themselves as a critical part of the campaign against missionaries, expressing discontent in a flurry of articles, editorials, and cartoons. A telling cartoon that appeared in *al-Lata'if al-Musawwara* on July 3, 1933 (see the illustration on p. 110), shows editors from leading newspapers—*al-Balagh*, *al-Jihad*, *Kawkab al-Sharq*, and *al-Siyasa* (the papers Turkiyya had visited when in Cairo)—all dressed similarly in suits and fezzes (signs of a Westernized professional class) sitting astride their respective newspapers. They ride their papers like horses on the "battlefield of the press," wielding swords and in one case a lance against an array of missionaries standing behind the walls of "the Capitulations." The four male and two female missionaries, whose national flags fly over the ramparts of the crusader-style walls, are French, Greek, Italian, Belgian, American, and British, with the last holding a Bible slightly aloft. Their headdress and robes mark them as affiliated with Protestant, Catholic, and Greek Orthodox churches and special orders, and include monks, priests, pastors, nuns, and evangelicals. The missionaries, some smirking, look down from the crusader walls on the journalists, indicating that this is an unfair battle. The caption reads, "Every one of the knights is a chivalrous hero . . . fighting those who are hidden in the fortress of colonialism."[5]

Under the authority of Section 153 of the Penal Code—which mandated penalties for incitement to hatred of one section of the community against another—the Parquet began investigating critical news periodicals. It interrogated editors and journalists, issuing warnings to periodicals that were seen as supporting the anti-missionary movement.[6] Many of those called before the authorities in these investigations were or would become active members of the League for the Defense of Islam. On Thursday, June 22, the day the league was launched, the Cairo Parquet summoned Hifni Bey Mahmud, the editor of *al-Siyasa*, and 'Abduh Effendi al-Zayyat, the editor of *Kawkab al-Sharq*, to appear before the tribunal to discuss an article on missionaries that had been published in the latter paper and commented upon in the former.[7] The head of the Parquet later had the offices of the two papers searched, and questioned Dr. Taha Husayn, a respected writer and the author of the *Kawkab al-Sharq* article.[8] Five days later, the chief of the tribunal summoned Hifni Mahmud to his office again, this time with Muhammad Husayn Haykal, who was on the higher committee of the League for the Defense of Islam.[9] The Parquet continued to summon journalists, questioning ʿAbbas Effendi Hafiz, editor of *al-Wadi*, in early July about articles on missionaries in his newspaper.[10]

The clampdown on the press came at the behest of the acting high commissioner Campbell, who spoke to the acting prime minister, Shafiq, about "the incitements contained in press articles." Using the language of liberalism, he told Shafiq "that the sort of thing that was going on could not but damage the reputation of Egypt abroad as an enlightened country with a constitution designed to consecrate its position as such."[11] In a discussion in late June with William Jardine, the head of the American legation, Campbell explained that he had taken measures to quiet or end the agitation, for "the whole of the Moslem population of Egypt had become thoroughly aroused." His measures included advising Egyptian authorities to take action "to prevent the Moslem press from publishing inflamatory [sic] articles as it has been doing for the past month."[12]

Campbell saw the press as stirring up anti-missionary sentiment rather than reporting it. He spoke with the American representative after isolated attacks in Cairo on American missionaries who worked with the Nile Evangelical Campaign and the American Church of God Mission. Yet the clampdown on the press had started even before scattered violence broke out, and a compiled list of attacks on missionaries showed that the number of such attacks was far fewer than the rhetoric of the colonial authorities would suggest. But for British colonial authorities, one attack, or the threat of one attack, was too many.[13]

Great Britain's man behind the scenes, Keown-Boyd, made sure that the Egyptian government followed through on Campbell's advice. "Nearly all the individual papers were warned that the Public Security Department had noted with concern that the press was full of missionary news much of which was fabricated or exaggerated," he reported in early July. Alluding to Article 153 of the Penal Code, he explained that because this missionary news "was likely to arouse hatred of a section of the community and cause disturbance of public order," any paper that repeated an offense was referred to the Parquet for trial and punishment.[14]

British and Egyptian officials framed the anti-missionary movement as the efforts of an angry opposition eager to discredit the government and dismissed claims of journalists and members of the League for the Defense of Islam of missionary improprieties as attempts to sell newspapers. But framing the opposition in this way ignored the very real concerns many Egyptians had about the threats that missionaries and other foreigners in Egypt presented to Muslims and to Islam as well as to national sovereignty. The league and Muslim Brotherhood had sought to articulate these concerns through the press.

The dance between the Parquet and the press continued through the summer, with warnings repeated and newspaper owners and editors facing trials. In late July, the Cairo Parquet summoned Sulayman Effendi Fawzi, the owner and editor of *al-Kashkul*, to question him on an anti-missionary cartoon that appeared in his periodical, and it ordered Taha Husayn and 'Abduh al-Zayyat of *Kawkab al-Sharq* to appear for questioning on an article that was considered defamatory to the rector of al-Azhar.[15] Some of these proceedings ended in trials: after completing an investigation of *al-Sarih*, the Parquet referred its owner, manager, and caricaturist to the 'Abdin Summary Court for a trial on charges of publishing libelous and defamatory material.[16] The Parquet referred another two newspapers covering the anti-missionary movement to trial for publishing libelous articles: *al-Siyasa* for an article carried in June that was considered offensive to the minister of interior, and *Kawkab al-Sharq* for insulting other cabinet ministers.[17]

The orphan scandal began to draw unwanted international attention, increasing the incentives to clamp down on the Egyptian press. The German government had launched a press campaign of its own against the anti-missionary movement, seeking to protect the privileges of its Protestant evangelicals. Forced to respond, acting prime minister Shafiq and the acting foreign minister used various channels to placate German officials and German public opinion about the Turkiyya Hasan affair.[18] Italians also closely followed the affair, with Catholic Church representatives pointing out that the Italian missions active in Egypt for a century were not involved in any of the recent conversion incidents. *Il Giornale d'Oriente* maintained that Catholic missions "have never had recourse to subversive means to influence the humanitarian, cultural and civilizing work, remaining firm in their attitude of absolute respect towards the religion and the traditions of Islam." In a stab at Protestants, Italian Catholics resented that their actions were placed "in the same basket" as the "incriminated activities of societies which are neither Italian nor Catholic."[19] International attention further forced an Egyptian state already concerned about the opposition to take strong action against the anti-missionary movement.

Under direct instructions from the British, who were acting in coordination with the Americans, and facing pressure from other foreign governments, the Egyptian state muzzled the Arabic press. Officials raised the specter of a "disturbance of public order," interpreting it broadly; they warned the press and then took disciplinary action against select papers. The government moved very quickly to rein in the press, but much less quickly to rein in missionaries. Threats and trials may have succeeded in subduing coverage of missionary affairs but did not dissipate Egyptian anger over proselytizing.

Tightening the Screws: The Banning of Public Meetings

The League for the Defense of Islam had tried to channel anger at missionaries into legitimate action, with leaders calling for the use of peaceful, nonviolent means to oppose missionaries. Since the league did not want to give the government an excuse to impose restrictions, its members were quick to condemn violence, especially after sporadic attacks on missionaries were reported in late June.[20] The event that gave the government the excuse to further tighten the screws on the anti-missionary movement and ban the right to assemble involved French Franciscan sisters in the Delta town of Kafr al-Zayyat and took place on July 11.[21] By that time, attacks may have been hard to prevent given the level of public anger at inaction on the part of the government in curbing missionary activity.

What exactly happened that Tuesday in the town near Tanta is not clear. The Mother Superior of the Sisters of the Franciscan order of Saint Marie had gone to the train station with two girls from the order's orphanage to travel to Alexandria. At the station a man approached the Mother Superior asking for the names of the girls, which could have signaled whether they were Muslims or Christians and thus possible converts. Refusing to give the girls' names, the Mother Superior boarded the train with her charges, but the two nuns who had accompanied the party to the station were roughed up on the way home. After a crowd gathered at the orphanage demanding the release of the children living there, the nuns surrendered some sixty or so youngsters, with one sustaining injuries. The nuns themselves fled to the nearby Franciscan monastery, where they remained until the police arrived to disperse the crowd.[22]

The British liaison for European affairs in the Egyptian government, Keown-Boyd, followed up quickly, going to Kafr al-Zayyat to investigate the incident.

Addressing his recommendations to the minister of interior, he called for punishing the guilty parties and better protecting the missionaries. At the same time, the acting high commissioner, Ronald Campbell, met with King Fu'ad to express his displeasure, calling for a public statement by the government that violence would not be tolerated.[23] Until then the French government had remained silent about the Turkiyya Hasan affair, trusting that Catholic missionaries would be distinguished from Protestant ones and exempt from public anger. Although the mission was under Italian protection, French officials broke their silence in the wake of this attack, demanding an explanation of injuries to French citizens.[24]

The attack on the nuns became an opportunity for Egyptian officials to legitimize a further crackdown on the League for the Defense of Islam. The day after these attacks Shaykh al-Maraghi, president of the league, traveled to Tanta only to find his planned meetings blocked. He had hoped to talk to local notables about peaceful strategies for resisting missionaries in a province that was home to French Catholic missionaries and a sizeable Protestant contingent. The Presbyterian American Mission had a hospital in the provincial capital, along with clinics and schools in and around the city. The YWCA also had a branch, whose American president, Miss Wright, was known to locals as "al-Shaytana" (the devil), and her deputy had recently affirmed in a newspaper interview that missionaries came to Egypt "for goals tied to one another: to teach and to proselytize," for it was "their duty to call others to their religion and persuade Muslims to adopt it."[25] The governor of Tanta, in consultation with the central government, banned al-Maraghi's meetings, ostensibly to prevent an escalation of events that might have harmed local missionaries.[26] The same scenario played out shortly thereafter when al-Maraghi traveled to Damanhur, accompanied by 'Abd al-Qadir Hamza, the editor of *al-Balagh*, and other league members. The group arrived to find that the mayor there, citing concern for public security, had banned the meeting under instructions from the capital.[27]

The government had effectively blocked the ability of the league to expand its reach, recruit new members, and build support for the anti-missionary movement. The next day the Egyptian Council of Ministers issued a definitive statement making its policy clear: "In view of the incidents which have taken place in some parts of the country especially at Tanta and Kafr el Zayat following on an invitation made by some notables for the holding of a meeting for the collection of funds for the establishment of homes for orphans and the waifs, the Government considers that such meetings should be forbidden, in order to maintain public security and to avoid disturbances."[28] The number of attacks in this period was actually quite limited, given the tensions and failure of the government to restrain missionaries. Nine attacks on missionaries or their institutions were reported in the period from June 7 (the day of the beating of Turkiyya) to July 31, 1933, with five reported before the July 14 communiqué was issued and four after it. The attacks included theft, stone throwing, and blows but no serious injuries.[29] The government pronouncement clearly blamed the league for the disturbances, though the league tried to prevent them and had no apparent role in the incident in Kafr al-Zayyat. Even though the league consistently advocated nonviolence, the government used the few isolated incidents that occurred around the country to block its ability to organize.

Evoking the need for "public security," the government soon extended the ban to include all of the league's public meetings.[30] The communiqué directed Egyptians who supported the anti-missionary campaign to cooperate with government-sanctioned representatives in the Body of Grand 'Ulama' of al-Azhar: "In view of the fact that the undertaking of this task by this responsible body will realise the objects desired by both the Government and the public, in so far as the protection of religion is concerned, the Government has decided to restrict the permission to hold such meetings to this body only in order to avoid trouble and in order to maintain public peace and order."[31] The government had unveiled its strategy, endorsing the Body of Grand 'Ulama' as the only body permitted to wage battle on the anti-missionary front and using it to silence its rival, the League for the Defense of Islam.

The Body of Grand 'Ulama' had met a few days after the founding of the League for the Defense of Islam but had done very little in the interim on the anti-missionary front. With the league continuing to organize, to call for funds, and to push the government to act, the government pressured the Body of Grand 'Ulama', to which the appellation "for the Protection of Islam and Muslims" had been added, to do more. The senior clerics reconvened on July 17 at al-Azhar to take the reins of a movement handed to it by government fiat. Seeking to protect "against the grave dangers of missionary activities," it set up a series of committees to study the problem, draw up regulations, and collect funds. Mimicking the League for the Defense of Islam, it established subcommittees in six provincial capitals.[32]

In the face of the ban on public gatherings of his group, al-Maraghi and his associates protested that Muslims were being prevented from meeting to discuss religious matters and to gather funds to help orphaned and abandoned children. But when al-Maraghi took up his concerns directly with the interior minister, al-Qaysi would not budge.[33] A writer in *al-Siyasa* summed up the contradictions in the government's policy, lamenting that opponents of the anti-missionary movement used the Kafr al-Zayyat event as an excuse to suppress what was essentially a peaceful effort to protect Islam and Muslims: "what never occurred to anybody's mind was that the Government would change its negative attitude towards the aggression of the missionaries to a positive attitude and would try to suppress the nation's peaceful movement organised to ward off the danger of the missionaries."[34] A writer in *al-Balagh* also complained against concerted government action to obstruct the activities of the League for the Defense of Islam.[35]

Starving the League: The Diversion of Funds

In addition to suppressing anti-missionary articles and cartoons in the press and banning public meetings, the government blocked the League for the Defense of Islam from raising funds. An official communiqué stated that while the government was attempting to increase the number and size of orphanages, "certain persons started on the formation of societies with the object of raising contributions for the establishment of national orphanages. These persons," by which was meant al-Maraghi and friends, "got in touch with each other and published articles in the newspapers," a reference to *al-Balagh*, *al-Jihad*, *Kawkab al-Sharq*, and *al-Siyasa*, "asking the public to take part in this work. Such an action is praiseworthy in itself," the communiqué continued, "had not some of the promoters of the movement deflected it into untrustworthy directions, in that they hold meetings and deliver speeches which abandon the appeal for funds and excite public feelings." As a result, the government said it was forced to move against unauthorized collecting of contributions.[36]

The Body of Grand 'Ulama' became the only group allowed to collect funds for orphanages. Whereas al-Maraghi's meetings "began by reviewing the misdeeds of the missionaries and working people up on this subject, and then, after the creation of a suitable excitement and indignation, asked for subscriptions," as Shafiq told Campbell, by contrast, "the Ulema's meetings would make no reference to the misdeeds of missionaries, but would merely ask for charitable subscriptions to help provide asylums and instruction for poor Moslem children."[37] Campbell subsequently confided to his French counterpart that al-Azhar 'ulama' "were of course completely under the control of the Government and would do as they were told."[38] The clerics were not completely passive, nor were they all on board with the plan, and some dissidents joined the League for the Defense of Islam. But the overwhelming majority seemed to back the government, which paid their salaries.

Still, the government was not all-powerful or necessarily acting in concert. With both Sidqi and Lorraine out of the country and replaced by less experienced officials as acting prime minister and high commissioner, Fu'ad seized the moment to expand his own power base and augment the financial resources at his disposal. The king quickly dispatched a chamberlain to Asyut to shore up a donation that the league had cultivated. In an early fundraising initiative, league members had approached al-Sayyid Ahmad Mustafa 'Amir, the son of grain traders and one of the largest landowners in the Egyptian south, for funds to help build an orphanage for Muslim boys and girls as an alternative to Lillian Trasher's Asyut Orphanage. 'Amir was a natural target for fundraisers, having accumulated 40,000 feddans and a great deal of capital. In the midst of the uproar over missionary attempts to convert poor girls, he promised to give 10,000 pounds to build a new orphanage and to put five hundred feddans into a trust to finance it.[39] The king's men siphoned the gift, ensuring that the funds were funneled through the Body of Grand 'Ulama' into the coffers of the Ministry of Religious Endowments, which the king controlled. In this way, Fu'ad, who sought to enhance his reputation as guardian of Islam, got the credit; the Ministry of Religious Endowments got the money; and the donor, whom the king named a pasha, got a title. Overnight 'Amir, a man who had avoided Cairo and its Westernized elite, became a national hero.[40] The League for the Defense of Islam was the loser.

'Amir's official letter to the head of the royal diwan detailing his gift placed it at the service of the king to be used for homes or hospitals for orphans and homeless children.[41] As the minister of religious endowments, 'Ali Bey al-Manzalawi, explained, the king had ordered that evangelizing "should be prohibited and that the poor orphans and waifs should be protected from any influence that may come from religious bodies."[42] Meanwhile, the League for the Defense of Islam, which had set the groundwork for the gift, lost an important donor and the opportunity to shape the project as it wished. The choking off of funds undermined the ability of the league to develop its own network of social welfare institutions.

The king's men sought to control other such gifts. After announcing 'Amir's donation, the press publicized another big catch: Sayyida Hafiza Hanim al-Alfiyya's donation of 2,500 square meters of land in Giza for a charitable purpose. An earlier supporter of the Islamic Benevolent Society, she decided this time to name the king as trustee of her gift, land that was valued at 5,000 pounds. In the midst of the orphan scandal, Fu'ad set aside the gift for a refuge for orphans and homeless children.[43] In this way, the king received great publicity for his benevolence, maintained the royal prerogative of overseeing charitable works, and reasserted his control over the Ministry of Religious Endowments.

Rather than work with those who sought to rein in the missionaries, the government chose to crush the league by suppressing its supporters in the press, forbidding its members to assemble, and diverting the funds it raised. The government used al-Azhar as a foil to achieve these ends. Al-Azhar's co-operation in suppressing the League for the Defense of Islam cost its clerics legitimacy in the eyes of many, including the Muslim Brothers and reformists such as Rashid Rida.

A Failed Exercise: Renegotiating Missionary Rights

Egyptian politicians at the helm of government in the wake of the Turkiyya Hasan affair found that their interests aligned with those of the British in suppressing the League for the Defense of Islam, which harbored members of the opposition. Yet men such as the acting minister of interior were genuinely alarmed by the pressure missionaries were putting on young Muslims to convert. After reading the letters that the founder of the Swedish Salaam Mission and other evangelicals had sent to Turkiyya Hasan, al-Qaysi had told Keown-Boyd that they now had proof that missionaries used "both cajolery and intimidation" to achieve their ends.[44] Having reined in the anti-missionary movement, the government began to tackle the missionaries to the extent possible.

Anti-missionary activists had called upon the government to exercise greater control over missionaries. At the same time, they acknowledged that the government was hampered by legal and political constraints: "the Egyptian nation was not unaware of the activities of the missionaries during the past seventy years: nor was it negligent," a columnist in *al-Siyasa* pointed out. "But the nation was fettered during most of this period with shackles which prevented it from rising to defend its religion and nationalism."[45] The shackles included the Capitulations and the protection of the British, who exercised special privileges in the country. After the Turkiyya Hasan affair, however, the status quo simply could not stand. As the writer in *al-Siyasa* asserted, "the danger of the missionary movement was not so serious then as it is now and their crimes were not so apparent as they have been recently."[46] Even the Coptic community protested the recent aggressive actions of missionaries, which made inroads into their community.

The Egyptian government sought to pass legislation that renegotiated the relationship between foreign missionaries and their hosts, making the former more accountable to a central authority and spelling out the conditions under which they could work in Egypt. A draft law prepared in late June giving the government authority to bring missionary organizations under its control was sent by al-Qaysi to the British residency for clearance. But there it met with a cool response, and the acting British high commissioner, Campbell, effectively thwarted the Egyptian attempt to curb missionary excess by stopping the bill. Campbell, according to the head of the American legation in Egypt, "as diplomatically as he could, had been instrumental in preventing such a measure from being passed."[47] For the moment, the British had successfully tabled plans for a law to control the missionaries. Similarly, a draft law for the regulation of private schools in Egypt did not progress. Killed by the British review, neither of the laws made it to a vote in the Egyptian Parliament.[48]

The British recognized at the same time that something had to be done to control the missionaries, and they continued conversations with the Egyptian Ministry of Interior. As Campbell later noted, he would like to see "some means adopted of sheltering *us* from the consequences of rash acts by the missionaries."[49] British officials in Cairo were under pressure after news of the Port Said orphan scandal reached the British Parliament, with the chairman of the Anglo-Egyptian Committee raising questions in the House of Commons about investigations into the assertion that a Muslim girl in Port Said had been beaten in an attempt to force her to accept Christianity.[50] In response to suggestions of evangelical excess, the British foreign secretary responded that the girl had been beaten as punishment for rudeness and disobedience, not to forcibly convert her, and then detailed the actions being taken by the British acting high commissioner in Egypt to explore greater supervision of missionaries.[51]

British authorities in Egypt preferred increased self-policing by missionary bodies to legislation, and pushed for an informal agreement between the Inter-Mission Council, which represented missionaries, and the Egyptian government. The head of the American legation, Jardine, reported after a conversation with Campbell that the British hoped to produce their own plan to control missionaries. Even the smaller organizations and individual workers, "who were usually less discreet," would be prevented from committing actions "offensive to Egyptian Moslems."[52] The American legation and the missionaries under its protection promised their complete cooperation with the British in devising such a voluntary plan. Toward this end, Keown-Boyd opened a correspondence with George Swan, head of the Egypt General Mission and the Inter-Mission Council, to explore a framework for controlling missionary actions. In this correspondence, Keown-Boyd technically acted on behalf of the Egyptian government but clearly promoted British interests.[53]

Not surprisingly, the missionaries Swan represented were not eager to renegotiate their rights, and he protested that since most members of the Inter-Mission Council were out of the country for the summer, it could not act in an official capacity. As a voluntary association, moreover, the council had little authority to impose its will on members and no authority over missionaries who were not affiliated with member organizations. Swan then went on the offensive, trying to gain ground from the missionaries' current disadvantage. He argued that the Egyptian Constitution ensured freedom of religion, which to the missionaries meant freedom to change religion, and that they hoped to see this right clarified and strengthened in law.[54]

Keown-Boyd remained firm and emphasized the gravity of the situation. Pointing to the recent attempts to convert children, he stated, "Here in all the maze of politics and religious enthusiasm, is the one place where you [missionaries] are up against real, true, sincere and conscientious feeling. I see it in my Moslem colleagues: they cannot bear the thought that children born Moslems should, because they are orphans or children of indigent parents, 'barter their religion for education and physical well-being.'" He allowed that the government may be mindful of the benefits of missionary education and health care, "but I can assure you that there is much that is real in this newly awakened consciousness of duty to provide for the orphan and destitute children of their own religion."[55]

Yet the most the Egyptian government got out of this correspondence was the promise that the missionaries would pursue negotiations in the fall when most evangelicals had returned from their summer leaves, and would come up with their own statement of policy. Under advisement from British and American authorities, Egyptian officials could not even publish documents on the missionary-government exchanges to demonstrate to the public that they were trying to curb the missionaries. The only concessions to which the British acquiesced were an announcement that negotiations were being held, that government representatives had issued warnings to the missionaries about the dangers of some of their actions, and that it would no longer tolerate the most brazen activities.[56]

Here and there provincial governments chipped away at the privileges of missionaries, cutting subventions to an institution where proselytizing was said to take place or issuing instructions to schools under their jurisdiction that they could not force girls to learn any religion other than their own unless their guardians had agreed.[57] Yet their limits were clear, as demonstrated by a meeting in mid-August between the deputy governor of the Canal Zone with the pastor of the Evangelical church in Port Said. According to *al-Fath*, this pastor was responsible for converting a number of Muslim girls to Christianity, was identified as "the one who had tempted the girl Turkiyya Hassan Yusuf to convert," and presided over the marriage of Nazli Ghanim to the missionary Zaki Isra'il "in spite of knowing she was Muslim."[58] The deputy governor attempted to persuade the pastor to exempt Muslim children from compulsory Christian prayer and lessons at school, but the pastor responded that missionary regulations covering evangelical schools in Egypt prevented him from doing so. Furthermore, he stated that those who enrolled their children in missionary schools knew this and were free not to enroll them. The deputy governor then pointed out that although the official religion of state was Islam, government schools did not force Christians to sit in on Islamic lessons, and Muslims respected Christian requests to leave during religious lessons. The deputy governor asked the pastor to show the same respect, but the pastor claimed he could not deviate from the guidelines of the union of evangelical schools in Egypt.[59]

In the summer of 1933, British colonial officials prevented the Egyptian government from enacting the sort of legislation that would have given it greater control over missionaries and challenged the way missionaries did business in Egypt. Rather than working through formal channels and reworking laws, the British preferred an informal route, allowing missionaries to voluntarily police themselves through the Inter-Mission Council. While missionaries had to be more careful in public, they did not face the same press restrictions, inhibitions against fundraising, or injunctions against meeting as the League for the Defense of Islam faced. Missionary periodicals and pamphlets continued to circulate, though not in high-profile areas like al-Azhar. Missionaries were free to fundraise, which they did with success, earmarking twenty thousand pounds to fight the anti-missionary movement.[60] And they were also free to assemble, much to the dismay of members of the league, whose own meetings were banned. As the Egypt General Mission prepared for a general two-day conference in early August at its headquarters in Zaytun, the league called for a ban of the meeting, with no success.[61]

Some of the vehemence of the anti-missionary movement in the summer of 1933 may well have been inspired by an opposition eager to exploit weakness on the part of the government and a press ready to capitalize on controversy. But it also went deeper and threatened the government and foreign missionaries on fundamental levels. The British, with tacit American support, intervened to protect evangelicals, giving the Egyptian government license to crack down on Egyptian dissent, indeed pushing it to do so, suppressing the League for the Defense of Islam. Freedoms of the press and assembly, as well as the freedom to fundraise, became victims of an effort to protect missionary personnel and property. Under the watchful eyes of British colonial officials, the Egyptian government utilized its energies to silence the opposition and re-channel the resources of the anti-missionary movement into its own coffers.

The clampdown on the movement combating conversion temporarily quieted dissent and shored up the king's position, but at the expense of democratic practices. In the summer of 1933, Egyptians did not see liberal democracy at work or the protection of their basic rights. They saw British and American imperial interests protecting evangelicals and stifling Egyptians' right to protest missionary excess. Americans, who were ostensibly in Egypt to promote the liberal values associated with Protestantism, had elevated their own safety and interests over the rights of Egyptians, and backed the king and his government over a popular grassroots movement. The Egyptian government was caught between a king who wanted to augment his own power, the British who called for a clampdown on anti-missionary forces, and an opposition eager to topple them.

While al-Qaysi and his colleagues cooperated with the British to crush the League for the Defense of Islam, they also hoped to curb some of the more egregious activities of missionaries. Yet the British prevented the government from enacting legislation that would have restrained evangelical practices and meaningfully limited proselytizing, effectively blocking efforts to rewrite the social welfare bargain between evangelicals and Egyptians. They did this at a time when many Egyptians had resolved that the price of missionary services had simply become too high and the risk of conversion of the young and vulnerable too great. Concerned to demonstrate that it cared, the Egyptian government identified the one place where it could take quick action: extracting Muslim children from missionary orphanages and finding them new homes.

THE BATTLE FOR EGYPT'S ORPHANS

Toward a Muslim Welfare State

IT WAS DIFFICULT FOR TURKIYYA HASAN to rebuild her life in Port Said in proximity to the missionaries who had raised and schooled her, for the town was simply not big enough for the teenage heroine to avoid chance meetings with affiliates of the Swedish Salaam Mission. On one occasion, the doorman from the Swedish Salaam Mission sought out Dr. Muhammad Sulayman, ostensibly to ask him to help find work in an orphanage, but he was really on a mission to find Turkiyya. When he came upon her after meeting with the physician, he asked Turkiyya to call on his wife, who he said was anxious about her. Turkiyya went to visit the family, for she "believed that this family loved her," and the doorman immediately went to inform members of the Swedish Salaam Mission that Turkiyya was at his home. A Bible woman, female preacher, and teacher came quickly to try to convince her to return to the fold: "Please come to the Lord's kingdom," one said, "for the Lord loves you and he chose you to be one of his disciples." After this incident, Turkiyya's sister appealed to the public prosecutor to completely sever missionaries' contacts with Muslim girls, sending her petition to the press.[1]

With Muslim citizens of Port Said again outraged, state officials decided to move Turkiyya to Cairo. In early July, the governor of Port Said, Hasan Fahmi Rif'at Bey, presented the teenager to the minister of interior, Mahmud Fahmi al-Qaysi Pasha. Taking an active role in the fate of the girl at the center of the orphan scandal, al-Qaysi had her enrolled at government expense in a nursing course at the King's Hospital, an institution under the authority of the Ministry of Religious Endowments, and it was expected that she would continue on at the hospital as a nurse once the course was completed. Al-Qaysi was hailed by supporters for the great deeds he was doing for Muslim girls extracted from missionary institutions.[2] By moving Turkiyya to the capital, government officials removed her from proximity to the missionaries as well as her patrons in Port Said and thereby appropriated the girl who had helped launch the League for the Defense of Islam for their own purposes.

The Port Said orphan scandal jolted government officials, who until that moment had provided only limited care of orphaned and abandoned children. Such care had generally been subcontracted to local benevolent societies and foreign missionaries, making a problem disappear at little or no cost. But now the cost in political terms had become prohibitive. In the wake of the Turkiyya Hasan affair, it became clear that Muslim children had to be removed from missionary homes, for leaving them there gave ammunition to the opposition that was simply too explosive. With the assistance of Muslim Brothers and other Islamic activists, the state moved to extract Muslim children from missionary institutions. Having remained vigilant to missionaries' attempts to convert Muslim children, these activists provided critical intelligence to state officials on the location of Muslim boys and girls in missionary refuges.

After removing Muslim orphans from the care of evangelicals, government officials had to immediately find new accommodations for them. They patched together a network of temporary housing and looked for more permanent solutions, including the expansion of state orphanages and the building of new structures. In the process, the state renegotiated the social welfare contract, taking on a benevolent activity that had long been the province of private religious groups, whether domestic or foreign. Yet in renegotiating the contract, it focused almost exclusively on the majority Muslim population. Copts and Jews were not included under its protective umbrella, and this had broad implications for further delineating boundaries between communities.

Turkiyya had set in motion a storm that put the fate of orphaned and abandoned Muslim children in missionary institutions on the political agenda. In the struggle to control the bodies and souls of these children, the responsibility of caring for the weak and the poor further shifted from society to the state. But many cases of "rescue" were not as seemingly straightforward as that of Turkiyya nor as simple as either missionaries or Islamists imagined. Often the children, and some grown women, became pawns in a three-sided tug of war between missionaries, Islamists, and the state. Some articulated their desires through actions, running away from missionary homes to sanctuary in police stations and government refuges; others fled relatives' homes to missionary institutions.

Custody of Converts

With the spotlight on the Swedish Salaam Mission, the saga of the Na'man siblings came to light, illustrating how missionaries, Islamists, and the state contested conversion and how some converts fought back. The children's father, a doorman, had died around the time of the 1919 Revolution, and their mother, a washerwoman, passed away a year later, leaving seven children behind. The family had few resources (uncles in Port Said included a gas seller, a milk merchant, and a waiter at a restaurant), and the children ended up in the care of Protestant missionaries. Of the three boys, the eldest, 'Isa, had converted to Christianity and left for the United States; the next, Ibrahim, worked as a porter and lived on his own; and the third, 'Abduh, was placed in a missionary refuge. Of the four girls, Maryam had married a baker and lived in Cairo. The second sister, 'Ayida, had converted to Christianity, taken the name Martha, and worked at the Swedish Salaam Mission, where she received room and board in addition to a salary. A third sister, Fathiyya, had rejected the life the missionaries had prepared for her, for she was "committed to Islam and hated proselytizing," according to Turkiyya, who helped her escape from the Salaam Mission in May 1931.[3] After taking sanctuary in a police station, Fathiyya married a cousin (Muhammad Khalil) who worked for the government. A fourth sister, Nabawiyya, was at the time of the Turkiyya Hasan affair aged nineteen and living in the Salaam School in Dikirnis.[4]

Prompted by news that missionaries were planning to move Nabawiyya from Dikirnis to Zaytun for baptism, Islamic activists—most probably Dr. Sulayman—pressed Ibrahim to remove his siblings from the Salaam Mission. This alarmed Martha, who was two years younger than him. On June 17 she wrote an appeal to the British judicial adviser in the Ministry of Justice making a case for the protection of her religious and civil liberties. Stating that she was born a Muslim on December 13, 1910, in Port Said and baptized in 1929 "by my own choice and upon my request," at which time she took the name Martha Bulus, she explained that her eldest brother was also a convert and that her parents were both dead. "Now because of the present agitation my other brother Ibrahim Naman [Na'man] is brought under the influence of some agitators who demand my recanting the Christian faith and embrace of Islam."

She appealed for protection of "guarantees and religious liberties assured to all citizens within the Constitution and all civil laws." Claiming she was "of age namely 23 years," she wanted no interference from any organization or person, and she appealed as well for religious freedom for her sister Nabawiyya, age nineteen, who asked for baptism.[5]

While the Ministries of Justice and Interior were deliberating her case, her brother Ibrahim filed a claim in the Islamic court in Port Said to gain custody over her. Behind the scenes, the British director general of the European Department in the Ministry of Interior, Keown-Boyd, tried to persuade the Ministry of Justice to urge the shari'a judges to "use common sense in such cases." With top government officials following the case, the governor of Port Said weighed in, advising that Martha be moved to safety. Keown-Boyd arranged for the Egypt General Mission to give her sanctuary at its home for female converts in Zaytun until the case could be resolved. "I consider that this is a case where the Ministry of Justice might well find means of ensuring that Martha be not forcibly handed over to her brother—a course of action which is manifestly unjust and absurd," wrote Keown-Boyd in a note.[6]

As it turned out, Keown-Boyd's optimism was unfounded. Three days before the hearing, Martha, accompanied by her good friend Kawkab Kamil from Suez (who also faced a custody battle with male relatives), came to see him, asking for his intercession with Muhammad Labib Bey 'Atiya, the advocate general and head of the Native Courts, whom she wanted to meet. Apparently coached by missionaries on the legal issues, Martha asked for an adjournment of the hearing until a decision could be reached on the conflict between civil and religious jurisdictions; she pointed in particular to the clash between clauses of the Egyptian Constitution and interpretations of shari'a law generally accepted in Egyptian religious courts. Failing an adjournment, she wanted to ask the advocate general, as the protector of civil rights, to send a representative to the Port Said court to ensure "the rights of an individual Egyptian guaranteed by the Constitution." As Keown-Boyd stated in his letter of introduction on behalf of Martha to Labib 'Atiya, "Her case is that she is a grown woman in full possession of her senses, a Christian, earning her living and with the right to shape her own life."[7]

Labib 'Atiya had a very favorable impression of the two women from his meeting with them, but told Keown-Boyd that although "Martha's Christianity was unshaken," there was little he could do, for "it was beyond his powers to intervene on her behalf." He could not stop or delay the Islamic court case and could make no arguments that would "have any effect upon the accepted interpretation of Sharia Law." He advised Martha to live with her brother and to continue her work at the school, returning home at night. If she agreed to this plan, he would have the brother instructed "not to subject her to any ill-usage or undue influence."[8] In a follow-up discussion with Keown-Boyd the next day, he confessed, "It weighed much on his conscience . . . that such things," by which he meant the fact that her brother would inevitably gain custody of her, "should be possible in a would-be advanced and civilized Egypt, and they must be remedied." Yet he recognized that reform of the law was impossible at that moment. As Keown-Boyd noted, "The Minister of Justice was already in a difficult position with his Sheikhs and others," so they agreed to a course of action, or inaction as it were.[9]

Islamic activists continued to advise Ibrahim and testified on his behalf. On June 28, 1933, Ibrahim's petition to have custody of 'Ayida (Martha) was heard in court in Port Said, with two witnesses coming forward to support his claim. The first was Muhammad Shirdi, a commercial clerk who worked for Muhammad Sarhan and had been among the party that escorted Turkiyya to Cairo. The second was 'Ayida/Martha's cousin, Muhammad Khalil, a clerk at the Port Said Municipal Council and the husband of her sister Fathiyya. Both witnesses attested that 'Ayida was an unmarried virgin, with one saying she was no more than twenty-one years of age, the other that she was about twenty or less, and asserted that her presence in the Salaam School constituted a danger to her religion, character, and chastity. They confirmed the good character of Ibrahim, her nearest male relative. Martha did not go to shari'a court to make her case, nor did government officials go to represent her interests, having decided that this would be futile. As expected, the judge awarded Ibrahim custody of 'Ayida/Martha, who as an unmarried woman remained in need of a male guardian in the eyes of Islamic law.[10]

In the meantime, Dr. Sulayman had directed Ibrahim to look for his younger brother, 'Abduh, at the Salaam Mission in Port Said. 'Abduh was eventually found at a boys' home run by the American Mission in the town of Qalyub to the north of Cairo and was transferred to a government orphanage in the capital.[11] His sisters had also been relocated to the vicinity of Cairo, pending the outcome of the trial and a resolution of their cases. Prompted by Islamists, Ibrahim picked up copies of the court's decisions awarding him custody of his sisters in early July and proceeded to Cairo to collect them.[12] Appearing with his lawyers in front of the advocate general, he responded to questions about his income and position, and then he and his brother-in-law signed a statement attesting that they would not interfere with 'Ayida's religious beliefs. In the statement they confirmed that they had prepared a place for her with the family, and that the "girl will have absolute liberty to work anywhere or in any place at Port Said," but added, "with the exception of the Evangelical schools, or hospitals, or institutions."[13] The advocate general had struck a bargain with Martha's male kin: we will deliver the girl to you if you promise to allow her to practice her religion; but Martha lost her right to work at the Salaam Mission or any other missionary institution.

Although Islamic activists had won this battle, cutting 'Ayida's ties to the Salaam Mission and putting her under the supervision of a male guardian, the victory may have been short-lived. In late July the two sisters fled their brother-in-law's home, setting the police on a chase. Fearing the press would claim that the missionaries had kidnapped the girls, the authorities immediately checked for them at the Salaam Mission in Port Said, speaking with the matron, Alice Marshall, only to learn that the girls had not been there; they proceeded to question missionaries the girls had visited in town, who reported that the pair planned to take a motor car to Isma'iliyya and possibly make their way to the American Mission in Asyut; they then alerted police in Isma'iliyya to be on the lookout for them. The sisters may have purposefully sown disinformation, for they later turned up in the YWCA in Cairo, claiming that they had been "smacked" by their brother-in-law, who prevented them from visiting the Salaam Mission. The League for the Defense of Islam branch at Port Said pressed Ibrahim to petition the governate to execute the shari'a court's decision and get the pair returned to his care.[14]

The case of the Na'man siblings showed how conversion cut across families, seeding family feuds. Martha and Fathiyya had clearly staked out positions: Martha had converted and advised her sisters to do the same; Fathiyya had chosen to remain a Muslim and fled the Salaam Mission. Nabawiyya's preference, like that of 'Abduh, was not clear, though she seems to have cast her lot with Martha. Baptism for Martha meant autonomy—freedom from interference— and a chance for a decent living. But the response of state officials and religious courts showed how converts, particularly unmarried female ones, were caught up in the backlash against the missionaries and could be disciplined through a legal regime of guardianship. In this, Martha's case seemed diametrically opposed to that of Turkiyya. While Turkiyya followed Fathiyya's footsteps and clung to her faith, becoming a celebrity among Egyptian Islamists, Muslim women who converted to Christianity often found that their missionary friends could not protect them at critical moments from the responses of the Muslim community.

In the Spotlight: The Swedish Salaam Mission and the Egypt General Mission

At the epicenter of the orphan scandal in the summer of 1933, the Salaam Mission of Port Said and its Home for Destitutes came under intense scrutiny in the wake of the beating of Turkiyya. Islamists accused Alice Marshall of rushing back from consultations in Cairo to disperse the resident Muslim girls to other institutions and of sending the friend of Turkiyya's who had testified at the Parquet, Nafisa 'Uthman, to Dikirnis to hide her there.[15] In the face of inquiries about the girl by Dr. Sulayman, Marshall told the commander of the Suez Canal police that Nafisa had been taken by a teacher to Dikirnis to collect her younger sister and that from there the girls would travel with the teacher to Cairo to be handed over to their mother "against receipt."[16] Amidst all the protests, the missionaries were concerned to have proof that children who had been under their care had been delivered into the right hands.

Under directions from the central government, the governor of Port Said moved quickly to have eight Muslim girls taken out of the Salaam Mission home. Four were escorted with great fanfare to Cairo, where they were turned over to the Ministry of Interior to be placed in state orphanages.[17] According to Marshall, six of the eight Muslim girls (out of a total of twenty residents in the home) were removed within two weeks, but the parents of the two remaining ones were away and had not responded.[18] Officials also withdrew two Muslim girls from the Salaam School in al-Manzala, where the Muslim Brotherhood had first sounded an alarm to Hasan al-Banna about proselytizing. Islamists continued to criticize a situation in which the state was only able to extract girls who wanted to leave the homes of their own accord.[19]

Elsewhere in the Canal Zone, the government attempted to extract Muslim children from orphanages run by the Egypt General Mission. In a possible attempt to thwart this plan, missionaries in Suez sent seven girls up the canal to Isma'iliyya, birthplace of the Muslim Brotherhood; four girls remained there, and three were dispatched further up the canal to Port Said. Members of the League for the Defense of Islam (most probably Muslim Brothers) notified the police about the movement of the girls; when the party arrived in Port Said, police met them. Upon questioning, the villager escorting the girls claimed to be the father of two of them (aged approximately seven and nine) and said he was delivering the third to her brother in Port Said. While investigating the case, the police took the three girls into custody, and the press called for freeing the four Muslim girls left in Isma'iliyya.[20]

The Salaam Mission had direct links with the Egypt General Mission headquarters in Zaytun, which contained a home for female converts that had become a popular spot for baptizing girls. After her release, one girl told a reporter from *al-Balagh* that many Muslim girls in various stages of conversion lived in the home, including her sister Nadila. Authorities removed the girl from the home, placing her in her brother's custody.[21] A delegation from the Society for Protecting the Holy Qur'an in Zaytun handed Bahiyya Muhammad al-Sa'ih, a fifteen-year-old who had spent nine years at the missionary orphanage in Zaytun, over to the League for the Defense of Islam for care.[22] And the group extracted a third girl, Hawa' 'Abbas Isma'il, from what a writer at *al-Fath* called a "nest of proselytizing in Zaytun," also handing her over to the league for care.[23]

Authorities did not always have a place ready to put children removed from missionary institutions. After Hawa' was reunited with her ten-year-old sister Ladida, who was taken out of the Salaam School in Suez, they were hosted by a pasha's wife, who set aside a room for them in her home. This sort of arrangement was provisional until the league or the state could find a more permanent residence for the girls.[24] As mentioned earlier, Hasan al-Banna's childhood friend Ahmad al-Sukkari provided shelter in his home to a young girl withdrawn from the care of missionaries.[25] Yet there was a limit to how many girls could be housed this way and for how long.

The extraction of boys from missionary institutions and sheltering them presented particular problems. This was in part because placing them in private homes, even temporarily, challenged norms of segregating unrelated men and women: Muslim men were concerned about protecting their wives. The Home for Destitutes in Port Said had sheltered a few young boys, leading Islamic activists to inquire into their backgrounds and petition authorities to have them removed. As secretary of the Muslim Society for the Welfare of Children, 'Ali Muhammad al-Alfi wrote the governor of the Canal at the end of July to inform him that there were still five Muslim boys, whom he named, at the Salaam School in Port Said. He requested that the governor withdraw them from the school "in order to save them from being converted."[26]

Responding to this appeal, the Suez Canal police inquired into the status of the boys "alleged to be still in the Salaam School" to ascertain their whereabouts. The police learned that in four out of the five cases, the boys had a father and in the fifth, a grandfather, still alive, and that the orphan scandal had prompted some of the fathers and the grandfather to reclaim these children. Yet some preferred to again place their child or grandchild into an orphanage, this time a government one, rather than raise them at home. The police learned that 'Abduh and 'Uthman Muhammad al-Qazzaz, aged nine and eleven, were still at the Salaam School orphanage for boys; their uncle had left them at the orphanage six years earlier; their father was a cook in Benha, and they had no local relatives. 'Izzat Ibrahim, an eight-year-old, had been removed by his father from the Salaam School in Port Said in June in the wake of the Turkiyya Hasan affair and had just been sent to the director general of public security to be placed in the government home in Cairo. The youngest of those mentioned in the inquiry, Fawzi Ahmad Hijazi Mirdan, aged five, had been taken out of an American Mission institution by his grandfather in the wake of the Turkiyya Hasan affair and was living with him until the government home opened. Only Ahmad Ibrahim Shinshin, a ten-year-old who had been removed from the Salaam School in Port Said by his father two months earlier, remained in the custody of his father to work.[27]

Ripples: American Mission Circles

In the wake of the Turkiyya Hasan affair, all missionary orphanages became suspect, including the American Mission's Fowler Orphanage in Cairo. According to the annual report, the anti-missionary campaign in the summer of 1933 "fell heavily upon us and our institution," and the inhabitants "passed through four strenuous months," during which time attackers tried to enter the residence. "In spite of the exasperating conduct of some of our persecutors and the attempts that were made to enter our compound by violence, our hearts were cheered by the faith and loving forbearance manifested by our girls and our staff," the report writer confessed.[28] That they escaped unscathed was lucky, for the home included six baptized converts as well as fifteen other girls of non-Christian origin, two of whom were ready for baptism. Government officials carefully checked the rolls of the Fowler Orphanage, removing and returning eight girls to their families.[29] This was not the first time Muslim girls had left the Fowler Orphanage for reasons related to anti-missionary sentiment. A year earlier two had to leave the home "on account of religious agitation stirred up by their relatives," but one returned within three weeks and the other remained under "Christian influences."[30] This time, however, the intervention of the state, the scale, and the repercussions were different: one-fifth of the inhabitants of the home were removed by state officials; they could not return nor could other Muslim orphans enter the home.

Authorities investigated the Qalyubiyya Orphanage after the press had reported that a Muslim boy in the home had converted to Christianity. Ahmad's odyssey, according to *al-Balagh*, had begun in Palestine when officials sent him from Haifa to the British Church Mission Society Hospital in Old Cairo for treatment of a leg disability. Upon his release, he had been sent to the refuge in Qalyub, which was under the control of the American Mission. When he told townspeople that he was forced to become a Christian and to change his name from Ahmad Sulayman to Sulayman 'Abd al-Masih, he was expelled from the home. Officials at the Qalyubiyya Orphanage had a different version of events, and, in any case, considered the boy self-sufficient, having taught him the trade of shoemaking.[31] (Other residents of the home had become shoemakers, which after clerks, merchants' assistants, and servants, alongside hospital assistants, were the most common jobs taken up by boys from the home.[32]) Revelations about Ahmad in the press sparked the police to investigate the orphanage, and more than eight Muslim boys were removed, according to the mission, "because of the anti-missionary agitation during the summer."[33]

Egyptians who had become savvy about the sort of proselytizing that was taking place in missionary institutions targeted American missionaries in Cairo and the countryside in protest. A group of students and others "besieged" Jane Smith, a member of the Fowler Orphanage staff, and an unnamed Bible woman at the child welfare clinic in Darb al-Ahmar at which they worked for two hours. The students asked them for their names and photographs and tried to take Smith and her assistant to the police station, threatening them with "dire results" if they continued their work. This work consisted of teaching the basics of hygiene and infant care to young mothers to combat high infant mortality rates, as well as of supplying basic instruction in Christianity. The pair of evangelists got away and decided to start their summer break early.[34]

In the towns that lay along the Nile to the south of Cairo, American Presbyterian missionaries and their assistants faced similar investigations and opposition. Newspapers in Bani Suwayf looked into the background of a Bible woman named Rose who visited the homes of secluded women to read to them. Originally a Muslim, Rose had entered the Fowler Orphanage at the age of ten under the name Na'ima and been baptized at the age of fifteen. The provincial governor called in her supervisor, who had already sent Rose to safety in Cairo, and advised her to close the station and take a vacation, which she did for the summer.[35]

Further to the south, authorities forced American missionary Jeanette Mc-Crory, a longtime resident of Egypt and head of the American Mission in Minya, to turn over Fatima Hassanayn, an eight-year-old Muslim girl she had raised from birth. McCrory gave the girl's history in a statement submitted to the acting director general of public security, who was looking into the matter. After Fatima's mother had died in 1925, her father, who worked at the school McCrory ran, asked the missionaries to take her in. The girl survived a three year struggle against tuberculosis; however, the father was not so fortunate and died two years later, having asked the missionaries before his death to keep the child and train her as a teacher. McCrory looked after the child, sending her for a few weeks every summer to visit aunts and cousins in a village outside of Benha, after which she would return to the school, where McCrory paid the fees.[36]

In the summer of 1933, Fatima's routine hit a snag. McCrory reported in her statement that in the midst of stories in the press about the girl's whereabouts, she had been called to Benha, where the girl's relatives had "made such a commotion that the child was afraid to go to her village." The missionary took the girl to the commissioner, who verified that the girl wanted to go to the village; he confirmed that if she so desired, she would be allowed to go back the American Mission's school in Asyut at the end of the summer.[37] In a different version of the affair, another American missionary noted that the girl's presence in a Christian school had created "a big fuss," and that the police had called in Fatima for questioning, at which time she "said openly that she was not a Moslem but a Christian" and wanted to continue at the missionary school.[38]

The outcome was not the one McCrory expected when she returned to Benha nearly two months later, in August, to retrieve Fatima for school. The commissioner, under instructions from the provincial governor, had, as he told his superior, "made all unobtrusive precautions which rendered it impossible for these missionaries to get into touch with the girl." When her "parents brought their daughter" to the station (in other accounts the parents are dead and male relatives appear in the commissioner's office), the missionaries attempted to take Fatima away, but the commissioner explained that the girl was a minor and could not decide for herself. The decision rested, he said, with her parents. In any case, the girl "flatly refused to go with them [the missionaries]," and the "parents" declared that they would not allow her to go with the missionaries. The matter seemed to end with the commissioner giving the girl a sum of money as instructed by the governor and sending her off to the director of education for placement in a provincial council primary school, where she would receive a free education.[39]

Whether the girl changed her mind about returning to the missionary school over the summer, or in the face of a financial reward, or was forced by her family to attend a local school, is not clear. Reverend A. A. Thompson, head of the American Mission in Benha, had his own version of events. In his telling, the missionaries had complied with the commissioner's order and handed the girl over to her relatives expecting that "at the end of the summer Fatma should be brought in from her village to go to school." When they went to "get a statement from authorities . . . guaranteeing that Fatma would not be molested during the school year, 1933–34, by any of her relatives," they faced three male relatives who said they did not want Fatima to return to the mission school. At that point, Thompson wrote, "both Miss McCrory and I considered the matter closed, and left Fatma with her relatives."[40]

But was the matter closed? For the governor and commissioner, who had achieved a victory by blocking the missionaries from taking the girl to the Asyut school, and for Thompson, who was not emotionally invested, no doubt it was. Clearly those involved had interpreted the facts, some of which seemed hazy (did the girl have living parents or were they dead? was she given an opportunity to voice her own views or was her voice suppressed?), as they saw fit. And all available tactics, including threats and bribes, were used to achieve desired outcomes. For McCrory, the forced separation from the girl she had raised from birth left a void, and she subsequently decided to "take on" another child. This time she found a Christian girl of five or six, Kamala, whose parents were dead and whose relatives were "relieved" to give her up. Since she was already a Christian, McCrory felt confident that the state would not take her away.[41] What about Fatima? Did she finish schooling and follow her father's dream for her of becoming a teacher? Or did she return to the village to start a family of her own? As an orphan who had become accustomed to life in missionary schools, she may well have been scared when relatives came to take her from those who had raised her; but she may also have been inclined to stay with family after spending a whole summer away from the missionary routine.

As with evangelicals from the Egypt General Mission and Salaam Mission, American Presbyterian missionaries did not understand the depth of Egyptian resentment against them. Rather, they saw the Turkiyya Hasan affair and the anti-missionary storm it unleashed as a passing phenomenon, which would not undermine their mission of sharing the gospel. After a tumultuous summer, they looked forward to opening their schools in the fall. "Let us pray most earnestly that our work may not be hindered in Egypt by these attacks on our missionaries, and that they may be kept in safety and abundantly blessed in all their service for the Master," one American evangelical wrote at the end of the summer.[42] Yet the affair had significant implications for many of the orphans in their care, wresting some from the only homes they had ever known, disrupting ties of intimacy for others, and reuniting still others with their extended families.

Great Joy, Sad Sight: Removing Muslims from the Asyut Orphanage

Amidst hot temperatures and prodding by the press, local officials visited Lillian Trasher's Asyut Orphanage in late June. They searched the premises, asking in particular after a twenty-something woman named Pauline. One of the hundreds of those raised in what was a veritable village of orphaned and abandoned children and widows, Pauline had a story, as related by Trasher, that diverged from the usual script. While many of the children there had been delivered to the orphanage's doorsteps, Pauline had been found wandering in the desert as a little girl by an Egyptian soldier, who handed her over to the American Hospital. At the age of six or so she ran away from the hospital to the orphanage, where she stayed and was later baptized, taking a Christian name. As a grown woman, Pauline had searched for and found her natal family, brought her younger sister Maryam to the orphanage, and asked to have her widowed mother placed on the orphanage charity list. Therein lay the problem. Trasher told her supporters that the charity list was taken as evidence by the police that she was "buying girls to make them Christians."[43] She feared that officials would "take away all of our Mohammedan children,"[44] and was not only worried about the children: "they may even send me home," she wrote, asking the faithful to "please pray for me."[45]

Under the terms of the trust that had been established for the Asyut Orphanage, the institution was supposed to provide Muslim children with Islamic lessons. A correspondent for *al-Jihad* had pressured authorities to determine whether this was indeed the case.[46] When questioned by investigators sent subsequently by the governor of Asyut, Trasher admitted that the Muslim children went to Christian services along with the other children. She explained that hers was a Christian faith-based enterprise—"the Lord supplies our needs"—

and told them about her own "call to the work," giving them copies of financial reports and pamphlets as well as a Bible.[47] The press accounts, visits by investigators, and possibility of leaving the home shook up the children, according to Trasher. "The little Mohammedan children are all praying and crying. . . . Many of them have never known any other home."[48]

Trasher's fears were soon confirmed: the governor of Asyut Province called her in to thank her for all she had done for the poor children of Egypt but told her that "they were going to build orphanages and take our Mohammedan children."[49] Once the investigation had been completed, the governor ordered the head of the police to remove the Muslim boys and girls.[50] Without giving Trasher any advance warning, the police chief and commissioner went to the home to extract the children: "July 8th, 1933 was a day of great joy at Asyut when about 64 Muslim boys and girls were taken away from Miss Lillian's Orphanage," the local correspondent for *al-Jihad* reported. Counting the widows, some seventy of the seven hundred children and women in the complex, or 10 percent of the population, left the Asyut Orphanage that day.[51] The scale of the operation dwarfed that at the Salaam Mission Home for Destitutes or Fowler Orphanage, where five to ten children were removed, though percentages of those taken out were actually higher in the smaller schools.

What to Islamists was a joyful sight of liberation, to Trasher and her orphanage family was seen as a great loss. "Words cannot describe the sad sight as they took them away!" Trasher wrote to supporters: "Pray that the teaching of years will go with them and not die."[52] As they left the orphanage before breakfast on the morning of July 8, 1933, the children faced the unknown. The sixty-four or sixty-five Muslim children extracted from the Asyut Orphanage that day were not given a choice. The only Muslim child left behind in the sweep was a physically disabled girl whom Trasher later claimed was left intentionally. And only converts over twenty-one—Pauline, whose reconnection with her natal family had raised suspicion, and Malazama, the woman in charge of the nursery—were allowed to stay.[53]

The extraction of a large group of Muslim children (and widows) did not end Islamists' questions about the Asyut Orphanage. The correspondent from *al-Jihad* who led the attack on the Asyut Orphanage and made it his mission to save Muslim children there doubted that "these were all the Muslim children in the orphanage," and feared "that there are some more still." He suggested that they may have been given Christian names to avoid detection and called for further investigation.[54] Later, the press focused on five Muslim babies who had been placed in the home by their impoverished fathers to be nursed and raised in the orphanage. This, in turn, piqued the interest of the central government. Mahmud Sadiq Yunis Pasha, deputy interior minister, charged provincial officials with removing these infants from the home and sending them to the Public Health Department's Center for Children in Asyut, and he appealed to Dr. Muhammad Shahin Pasha, deputy interior minister for health affairs, to give the order to complete the transfer. The five nursing infants were removed from Trasher's care.[55]

Although disappointed by the challenges that summer, Trasher felt relieved that she had not been forced out of Egypt. Her fate was not the same as the Swiss missionary in the Port Said orphanage whose disciplinary action had sparked the wave of anti-missionary activity that summer. The authorities had also allowed Pauline to stay on, for there were no male relatives who made a claim for her or Muslim Brothers on hand to urge them to do so. Still, Trasher lamented the loss of the babies, whose care she had personally supervised in her home, and of the children who had been taken away. The latter were temporarily lodged in educational institutions, and were, according to *al-Jihad*, "well looked after and supplied with food and clothing and all means of comfort."[56] But they, like many of the other displaced Muslim orphaned and abandoned children taken from Christian missionary institutions, remained in limbo, as the state reviewed the options for housing them.

Competing Ministries: Building, Expanding, and Regulating Orphanages

Having extracted Muslim children from missionary orphanages, the Egyptian state now had to find shelter for them. Some were turned over to siblings who had become old enough and had sufficient means to care for them or were handed to other willing relatives, which were the simplest solutions whatever the outcomes, but many had no known relatives and needed a home. Some of the children were given refuge in the network of private institutions started by Egyptian organizations such as the Islamic Benevolent Society. Yet the number of children that these associations could accommodate proved limited. Simply put, the state faced a shortage of beds: it ran few refuges of its own, and the few it administered were cramped. The housing crisis would provide opportunities for the growth of state welfare.

Under the direction of 'Ali Bey al-Manzalawi, the Ministry of Religious Endowments used the orphan scandal as an opportunity to expand the number and size of institutions it controlled. In the wake of the Turkiyya Hasan affair, the ministry revived discussions to build an orphanage for one thousand children on twelve and a half feddans on the banks of the Nile at Imbaba, drawing up plans and seeking funding.[57] It also developed plans for the children taken out of Lillian Trasher's Asyut Orphanage, with al-Manzalawi announcing that the funds donated by al-Sayyid Ahmad Mustafa 'Amir would be used to establish a home in Asyut for the sixty-five Muslim children who had been in an orphanage "managed by a foreign lady."[58] Under al-Manzalawi, the ministry also discussed the expansion of already existing orphanages, planning to enlarge the Rawd al-Faraj Orphanage, the main government refuge in Cairo, from 459 boys to a capacity of 650, and to add an annex to the Qabbari Home for the Aged to house children there. And the minister promised to find work in refuges and hospitals for older orphans under the care of his ministry.[59]

Although the Ministry of Religious Endowments ran a number of refuges, over the course of the summer it ceded control of the orphan question to the Ministry of Interior, which took the lead in the government's effort to house Muslim orphans. The new orphanages set up with state funds, or private ones taken over by the state, came under the administration of the Ministry of Interior. This shift is apparent in the case of Asyut: while the minister of religious endowments had announced plans to build a new orphanage in Asyut in July, officials in the Ministry of Interior cut the ribbon at the opening in August.[60] And after al-Sayyida Hafiza al-Alfiyya gave 2,500 square meters of land valued at 5,000 pounds to the king to use at his discretion, the king issued an order to the minister of interior, not to the minister of religious endowments, to set aside the entrusted land for a charitable purpose, later identified as a refuge for orphaned and abandoned children.[61]

The Ministry of Interior got the upper hand on child welfare for a variety of reasons. The Port Said orphan scandal had landed on the lap of its minister, al-Qaysi, who was charged with bringing it under control. His ministry contained the European Department, whose head (Keown-Boyd) served as a liaison between the government and missionaries. And al-Qaysi's ministry controlled the distribution of funds—70,000 pounds—set aside for refuges for orphaned and abandoned children. To figure out how best to distribute these funds, it solicited reports from provincial governors on the condition of homes under their control and weighed proposals submitted by benevolent societies detailing how they would expand homes or erect new ones. The Ministry of Interior sought to standardize the network of private and public refuges run

THE BATTLE FOR EGYPT'S ORPHANS   183

by different outfits. Toward this end, al-Qaysi visited refuges such as the ʿAb-basiyya Orphanage of the ʿUrwa al-Wuthqa Society in Alexandria to have a better sense of its operations and services. That society had decided to increase the capacity of the home from four hundred to seven hundred by building a new wing and hoped the minister's tour would result in increased government aid. The governor of Alexandria and vice-president of the society followed up on al-Qaysi's visit with a personal appeal to him to fund the expansion, and, to their delight, the minister promised funds.[62]

Deputy Minister Yunis headed an Orphanages Committee, which sought to gain greater control of the refuges operating throughout Egypt, whether run by provincial councils or private bodies, as well as the new ones being built. The committee reviewed proposals submitted by provincial officials. The governor of the Canal Zone, for example, presented a plan for two temporary orphanages: a small one in Port Said for fifty girls, which could replace the Salaam Mission Home for Destitutes, and a second one in Ismaʿiliyya for fifty boys, which could replace the Egypt General Mission home for boys. The two would house orphans temporarily while the new government orphanages in Port Said were being built, which was expected to take a year.[63] The governor of the Canal Zone had met in July with members of Port Said's League for the Defense of Islam branch to dis-cuss the provincial government's interest in building orphanages for poor chil-dren who had been forced by circumstances to enroll in missionary schools and orphanages. He noted that engineers had already begun work on erecting struc-tures on 9,000 square meters of land designated for the building of orphanages, and that until the buildings were completed, two big houses would be rented.[64]

Different groups jostled for state funds to build homes for orphaned and abandoned children, with the Ministry of Interior releasing allotments at the end of July. The 70,000 pounds originally set aside was distributed to provin-cial and governorate offices throughout the country for the express purpose of renting buildings for separate homes for boys and girls, subsidizing or enlarg-ing existing homes, or in one case (Damietta), creating two new homes where it looked like a provincial government could act quickly. Allocations ranged from as little as 1,167 pounds (Qalyub) to as much as 13,700 pounds (Cairo), with Port Said somewhere in the middle, getting 4,167 pounds for the year. The allocations provided an opportunity for builders, especially because in addition to the original 70,000 pound allotment, the ministry set credits for the follow-ing year that totaled 106,000 pounds. These were designated for the creation of one or two new homes in eleven locations, the largest amount (20,000 pounds) promised for two new homes in Asyut. Provincial governments also joined the building spree. In Alexandria, the municipality opened its own credit of 16,000 pounds for the purpose of constructing homes for boys and girls, entrusting two contractors with erecting the buildings on government land.[65]

The Orphanages Committee met to review regulations for running orphanages throughout Egypt. Among its considerations, the committee studied rules pertaining to medical examinations, contagious diseases, and inspections by physicians. The new regulations drew different government agencies, particularly the Public Health Department of the Ministry of Interior, deeper into the operation of refuges. Members of the committee came up with all sorts of schemes for making orphanages more self-sufficient. The head of the Department of Spinning and Weaving in the Agency of Trade and Manufacture suggested, for example, that the residents of the homes make children's toys, such as small wooden wagons, that could be sold at a profit to benefit the orphanage.[66]

The Orphanages Committee also looked into the problem of abandoned infants. Some missionary orphanages, such as the Asyut Orphanage, took in foundlings, as did some hospitals, such as Qasr al-'Ayni in Cairo. The Ministry of Interior decided to open four new foundling homes throughout the country, locating them in Cairo, Alexandria, Wahj al-Bahri, and Upper Egypt. Each home was to have a window with an electrical button so that when the infant was left, the bell would signal a wet nurse. By giving anonymity, this plan would encourage those leaving the infants to deposit them in a safe place and not abandon them in dangerous surroundings. Wet nurses would breast-feed the foundlings in their homes for ninety piasters a month per infant until the infants reached the age of weaning, at which point the wet nurses would return them to the foundling home. At the age of six, the child would be old enough for integration into an orphanage and would be sent to a separate facility for education and socialization.[67]

Given the new regulations proposed by the Ministry of Interior's Orphanages Committee, some societies decided to hand their institutions over to the government for administration. It is also possible that some societies thought their institutions had a greater chance of getting funding if they were subsumed under the aegis of the government, which looked with favor upon such gifts at a time when it was racing to erect enough housing for children removed from missionary homes. The governor of Suez informed Yunis that the local Islamic Benevolent Society had handed over its orphanage, which had two branches of one hundred girls and boys each, to the state to administer.[68]

By the end of summer, new orphanages in the Delta began to open their doors to Muslim children. In Shibin al-Kawm, a city north of Cairo, the Provincial Council of Minufiyya launched a refuge for one hundred girls, who received health checks and an education that included reading, writing, religion, and domestic arts. The provincial government hoped to double the number of girls in the coming year. Nearby, a new wing was being added to a home that sheltered eighty-eight boys, with the goal of increasing the capacity to two hundred. Once opened, it would add broom- and carpet-making to a curriculum of reading, writing, religion, music, and saddle- and chair-making.[69] An orphanage named and sponsored by Princess Fawziyya was set to open that August in Tanta. The modern building and land on which it was erected cost 15,000 pounds and took nearly two years to complete. The planned curriculum included "useful sciences" as well as sewing, handicrafts, carpet-making, and millinery.[70] Whether or not they had been in the works for some time, the orphan scandal gave new urgency to opening these homes and accelerated the construction timetable.

At the end of August, Yunis took a swing through southern Egypt on a tour of new orphanages. He stopped in al-Minya, where he celebrated the opening of the provincial council's Queen Nazli Orphanage for Girls. Its sixty-five female residents were on hand for the ceremony in new white cotton dresses, head-coverings, and sandals. The new orphanage for girls, which provided an elementary education, joined the King Fu'ad Orphanage for Boys, which Yunis had launched in 1920 when he governed the town. The deputy minister continued on his tour, stopping in Manfulat to open a home there for orphans. Such openings had become carefully orchestrated and well-attended events.[71]

When he arrived in Asyut to inaugurate two homes rented with a generous federal allotment, Yunis was escorted by the governor and a police detail on motorcycles. At the site of the homes, the deputy minister of interior found a gathering of town notables, mayors of nearby villages, a detachment of soldiers, a military band, and facilities decorated by flags. The governor of Asyut spoke, expressing deep gratitude to the minister of interior for supporting this charitable cause in Asyut and throughout Egypt. Although he stated that the homes would be open to orphans regardless of religion or creed, no doubt out of respect for the large local Coptic population, the circumstances under which these homes had been founded made this claim sound hollow. His concern for including minorities came up against the reality that the new homes had been opened to shelter Muslim children extracted from Lillian Trasher's orphanage.[72]

The governor was followed by a parliamentary deputy and then by the rector of the Asyut Religious Institution, with Yunis having the final word. Declaring the home officially opened, he acknowledged the work of the government, which had energetically pursued the opening of refuges throughout the country. "The success of the scheme," he said, "was entirely due to the Minister of the Interior by whose efforts so many homes were opened in so short a time."[73] Speakers credited the minister of interior for sheltering and safeguarding the nation's children. The role of Turkiyya Hasan and other young women in bringing attention to the problems Muslim children faced in missionary orphanages as well as the advocacy of the League for the Defense of Islam on behalf of orphaned and abandoned children were lost. Also lost in the noise of the celebration was the fact that the "new" homes were often temporary ones where the children would stay while more permanent facilities were being built. Children who had been removed from familiar surroundings would face repeated dislocations.

Amidst the celebrations of the openings of new state orphanages in northern and southern Egypt that August, something else may have been lost as well. In moving out of missionary orphanages and into old, expanded, or new state or state-supported institutions, Muslim children generally went from homes of roughly fifty girls or boys, a scale that most missionaries found manageable and children may have too, to institutions of much greater size. (The missionary orphanage at Asyut was truly exceptional, and functioned more as a village than a single home, or rather a series of smaller homes.) The state took children from homes in which they may have known or recognized all of the residents and caregivers, and placed them in settings that had a greater resemblance to a factory. In order to accommodate the children taken from missionary institutions, state authorities envisioned expansions of, for example, up to 650 children in Cairo, up to 700 in Alexandria, and up to 400 in Shibin al-Kawm; a home in Suez already sheltered 400 boys and girls. In short, the state may have protected orphans' Muslim identities by extricating them from missionary homes, but this may have sometimes come at the price of becoming lost in their new surroundings.

The move to extract Muslim children from missionary orphanages made sense to Islamic advocates, but children who had already had a rough ride in life often faced uprooting with fear. The orphans and abandoned children taken from the only homes some of them had ever known became pawns between missionaries, anti-missionary activists, and state authorities. Although some may have felt relief at having been removed from a Christian environment, others may have experienced regret, having formed emotional attachments and found spiritual sustenance within the orphanage. Once extracted, their fates varied depending on the availability of relatives to care for them or the readiness of alternative institutions to receive them. For older female converts, the path was particularly rocky, as they often lost their autonomy, mobility, and the right to work and pray in missionary institutions. Removing children and young adults from missionary orphanages had varying impacts on those left behind, too. Missionaries faced the painful process of having to hand over those who had sometimes been in their care for years.

The anti-missionary movement, which peaked in the summer of 1933, transformed missionary orphanages from heterogeneous homes into institutions opened only to non-Muslims (although one could not be certain of the identity of a foundling or abandoned child). This shift demonstrated the state's concern for its Muslim population but not its Coptic Orthodox and Jewish citizens, some of whom were left exposed to the proselytizing that took place in evangelical institutions. Creating separate homes for Muslim children affirmed religious difference, placing new boundaries between Christians, Jews, and Muslims and driving a wedge into the Egyptian body politic. Along with affirming difference, this development reflected shifts in the relationships of religious minorities to the state, since Muslims were seen as deserving of state protection, and Christians and Jews were increasingly seen as less deserving of such protection.

The Turkiyya Hasan affair provided the catalyst for rethinking the "social welfare bargain" in which foreign missionaries provided crucial medical, educational, and child welfare services that the state had underfunded in return for access to the young. Egyptians saw the orphan scandal as an impetus to contest terrain ceded to foreigners and used the moment to rethink the role of the state in providing social welfare. The presence of girls at the center of so many of these stories reflected the fact that the state had been particularly negligent when it came to providing girls with services, and that missionaries, most of whom were women, had found a need. In the wake of the beating of Turkiyya, the League for the Defense of Islam pressured the state, as the only entity large enough and with sufficient resources, to take greater control of social services. The state intervened in an arena—orphan care—that had previously been autonomous and unregulated, and in the process became more vigilant about the fate of orphaned and abandoned Muslim children. The Egyptian state gradually came to see Muslim social welfare as part of a means of establishing its legitimacy, or at least an area that should not be ceded so easily to competitors, whether they were foreign missionaries or local Islamists, and moved one step closer to becoming a welfare state.

EPILOGUE

WHEN FIFTEEN-YEAR-OLD TURKIYYA HASAN stood up to the matron at the Port Said Swedish Salaam Mission in June 1933, she unleashed a storm with broad reverberations, putting orphaned and abandoned Muslim children in missionary institutions on the political agenda. Turkiyya quickly became a celebrity, appearing in pictures in the leading newspapers, giving speeches, and traveling to Cairo to be feted by the press. The girl who had stood up for Islam and withstood a missionary beating became the hero of a burgeoning anti-missionary movement. Fallout from her beating helped fertilize the seeds of a welfare state, caused the retreat of missionaries, spurred the spread of the Muslim Brotherhood, and brought attention to the plight of orphans and abandoned children in Egypt. This was no small feat for a teenage Muslim orphan girl.

A Government Falls, Social Welfare Rises

Prime Minister Isma'il Sidqi watched the "missionary incident" unravel from abroad, where he had gone to recover from a mild stroke, leaving acting ministers at the helm of the state. His view, expressed in an overseas meeting with the departing British high commissioner, Sir Percy Lorraine, was that "missionary activities had caused an explosion of feeling in Egypt, and the King used this to gain credit as the first defender of Islam."[1] Sensing his power slipping, particularly now that the high commissioner who had been his ally had been replaced, he saw that it would be difficult to reestablish his former authority. When he returned to Egypt in September 1933, he tendered his resignation to King Fu'ad, who found the once powerful prime minister expendable. Sidqi's first stint as prime minister was over; he would return for an encore thirteen years later under a different king. Amongst other things, Turkiyya seems to have toppled a government.

King Fu'ad used the affair to assert his Islamic credentials and tighten his hold on power. However, a little over a year later, in November 1934, nationalists forced a revoking of the 1930 Constitution, which they considered to have given state authorities dictatorial powers, and, in December 1935, they won the restoration of the more liberal 1923 Constitution. After that, Fu'ad appointed a multiparty delegation to negotiate with Great Britain for the resolution of Egypt's status; he did not live to see the signing of the Anglo-Egyptian Treaty of 1936 by his son and heir, Faruq. The treaty led to an expansion of government ministries that included, in 1939, the creation of a Ministry of Social Affairs. That ministry grew in part out of calls generated during and after the orphan scandal for the expansion of state social welfare services for the young and vulnerable. This helped pave the way toward the Egyptian welfare state realized more fully after the 1952 Revolution.

British officials had watched the "missionary incident," which raised concerns in the British Parliament, with alarm. Although they tried to curb the enthusiasm of the more aggressive missionaries, colonial officials had a duty to protect foreigners and respect the Capitulations. In the wake of the Turkiyya Hasan affair, the British pushed Egyptian authorities to crack down on anti-missionary activity and at the same time tried to get missionary institutions to better police themselves. Debates in the Egyptian press over the danger of missionaries intersected with demands, which peaked in the 1930s, to end the Capitulatory regime. The negotiation of the Anglo-Egyptian Treaty in 1936 led to the signing of the Montreux Convention of 1937, which phased out the Capitulations. While British forces remained in the Canal Zone, the new agreement gave the Egyptian government more leverage to rein in missionaries.

Missionaries in Retreat

The women who ran faith-based orphanages had looked for a project to give meaning to their lives as single Christian women working abroad. They came to "spread the gospel" and "word of God," whether of a Presbyterian or Pentecostal variety, and in starting orphanages, they answered their calling. Fulfilling spiritual needs and caretaking ambitions at the same time, they often achieved far more professionally than they could have at home: Maria Ericsson and Margaret

Smith mothered hundreds of girls over the years; "Mama" Trasher gave refuge to thousands. These evangelicals perceived the orphans in their care to be empty slates, ready to receive the word of God, and the percentages of those who came into their care who were converted attest to the fullness of their "harvests."

The impact of the Turkiyya Hasan affair on missionary institutions rippled throughout Egypt. State authorities watched carefully for the illegal conversion of Muslim minors in missionary schools and health facilities, and withdrew Muslim children from evangelical orphanages in an effort to preserve their Muslim identity. Although authorities claimed that state institutions were open to all, they had withdrawn only Muslim children from missionary orphanages and sought to house them in expanded or new facilities, which in effect segregated orphans by religion. This segregation reinforced a divide in Egyptian society and a perception that the nation was not homogenous but made up of parts. But only one—the Muslim part—had its social welfare increasingly provided by the state. The Coptic and Jewish communities still administered much of their own social welfare needs. In short, segregation of orphans in the wake of the orphan scandal deepened religious divides in Egypt.

Moves by the Egyptian government to more carefully control missionary educational and medical enterprises failed in the short term due to British colonial protection, but new regulations for such institutions emerged after the legal hurdles had been cleared. These stipulated that missionary schools had to obtain parental consent to allow the students to receive Christian instruction and/or provide Islamic lessons for Muslim pupils. The new regulations made the mission of spreading the gospel in Egypt increasingly difficult.[2]

After the summer of 1933, the Swedish Salaam Mission hobbled along but with depleted numbers. In October of that year, when Anna Eklund returned to Port Said from her trip to Finland, she found that the Muslim girls who had been removed from the Salaam Mission had been placed in a new orphanage right across the street from their former home; only Coptic children remained in the Home for Destitutes. The school in Port Said was opened, but enrollment had dropped to eighty students, about a third of the total at its peak.[3]

The mission founder, Maria Ericsson, who turned sixty-nine that year, lived out her retirement in Boulder, Colorado, where she had established the headquarters of the mission.[4] With the Egyptian government preventing new missionaries from replacing those who retired or left—a few missionaries had returned home due to "illness and stress"—the mission continued to shrink.[5] In 1937 a male missionary from the Filadelfia Church of Stockholm took over the mission and within a year reorganized it as a Pentecostal church with a "full gospel" emphasis, renaming it the Salaam Church. By the mid-1940s, all of its foreign workers had left the country and membership in the church was entirely Egyptian. In the 1950s, the mission building had yet another reincarnation as the Middle East Bible School of the Assemblies of God at Port Said.[6]

At the Fowler Orphanage, repercussions from the Turkiyya Hasan affair resounded in the summer of 1933 and into the following year. "During the early months of the year [1934] we had to cope with some difficult problems resulting from the anti-missionary campaign of last year," one of the missionaries wrote, referring to the ten girls who had been "compelled to leave this year for various reasons."[7] The orphanage committee replaced almost all of them, and American evangelicals dedicated themselves to accepting and raising Christian orphans. They enjoyed support from individuals as well as collectives, including the Friends of Fowler, an Ohio Quaker group that met annually after the deaths of the original benefactors and followed the affairs of the orphanage closely. Later renamed the Fowler Home for Girls, "since so many of them are not truly orphans," the refuge continued as a pivotal part of the American Mission.[8]

Yet the American Presbyterian mission had already peaked. In view of decreasing support at home and increased antipathy in the field, Presbyterian evangelicals reassessed the purpose of their mission in Egypt and planned their retreat. They gradually transferred their schools, hospitals, and other properties to the Egyptian Evangelical Church, which they had founded and nurtured, in a process of indigenization. The Fowler Home was among those properties handed over to avoid confiscation and nationalization after the 1952 Revolution, as American Presbyterians phased out their century-long mission. The home had left its imprint on the girls who had passed through its doors, on the women who worked there, and on those who had funded and served it.[9]

In contrast to the United Presbyterian Church of North America, the Assemblies of God Church was on the upsurge in the United States, with foreign missionary zeal still strong. Support from abroad and the field helped the Asyut Orphanage overcome the temporary setback of the removal of its Muslim children in the summer of 1933. In the wake of the Port Said affair, numbers in the orphanage had dropped from about 700 to 630 children and widows; six years later, the numbers had climbed back, with 647 children and 74 widows, for a total of 721.[10] The village home continued to expand steadily under Trasher's leadership. Although most American missionaries were evacuated during World War II, she received permission to stay on, providing shelter to graduates who had become refugees when the cities they lived in had been bombed. And when more orphans were generated by the cholera and malarial epidemics that ravaged Egypt at this time, Trasher welcomed them into the home, calling for missionary reinforcements to help.[11]

Just as the Presbyterian American Mission was pulling up its roots in Egypt, Lillian Trasher set hers deeper, successfully navigating Egypt's transition from monarchical to military rule. In a bit of luck (or, as she would have it, providence), Jamal 'Abd al-Nasir, chief architect of the Free Officers Revolution that toppled King Faruq, had spent summers and a few school years in his father's natal village, Bani Murr, which was adjacent to the village where the orphanage was based, Abnub.[12] In a publicity coup for Trasher, the Free Officers visited the orphanage, recasting her as a model social worker, and they later exempted her from the evacuation of Americans in 1956 in the midst of the Suez Canal crisis.[13] Nasir conveyed the esteem Egyptians had for Trasher when waiving duties on a car held up in customs for her: "I would like to tell you that your work for the orphans is very much appreciated by everyone in this country."[14]

That Trasher was permitted to stay on in Egypt as others were expelled reflects the acceptance of her enterprise by the new elite. At the start of 1957, the orphanage headcount stood at 1,035, a number that did not include refugees from the Suez War a year earlier or the twenty-five to thirty new orphans from Port Said whom Trasher had pledged to accept.[15] Yet the indomitable missionary was not immortal. Cutting short a trip to the United States in 1960 when she grew ill, she returned to Egypt, not wanting to die and be buried away from her orphans; by then, the orphanage housed 1,340 children, widows, and workers. In February 1961, Trasher was on hand at the orphanage to celebrate its fiftieth anniversary. When she died later that year, in December, the Egyptian and Pentecostal press mourned the passing of the woman called a "saint," "virgin mother of thousands of Egyptians," "Nile Mother," and "Mama" Lillian. Many of the former residents of the orphanage—some eight thousand had passed through its doors—returned to pay their respects. A six-horse carriage pulled the body through the streets of the city to a plot in the orphanage cemetery where she was buried alongside some of her helpers and many of her "children."[16]

After Trasher's death, the orphanage was rechristened the Lillian Trasher Orphanage. Run by a handpicked group of orphans groomed for the job and assisted by Assemblies of God Foreign Board advisors, the orphanage came under the umbrella of the Ministry of Social Affairs, which regularly inspected and certified it. By then, the ministry had begun to promote fostering, and

Trasher's successors downsized the orphanage to make it more manageable. The home continues to provide a refuge for Upper Egyptian orphans, disabled children, and blind women as well as a spiritual focal point for the Assemblies of God Church.

Taken together, the stories of the three missionary orphanages in Asyut, Cairo, and Port Said show that while evangelicals on the Nile shared an impulse to spread the gospel, they were a diverse lot whose Christian practices and beliefs ran a gamut and whose scripts for salvation diverged at critical moments. Presbyterians favored order and methodical planning, and focused on learning and proving faith over time, often delaying baptism and membership in the church. Pentecostals stressed a religious experience that included exuberant revivals and welcomed new believers with open arms. While the Presbyterians mobilized physicians from their medical missions to help screen and treat orphans, Pentecostals initially relied on faith healing and only later turned to medical personnel for help with infirm children. American Presbyterians championed girls' education, starting secondary schools and colleges for girls in Asyut and Cairo; Pentecostals valued marriage over education, which is ironic given the single status of many female missionaries. The difference between practices at the orphanages highlights the diversity of missionary projects, which were shaped by the religious visions of their founders as well as by the communities that supported them and the children they served.

The view from the ground suggests that the theory and practice of mission often diverged, as missionaries adapted to challenges in the field and rewrote scripts for their specific evangelical agendas. Scholars of missionaries have often focused on a shift from evangelizing to civilizing, but the lines and intentions were never that clear, and missionaries in Egypt never gave up on the dream of converting those who crossed their paths. And Egyptians did not see this purported shift from Christianizing to service providing. Nineteenth-century rulers like 'Abbas and Isma'il tolerated missionaries, and even encouraged them, as bearers of education and medicine. Although locals critiqued missionaries, their critiques did not become a roar until the 1930s, when the perceptions of Egyptians changed, and they began to see the missionaries as proselytizers rather than just service providers.

The brigades of American and other missionaries sent to the Middle East carried the gospel in order to convert the inhabitants to Protestantism. That the effort failed to transform large numbers of Muslims into Christians does not mean that it did not leave an imprint in the region or at home. Foreign missionaries came to Egypt with what they thought were the best of intentions, building schools, hospitals, and orphanages to give them the means to spread their versions of Christianity. Their open attempts to convert Muslims as well as Christians and Jews through disciplining and other measures led to a record number of revivals, baptisms, and conversions in the late 1920s and early 1930s. But evangelical actions had unintended consequences, causing a backlash that peaked in the summer of 1933, leaving a lasting impact on Egyptian society and politics.

The League for the Defense of Islam and the Muslim Brotherhood

In early August 1933, the League for the Defense of Islam announced the founding of a Ladies' Committee, which looked a lot like the Muslim Sisters associated with the Muslim Brotherhood, except that it was made up of a circle of women from elite families whose menfolk were pashas and beys, not the effendis and doctors of the Brotherhood. Committee women visited the homes of poor women to propagate Islam, hoping to spiritually strengthen them, in this way copying and countering the work of Bible women. The "missionaries" of the Ladies' Committee for the Defense of Islam also sought to raise funds for an orphanage, aiming to shelter poor girls and find respectable work for them.[17] The founding of the Ladies' Committee was a valiant final effort by the league to remain relevant in the face of government edicts that prevented it from publicizing its positions, assembling at meetings, and raising funds. In the summer of 1933, the Egyptian state used the resources at its disposal to empower the Body of Grand 'Ulama' and suppress the league. After a burst of activity, and a last gasp in founding the Ladies' Committee, the league disappeared from the political scene.[18]

For the moment, Shaykh Muhammad al-Ahmadi al-Zawahiri, the rector of al-Azhar, had bested his rival, the former rector and president of the league, Shaykh Muhammad Mustafa al-Maraghi. Al-Zawahiri issued a *fatwa* in September that condemned Muslims who registered their children in missionary schools. But by then, al-Zawahiri had resigned as head of the government's anti-missionary committee, whose main goal—undermining the League for the Defense of Islam—had been accomplished, and he disbursed the funds collected over the course of the summer for other purposes.[19] The collaboration of the leadership of al-Azhar with the government, which identified al-Azhar as the only body authorized to carry on anti-missionary activities, damaged the legitimacy of al-Azhar in the eyes of Islamic reformers and activists. In

April 1935, disgruntled students and teachers in al-Azhar forced the resignation of al-Zawahiri as rector, calling for the return of al-Maraghi, who had a personal friendship with Hasan al-Banna. Backed by British officials, who felt they could work with him in spite of his role in the league, and Islamists, whose support he had won in fighting missionaries, al-Maraghi regained his post as rector, serving until his death ten years later.[20]

Although the league had been effectively blocked, the Islamic organizations that had banded together in a coalition to fight missionaries continued to pursue their own reformist agendas. The Muslim Brotherhood became the most prominent of these societies, eluding British colonial authorities in the summer of 1933 and for a few years after. Hasan al-Banna used the summer school break to visit branches on the frontlines with missionaries. Tapping into the sentiments unleashed by the Turkiyya Hasan affair, he shored up support, and throughout that summer and fall, more than doubled the number of Muslim Brotherhood branches. At the time of the Brotherhood's second conference in January 1934, held in Port Said to mark the city's importance as a citadel against missionaries, the Brotherhood announced that the number of its branches totaled thirty-two. Branches began to spread across the Delta and into Upper Egypt, and within another half year, al-Banna proclaimed that the Brotherhood had reached fifty villages and towns in Egypt.[21]

The Muslim Brotherhood learned tactical and strategic lessons from the missionaries they encountered. The first branches of the Brotherhood emerged in Canal Zone towns in which evangelicals from the Swedish Salaam Mission and the Egypt General Mission had been aggressively proselytizing among Muslims, particularly poor, abandoned, and orphaned children. The Brotherhood fought back by building competing social welfare institutions—orphanages, workshops, schools, and later clinics—to provide services to the local population so it would not need to turn to Christian institutions. To "fight them with their own weapons," branches launched Islamist social welfare projects, recognizing the importance of taking the message to the community. The lesson of the significance of social welfare outreach in recruiting members became engrained in Islamist organizations. Muslim proselytizing (da'wa) took on new meaning, becoming central to the Muslim Brothers, who sent missionaries to villages and towns throughout Egypt to recruit members. The Brotherhood also honed the political skills of organizing campaigns around particular issues. Leaders gathering at their first conference in June 1933 to discuss how to battle the missionaries developed a template for action, including the penning of petitions and launching of publications. The Muslim Brotherhood subsequently fought campaigns against prostitution, alcohol, and other forbidden practices using similar tools.

One of the first and most prominent Islamist organizations in the Arab world arose in reaction to missionaries as well as in their image, leading the anti-missionary movement on the ground and providing information to government officials about missionary activities. In the summer of 1933, the Muslim Brothers acknowledged their conscious borrowing from missionaries, but over time came to emphasize the threat of missionaries rather than their importance as a model. Moreover, unlike the Christian missionaries who proselytized extensively among non-Christians, Muslim Brothers did not proselytize among non-Muslims. From their side, the missionaries disavowed any responsibility for inspiring Islamist organizations, though missionaries and colonial authorities came to recognize the Muslim Brotherhood as one of their staunchest adversaries.

The debt Islamists owed Protestant missionaries went beyond issues of organizing into ways of understanding religious knowledge and authority. The armies of Protestant missionaries active in Egypt depended upon literacy and personal interpretation of texts to spread their gospel message. They castigated the Coptic Orthodox priesthood, built schools and presses, and peddled and pushed Bibles throughout the country, challenging the religious establishment. The evangelicals closely examined the Islamic reform movement, seeing in it parallels to the Protestant Reformation. Men such as Reverend Charles Adams, the chairman of the faculty of the Theological Seminary in Cairo, contributed important works to the English language literature on Islamic reform, interpreting it through the prism of Protestantism.[22] But they missed the intimate connections between their own activities and those of Islamists, whom they came to see as extremists, as well as the links between Islamic reform and Islamism.

Egyptian Muslim encounters with Protestantism transformed Islam. The seeds for Islamist challenges to the 'ulama' of al-Azhar may have been spread in part by the example of independent Protestant preachers. The Muslim Brotherhood learned from missionaries that in an age of print culture and increasing literacy laymen could interpret religion and preach. This would completely transform the relationship of believers to scholars, challenging the authority of clerics and institutions such as al-Azhar in their leadership of the community. Hasan al-Banna was careful not to challenge the religious knowledge of Muslim clerics, but his movement ultimately undermined the hegemony of al-Azhar, and spin-offs encouraged even more independent religious interpretation. A new generation was reinventing Islam, with new goals and leaders, men like al-Banna who had grown dispirited by the lack of fight in older institutions. Missionaries brought Protestantism with them, but their mission worked in unpredictable ways, generating unintended consequences; in the end, evangelicalism helped to unleash reformers such as Hasan al-Banna, who came from outside the religious establishment. Islamism would ultimately bear an uncanny resemblance to Protestant evangelicalism: in the close encounter with Protestant missionaries and British occupiers, Islamic activists reshaped Islam to position it for survival.

Within a decade of its founding in 1928, the Muslim Brotherhood had become the largest Islamist organization in Egypt. By World War II its rolls recorded over half a million members, with a million more counted as supporters, making it the most popular group in Egypt. Although women formed only a fraction of the members, the number of Muslim Sisters far exceeded those who joined secular women's organizations such as the Egyptian Feminist Union. The Muslim Brotherhood also became the progenitor of the most important Sunni Islamist groups in the Arab world, with affiliates in Iraq, Jordan, Palestine, Syria, and elsewhere. Methods adapted from the missionaries became a blueprint for building support for Islamist organizations throughout the world.

The Fate of Egypt's Orphans

After leaving the Swedish Salaam Mission, Turkiyya had a relatively smooth landing, allowing her to push for removing the Muslim boys and girls left behind in missionary institutions. The state could not fully constrain the missionaries, who were protected by the Capitulations, but it could extract Muslim children from missionary refuges, which it did. Yet after the protests of the summer of 1933 died down, many of the efforts to build better lives for orphans and abandoned children had fallen short. According to *al-Jihad*, the newspaper that took credit for having "started the great movement against missionaries and proselytizing in Port Said, which spread to every quarter of Egypt and . . . the whole Islamic world," preachers and activists had raised more than 8,000 pounds for a new orphanage in Port Said. But a few years later the refuges for boys and girls in Port Said were "crowded to overflowing."[23]

The situation for the Muslim orphans extracted from the Asyut Orphanage was not much better. Government officials, army personnel, notables, and others had turned out to celebrate the opening of temporary homes in late summer 1933. But the building of a more permanent home with the funds donated by al-Sayyid Mustafa ʿAmir stalled, with the government taking two years to break ground on a large three-story home for Muslim orphans and abandoned children. Officials situated the new home just a hundred feet away from the Asyut Orphanage, which some locals thought was "a great shame for them to do," according to Lillian Trasher. Yet she did not mind the proximity, because "most of their children are really my children, those whom they took away from us." Trasher kept in contact with some of the younger children, who phoned, and older boys, who visited when they could. "They seem well treated but that is not what counts most."[24] What counted most to her was saving them spiritually.

Until the orphan scandal in the summer of 1933, few Egyptians competed with missionaries to provide needed social services to a group—orphaned and abandoned Muslim children—on the margins of society. Egyptian social activists began to challenge their marginalization, promoting them as good Muslims and citizens of the nation, which had a responsibility to care for them. Zaynab al-Ghazali, an heir to Labiba Ahmad, founded an Islamist women's association in the 1930s that started an orphanage for girls sometime after the Turkiyya Hasan affair.[25] Other elite women started homes for abandoned children: Leila Ahmed tells the story of her Aunt Karima, who "further added to her reputation for unconventionality when she founded an orphanage for illegitimate children." Ahmed continues, "It was scandalous to men like Grandfather for respectable women even to mention such a subject, let alone to be founding a society and openly soliciting funds from him and his cronies to support an organization addressing the matter."[26] This must have been in the 1940s.

Throughout the twentieth century, the care of orphans shifted from missionaries to government or nongovernmental organizations under the watchful eye of the state, and their care became more bureaucratized, as the state sought to regulate procedures. In 1946, a provision was dropped from a 1912 law that had allowed private individuals to claim foundlings after presenting them to authorities and demonstrating their moral character and ability to provide for the child. This law had enabled missionaries such as Trasher, whose orphanage was founded the year before, to keep the children deposited on their doorsteps. In 1965, a new law overriding previous legislation stipulated that all foundlings had to be brought to the nearest center or refuge, where the police registered the child, often creating a false pedigree with made-up names, dates, and time of birth, and the infants were then placed in institutions. Throughout, informal adoption continued away from the watchful eyes of the state.[27]

From the late 1950s, social workers promoted fostering or "the gift of care," which was sanctioned by Islamic law and regulated by the state, as the best solution for abandoned and orphaned children. Toward this end, the Ministry of Social Affairs established a foster families program, setting informal adoption in a administrative frame to regulate the procedure and find homes for children without families and find children for families without offspring. But the supply of orphans continued to far exceed the demand for foster children, and the majority of Egypt's orphans remained residents in institutional settings.[28] When the Mabarrat Muhammad 'Ali (Muhammad 'Ali Benevolent Society), which ran an extensive network of clinics and hospitals, and the New Woman Society, which specialized in training schools, merged in the 1960s, the new union turned its attention and what remained of its assets after nationalization to developing orphanages and childcare centers. By the late 1960s, the number of orphanages had reached 179, half of which were Christian, though Copts were a minority estimated at 5 to 15 percent of the general population.[29]

In the 1970s, SOS Children Villages emerged in Egypt, introducing a family-centered model of caring first tried in Austria of placing orphans in group homes.[30] With the open door policy of the 1970s, the government began to pull back from tight control on orphanages and other social welfare institutions, and structural readjustment in the 1990s further reduced the state's role in running orphanages. The numbers of street children increased, becoming in the eyes of some a problem, in the eyes of others a sign of their empowerment.[31] By 2004, the official number of orphanages run by nongovernmental organizations and monitored by the Ministry of Social Affairs stood at 232, in addition to the 62 residential nurseries for children under age six.[32]

Seventy years after the Port Said orphan scandal, officials in Dar al-Urman, an orphanage specializing in the care of special needs children, decided to launch a National Orphan's Day, which came to fruition on April 2, 2004. Aiming to break down the social stigma still attached to children without parental care, the event had its detractors, who recognized the organizers' noble intentions but criticized a name that drew attention to orphans' difference rather than normalize their lives.[33] Since its launch, the event has mushroomed in size and scope: in Egypt the number of sponsoring companies and organizations has continued to grow, and organizers persuaded the Arab League to sign on, launching celebrations of Arab Orphan's Day.[34] What would Turkiyya think?

Turkiyya: A Final Note

When Turkiyya took her press tour of Cairo, leaders of the anti-missionary movement discussed her future. 'Abd al-Qadir Hamza, editor of *al-Balagh*, suggested the possibility of her marrying one of the editors at his paper, Muhammad Effendi Khalil. The thirty-five-year-old Khalil, twenty years Turkiyya's senior, was not the only candidate interested in marrying her. In late June when she was back in Port Said, her de facto guardian, Dr. Muhammad Sulayman, received a letter from Murad Khalifa of al-Fayyum Province expressing his interest in marrying Turkiyya, and Dr. Sulayman sent an acquaintance to the town to assess Khalifa's moral conduct and financial position. Shortly after that, Turkiyya returned to Cairo, where she started training as a nurse in a government hospital and seems to have gotten married later that summer.[35] Turkiyya then disappeared from the public eye and the historical record, having left her mark on Egyptian society and politics.

REFERENCE MATTER

NOTES

Preface

1. The terms Muslim Brotherhood and Muslim Brothers are used for the organization and the membership respectively.

2. Richard P. Mitchell, *The Society of the Muslim Brothers* (Oxford: Oxford University Press, 1969; repr. 1993); Brynjar Lia, *The Society of the Muslim Brothers in Egypt: The Rise of an Islamic Mass Movement, 1928–1942* (Reading, UK: Ithaca Press, 1998); Gudrun Kraemer, *Hasan al-Banna* (Oxford: One World, 2010). Mitchell and Lia both called the organization the Society of the Muslim Brothers, but most writers now call it the Muslim Brotherhood.

3. For an example of a book that attempts to shift focus to the south of the country, see Nicholas Hopkins and Reem Saad, eds., *Upper Egypt: Identity and Change* (Cairo: American University in Cairo Press, 2004).

4. Heather J. Sharkey, *American Evangelicals in Egypt: Missionary Encounters in an Age of Empire* (Princeton, NJ: Princeton University Press, 2008); Paul Sedra, *From Mission to Modernity: Evangelicals, Reformers and Education in Nineteenth Century Egypt* (London: I. B. Tauris, 2011). See too the recent study by Samir Boulos, "Cultural Entanglements and Missionary Spaces: European Evangelicals in Egypt (1900–1956)" (PhD diss., University of Zurich, 2012).

5. For theoretical debates on conversion, see Robert W. Hefner, ed., *Conversion to Christianity: Historical and Anthropological Perspectives on a Great Transformation*

(Berkeley: University of California Press, 1993); Peter van der Veer, ed., *Conversion to Modernities: The Globalization of Christianity* (New York: Routledge, 1995); Andrew Buckser and Stephen D. Glazier, eds., *The Anthropology of Religious Conversion* (New York: Rowman & Littlefield, 2003).

6. See Sharkey, *American Evangelicals in Egypt.*

7. See Heather J. Sharkey, ed., *Cultural Conversions: Unexpected Consequences of Christian Missionary Encounters in the Middle East, Africa, and South Asia* (Syracuse, NY: Syracuse University Press, 2013).

8. Ussama Makdisi, *Artillery of Heaven: American Missionaries and the Failed Conversion of the Middle East* (Ithaca, NY: Cornell University Press, 2008); Hans-Luker Kieser, *Nearest East: American Millennialism and Mission to the Middle East* (Philadelphia: Temple University Press, 2010); Mehmet Ali Dogan and Heather J. Sharkey, eds., *American Missionaries and the Middle East: Foundational Encounters* (Salt Lake City: University of Utah Press, 2011); Barbara Reeves-Ellington, *Domestic Frontiers: Gender, Reform, and American Interventions in the Ottoman Balkans and the Near East, 1831–1908* (Amherst: University of Massachusetts Press, 2013). Gender scholars have taken a lead in documenting the impact of American missions globally. See Barbara Reeves-Ellington et al., eds., *Competing Kingdoms: Women, Mission, Nation, and the American Protestant Empire, 1812–1960* (Winston-Salem, NC: Duke University Press, 2010).

9. See Norbert Friedrich, Uwe Kaminsky, and Roland Loffler, eds., *The Social Dimension of Christian Missions in the Middle East* (Stuttgart: Franz Steiner Verlag, 2010).

10. For an exemplary model of how a history of orphans gives broad insight into American history, see Linda Gordon, *The Great Arizona Orphan Abduction* (Cambridge, MA: Harvard University Press, 1999).

11. Jamila Bargach, *Orphans of Islam: Family, Abandonment, and Secret Adoption in Morocco* (Lanham, MD: Rowman and Littlefield, 2002); see also Kamal Fahmi, *Beyond the Victim: The Politics and Ethics of Empowering Cairo's Street Children* (Cairo: American University in Cairo Press, 2007).

12. Amira al-Azhary Sonbol, "Adoption in Islamic Society: A Historical Survey," and Andrea B. Rugh, "Orphanages in Egypt: Contradiction or Affirmation in a Family-Oriented Society," in *Children in the Muslim Middle East*, ed. Elizabeth Warnock Fernea (Austin: University of Texas Press, 1995), 45–67, and 124–41, respectively; Nazan Maksudyan, "Modernization of Welfare or Further Depriving? State Provisions for Foundlings in the Late Ottoman Empire," *Journal of the History of Childhood and Youth* 23 (2009): 361–92; idem, "Hearing the Voiceless—Seeing the Invisible: Orphans and Destitute Children as Actors of Social, Economic, and Political History in the Late Ottoman Empire" (PhD diss., Sabanci University, 2008).

13. Missions in Egypt pooled resources and regularly generated summaries of press articles, some from newspapers that are hard to locate, on topics related to evangelizing. These translations tend to be quite accurate, though the pieces selected for translation obviously reflect the interests of the missions. In addition, the *Egyptian Gazette* carried long translations of articles in the Arabic press, including pieces from *al-Ahram, al-Balagh, al-Jihad,* and *al-Siyasa,* to better inform its English reading public of debates in the Arabic press.

Prologue

1. TNA, FO 141/760/19–21, Keown-Boyd, "Case of Turkia of the Salaam School, Port-Said," 13 June 1933, 3; NARA, RG 59, SD 883.00/768, Enclosure 1, Maria Ericsson to Turkya, 8 September 1932. Turkiyya's mother does not figure in any other reference and may have died after Ericsson traveled to the U.S. NARA, RG 84, 350/37/13/04, Egypt, 1931–1935, Port Said Consulate, Strictly Confidential Files, Vol. 98, Horace Remillard, American Consul, Port Said, to William Jardine, American Minister, 26 June 1933, "The So-Called 'Missionary Incident' at Port Said." I would like to thank my colleague Craig Daigle for helping me to locate this report. PHS, RG 209, Box 26, Folder 12 (hereafter RG 209/26/12, with other PHS records being shortened in a similar fashion), "Preaching by Aggression," al-Siyasa, 14 June 1933.

2. "Anisa Turkiyya Hasan Yusuf fi Dar al-Jihad," al-Jihad, 24 June 1933, 5.

3. YDS-Salaam, Maria Ericsson, *The Swedish Mission Story: Egypt* (n.p., [1924]); NARA, RG 59, SD 883.00/768, Enclosure 1, Maria Ericsson to Turkya, 8 September 1932; Remillard, "The So-Called 'Missionary Incident' at Port Said," 1.

4. Quote from "Anisa Turkiyya Hasan Yusuf fi Dar al-Jihad," al-Jihad, 24 June 1933, 5; PHS, RG 209/26/12, "al-Balagh Investigation in Port Said Incident," al-Balagh, 16 June 1933; PHS, RG 209/26/12, "The Calamity of a Moslem Family Dispersed by the Evangelists in Port Said," Kawkab al-Sharq, 21 June 1933; TNA, FO 141/760/19–41, A. W. Keown-Boyd, "Note on the Case of Martha Bouloss, alias Aida Mohammed Neman, of the Salaam Institution, Port Said," 22 June 1933.

5. NARA, RG 59, SD 883.00/768, Enclosure 1, Maria Ericsson to Turkya, 8 September 1932.

6. NARA, RG 59, SD 883.00/768, Keown-Boyd to George Swan, 14 June 1933.

7. "Anisa Turkiyya Hasan Yusuf fi Dar al-Jihad," 5.

8. Ibid.

9. Quote from ibid.; PHS, RG 209/26/12, "Regrettable Incident of Missionaries at Port Said," al-Siyasa, 20 June 1933; Remillard, "The So-Called 'Missionary Incident' at Port Said," 2.

10. Quote from "Anisa Turkiyya Hasan Yusuf fi Dar al-Jihad," 5; "al-Mujrim al-Akbar," al-Fath, 22 June 1933, 8.

11. "Anisa Turkiyya Hasan Yusuf fi Dar al-Jihad," 5.

12. Ibid.

13. Ibid.; Remillard, "The So-Called 'Missionary Incident' at Port Said," 2; TNA, FO 141/760/19/13, Keown-Boyd to Booth, "Second Incident at the 'Salam' School of the Swedish Mission at Port Said," 11 June 1933, Attachment: "Result of medical examination in connection with the incident which occurred at Port Said on 8.6.33." The medical examiner misdates the incident to June 8. PHS, RG 209/26/12, "Preaching by Letters," al-Balagh, 16 June 1933.

14. TNA, FO 141/760/19/22, Keown-Boyd, "Case of Turkia of the Salaam School, Port-Said," 13 June 1933, 2; "70,000 Guinea," al-Fath, 22 June 1933, 7; "The Port Said Missionary Incident: Minister of Interior's Statement," Egyptian Gazette, 16 June 1933, 6.

15. *Al-Ahram*, 13 June 1933, 1; al-Jihad, 13 June 1933, 1; TNA, FO 141/760/19–32,

Keown-Boyd, "Case of Turkia of the Salaam School, Port-Said," 13 June 1933, Attachment: Summary of press comments; see also *al-Balagh*, *Kawkab al-Sharq*, and *al-Siyasa* for the third week of June 1933.

16. TNA, FO 141/760/19/40, W. J. Ablitt, Commandant, Suez Canal Police, to K. B., 15 June 1933, Attachment of text of speech delivered by Turkia Hassan Youssef on the 14th of June 1933. The file does not contain the Arabic original of the speech; I have re-worded parts of the English translation where it appeared too literal.

17. Ibid.

18. TNA, FO 141/760/19/40, Ablitt to K. B., 15 June 1933; PHS, RG 209/26/12, "The Speech of Turkeya in Yesterday's Meeting," *al-Balagh*, 16 June 1933.

19. TNA, FO 141/760/19/14, Keown-Boyd to Booth, 11 June 1933, "Second Incident at the 'Salam' School of the Swedish Mission at Port Said," 2.

20. Ibid.

21. TNA, FO 141/760/19/18, W. J. Ablitt to K. B., Confidential, 13 June 1933; TNA, FO 141/760/19–33, *al-Balagh*, 12 June 1933.

22. TNA, FO 141/760/19/18, W. J. Ablitt to K. B., Confidential, 13 June 1933. Shaykh Jum'a Hilba and Muhammad Sulayman represented Port Said at the Muslim Brotherhood conference in Cairo in 1934. See Hasan al-Banna, *Mudhakkirat al-Da'wa wa-l-Da'iya*, 2nd ed. (Cairo: n.p., 1966), 178.

23. TNA, FO 141/760/19/32, Keown-Boyd, "Case of Turkia of the Salaam School, Port-Said," 13 June 1933, Attachment: Summary of press comments: *al-Jihad*, 11 June 1933, and *al-Balagh*, 12 June 1933.

24. TNA, FO 141/760/19/18, W. J. Ablitt to K. B., Confidential, 13 June 1933.

25. TNA, FO 141/760/19/27, Keown-Boyd, "Case of Turkia of the Salaam School, Port-Said," 13 June 1933, 7; *al-Jihad*, 22 June 1933, 1; PHS, RG 209/26/12, "Scandals of the Evangelists: Fighting Evangelisation at Port Said," *al-Jihad*, 21 June 1933; Remillard, "The So-Called 'Missionary Incident' at Port Said," 3.

26. Remillard, "The So-Called 'Missionary Incident' at Port Said," 3–4, quote from 4; Helmi Pekkola, *Jumalan Poluilla Islamin Eramaassa* (Porvoo: Werner Soderstrom Osakey-hitio, 1934), 223. Merja Jutila translated sections of the work from Finnish to English.

27. TNA, FO 141/760/19/21, Keown-Boyd, "Case of Turkia of the Salaam School, Port-Said," 13 June 1933, 1.

28. *Al-Ahram*, 13 June 1933, 1; *al-Jihad*, 13 June 1933, 1; PHS, RG 209/26/12, "The Evils of the Missionaries," *al-Jihad*, 12 June 1933; "The Policy that Supports Evangelism," *al-Siyasa*, 12 June 1933; "Teaching by Aggression," *al-Siyasa*, 14 June 1933.

29. For more on the debate over freedom of religion, see Heather J. Sharkey, *American Evangelicals in Egypt: Missionary Encounters in an Age of Empire* (Princeton, NJ: Princeton University Press, 2008); see also NARA, RG 59, SD 883.404/43, Enclosure 3, Swan to Keown-Boyd, 26 June 1933, for the Inter-Mission Council's position.

30. See Malak Badrawi, *Isma'il Sidqi, 1875–1950: Pragmatism and Vision in Twentieth Century Egypt* (Richmond, Surrey: Curzon, 1996).

31. TNA, FO 141/760/19/21, Keown-Boyd, "Case of Turkia of the Salaam School, Port-Said," 13 June 1933, 1.

32. NARA, RG 59, SD 883.404/43, Enclosure 4, Keown-Boyd to George Swan, 1 July 1933, 2.

33. TNA, FO 141/760/19/28, Keown-Boyd, "Case of Turkia of the Salaam School, Port-Said," 13 June 1933, 8.

34. "Hadith al-Tabshir fi Bur Sa'id," *al-Jihad*, 15 June 1933, 4; "70,000 Guinea," *al-Fath*, 22 June 1933, 7. See TNA, FO 141/760/19/28, Keown-Boyd, "Case of Turkia of the Salaam School, Port-Said," 13 June 1933, 8, for a rough translation, and "The Port Said Missionary Incident: Minister of Interior's Statement," *Egyptian Gazette*, 16 June 1933, 6, for another translation.

35. TNA, FO 141/760/19/21–29, Keown-Boyd, "Case of Turkia of the Salaam School, Port-Said," 13 June 1933, 1–9.

36. "A Port Said Missionary Incident," *Egyptian Gazette*, 15 June 1933, 4.

37. "The Port Said Missionary Incident: Minister of Interior's Statement," *Egyptian Gazette*, 16 June 1933, 6; "70,000 Guinea," *al-Fath*, 22 June 1933, 7; "Mas'alat al-Tabshir fi Majlis al-Nuwwab," *al-Fath*, 29 June 1933.

38. San-Eki Nakaoka, "Keown-Boyd and the British Policy towards Egypt," *Orient* 12 (1976): 89–102.

39. TNA, FO 141/760/19/13, Keown-Boyd to Booth, "Second Incident at the 'Salam' School of the Swedish Mission at Port Said," 11 June 1933, 1.

40. Ibid., 1–2.

41. TNA, FO 141/760/19/15, Keown-Boyd to Booth, "Second Incident at the 'Salam' School of the Swedish Mission at Port Said," 11 June 1933, 3; TNA, FO 141/760/19/17, "Result of medical examination in connection with the incident which occurred at Port Said on 8.6.33."

42. TNA, FO 141/760/19/19, W. A. Smart, 14 June 1933.

43. Nizarat al-Ma'arif al-'Umumiyya, *Qanun Nizam al-Madaris, 1902, Nimra 898* (Cairo: al-Matba'a al-Kubra al-Amiriyya, 1902), 38–39; see Ahmad Qasim Jawda, "al-'Uquba al-Madrasiyya wa-Tatawwuruha khilal al-Qarn al-Akhir," *al-Hilal*, 1937, 709–12.

44. TNA, FO 141/760/19/15, Keown-Boyd to Booth, "Second Incident at the 'Salam' School of the Swedish Mission at Port Said," 11 June 1933, 3–4.

45. TNA, FO 141/760/19/22, Keown-Boyd, "Case of Turkia of the Salaam School, Port-Said," 13 June 1933, 2.

46. TNA, FO 141/760/19/23–24, Keown-Boyd, "Case of Turkia of the Salaam School, Port Said," 13 June 1933, 3–4.

47. TNA, FO 141/760/19/24–25, Keown-Boyd, "Case of Turkia of the Salaam School, Port Said," 13 June 1933, 4–5.

48. TNA, FO 141/760/19/25–27, Keown-Boyd, "Case of Turkia of the Salaam School, Port-Said," 13 June 1933, 5–7.

49. TNA, FO 141/760/19/26, Keown-Boyd, "Case of Turkia of the Salaam School, Port Said," 13 June 1933, 6.

50. TNA, FO 141/760/19–29, Keown-Boyd, "Case of Turkia of the Salaam School, Port Said," 13 June 1933, 9.

51. TNA, FO 141/760/19–35, Ronald Campbell, Minute Sheet.

52. "Questions in House of Commons," *Egyptian Gazette*, 6 July 1933, 6.

53. Remillard, "The So-Called 'Missionary Incident' at Port Said," 2.

54. Ibid., 3.

55. TNA, FO 141/760/19–23, Keown-Boyd, "Case of Turkia of the Salaam School, Port-Said," 13 June 1933, 3–4.

56. Remillard, "The So-Called 'Missionary Incident' at Port Said," 3.

57. TNA, FO 141/760/19, Keown-Boyd, "Case of Turkia of the Salaam School, Port-Said," 13 June 1933, 4–7; NARA, RG 59, SD 883.404/43, W. M. Jardine to Secretary of State, 8 July 1933, 7; *Conferences of Christian Workers among Moslems 1924* (New York: International Missionary Council, 1924), 98.

58. TNA, FO 141/760/19–81, W. J. Ablitt, Suez Canal Police, 23 July 1933; Remillard, "The So-Called 'Missionary Incident' at Port Said," 3–4; PHS, RG 209/26/38, C. C. Adams to Dr. Anderson, 26 June 1933, 2; Pekkola, *Jumalan Poluilla*, 223.

59. NARA, RG 84, 350/37/13/04, Horace Remillard to Alice Marshall, 26 June 1933.

60. NARA, RG 84, 350/37/13/04, Egypt, 1931–1935, Port Said Consulate, Strictly Confidential Files, Vol. 98, Alice Marshall, Acting Principal, Salaam Mission Girls School and Orphanage, Port Said, to American Consul, Port Said, 24 June 1933.

61. George Swan, *"Lacked Ye Anything?" A Brief Story of the Egypt General Mission*, rev. ed. (London: Egypt General Mission, 1932); idem, *In Troublous Times: Sequel to "Lacked Ye Anything?"* (London: Egypt General Mission, 1923).

62. Quote from NARA, RG 59, SD 883.404/43, Enclosure 4, Keown-Boyd to Swan, 1 July 1933, 1; NARA, RG 59, SD 883.00/768, Enclosure 1, Maria Ericsson, Flint, Michigan, to Turkya, 8 September 1932.

63. NARA, RG 59, SD 883.404/43, Enclosure 3, Swan to Keown-Boyd, 26 June 1933, 3.

64. NARA, RG 59, SD 883.404/43, Enclosure 4, Keown-Boyd to Swan, 1 July 1933, 3.

65. C. C. Adams, *Islam and Modernism in Egypt: A Study of the Modern Reform Movement Inaugurated by Muhammad 'Abduh* (New York: Russell and Russell, 1933); Sharkey, *American Evangelicals in Egypt*, 103–4.

66. PHS, RG 209/26/38, C. C. Adams to Dr. Anderson, 26 June 1933, 1.

67. Ibid.

68. Ibid., 1–2.

69. Ibid., 1.

70. Remillard, "The So-Called 'Missionary Incident' at Port Said," 1–3; NARA, RG 59, SD 883.404/43, W. M. Jardine to Secretary of State, 8 July 1933, 3.

71. Remillard, "The So-Called 'Missionary Incident' at Port Said," 4.

72. NARA, RG 84, 350/37/13/03, Egypt, Port Said Consulate, J. Rives Childs, Second Secretary of Legation, to Horace Remillard, 22 June 1933.

73. NARA, RG 84, 350/37/13/04, Egypt, Port Said Consulate, Alice Marshall, Acting Principal, Salaam Mission Girls School and Orphanage, Port Said, to American Consul, Port Said, 24 June 1933.

74. Remillard, "The So-Called 'Missionary Incident' at Port Said," 2.

75. Ibid., 4.

76. Ibid., 5.

77. Ibid., 2.

78. Ibid., 4.

79. Ibid., 5.

80. Ibid., 6.

81. Pekkola, *Jumalan Poluilla*, 7. The quotes throughout are Merja Jutila's translations.

82. Ibid., 218–20; Sharkey, *American Evangelicals in Egypt*, 127–28.

83. Pekkola, *Jumalan Poluilla*, 220–21.

84. Ibid., 221.

85. Ibid., 222.

86. Ibid.

87. Ibid., 224.

88. NARA, RG 59, SD 883.404/43, Enclosure 4, Keown-Boyd to Swan, 1 July 1933.

89. Al-Banna, *Mudhakkirat*, 91–92, 138, 141–45, 178.

90. "Jam'iyyat al-Ikhwan al-Muslimin wa-l-Tabshir," *Jaridat al-Ikhwan al-Muslimin* 1, no. 3 (6 Rabi' I, 1352/29 June 1933): 15–18.

91. Quote from "al-Mujrim al-Akbar," *al-Fath*, 22 June 1933, 8; "Jam'iyyat al-Ikhwan al-Muslimin wa-l-Tabshir," 15–18; TNA, FO 141/752/3, Suez Canal Police to Roche, 10 August 1933.

92. TNA, FO 141/760/19/18, Confidential, Ablitt, 13 June 1933; TNA, FO 141/760/19/32, Keown-Boyd, "Case of Turkia of the Salaam School, Port-Said," 13 June 1933, Attachment: Summary of press comments: *al-Jihad*, 11 June 1933, and *al-Balagh*, 12 June 1933.

93. TNA, FO 141/760/19/37, W. J. Ablitt to K. B., 15 June 1933, Attachment of text of speech delivered by Turkia Hassan Youssef on the 14th of June 1933; PHS, RG 209/26/12, "The Speech of Turkeya in Yesterday's Meeting," *al-Balagh*, 16 June 1933; "al-Mujrim al-Akbar," *al-Fath*, 22 June 1933, 8; al-Banna et al., "Surat al-'Arida," *Jaridat al-Ikhwan al-Muslimin* 1, no. 3 (6 Rabi' I, 1352/29 June 1933): 19–20; al-Banna, *Mudhakkirat*, 138, 140.

94. TNA, FO 141/760/19/83, Suez Canal Police, Special Branch, Daily Report No. 428, Port Said, 24 June 1933; TNA, FO 141/760/19/84, Special Section, 25 June 1933, 1–3; "Nahda Mubaraka wa-Ijtima'i Hafil bi-Dar," *Jaridat al-Ikhwan al-Muslimin* 1, no. 3 (6 Rabi' I, 1352/29 June 1933): 22.

95. *Al-Lata'if al-Musawwara*, 3 July 1933, 1.

96. "Al-Mujrim al-Akbar," *al-Fath*, 22 June 1933, 8.

97. TNA, FO 141/760/19/85, Suez Canal Police, Special Branch, Daily Report No. 428, Port Said, 24 June 1933.

98. FO 141/760/19/67, Suez Canal Police Special Branch, Port Said, 22 June 1933, Daily Report No. 427; FO 141/760/19/95, Ablitt, Suez Canal Police, Special Branch, to K. B., 26 June 1933; FO 141/752/1, Commandant, Suez Canal Police, to D.G.E.D., 6 July 1933; FO 141/760/19/109, Suez Canal Police, 23 July 1933; FO 141/752/3, Roche to Smart, 26 August 1933; FO 141/752/3, Ablitt to Roche; all in TNA.

Chapter 1: Forgotten Children

1. See Beth Baron, "Orphans and Abandoned Children in Modern Egypt," in *Interpreting Welfare and Relief in the Middle East*, ed. Nefissa Neguib and Inger Marie Okkenhaug (Leiden: Brill, 2008), 13–34.

2. Muhammad 'Azmi Salih, *al-Ri'aya al-Ijtima'iyya li-l-Yatama fi al-Islam* (Cairo: Maktaba Wahba, 1977).

3. See Amira al-Azhary Sonbol, "Adoption in Islamic Society: A Historical Survey," in *Children in the Muslim Middle East*, ed. Elizabeth Warnock Fernea (Austin: University of Texas Press, 1995), 45–67; Jamila Bargach, *Orphans of Islam: Family, Abandonment, and Secret Adoption in Morocco* (Lanham, MD: Rowman and Littlefield, 2002). Bargach, who writes movingly of the experience of "bastards," as she provocatively calls them, explores secret adoption, in which a couple, longing for a child but unable to conceive or deliver, takes the infant from a mother who is unable to raise it for social or financial reasons. The secrecy in many of Bargach's cases often unraveled at the moment of the father's death, when relatives stepped forward to contest the "adopted" child's right to the patrimony.

4. See writings by Marcia C. Inhorn, esp. *Infertility and Patriarch: The Cultural Politics of Gender and Family Life in Egypt* (Philadelphia: University of Pennsylvania Press, 1996); *Quest for Conception: Gender, Infertility, and Egyptian Medical Traditions* (Philadelphia: University of Pennsylvania Press, 1994).

5. See Beth Baron, "Women, Honour, and the State: Evidence from Egypt," *Middle Eastern Studies* 42, no. 1 (2006): 1–20.

6. See Heather J. Sharkey, *American Evangelicals in Egypt: Missionary Encounters in an Age of Empire* (Princeton, NJ: Princeton University Press, 2008); Paul Sedra, *From Mission to Modernity: Evangelicals, Reformers and Education in Nineteenth Century Egypt* (London: I. B. Tauris, 2011).

7. Gabriel Baer, *Studies in the Social History of Modern Egypt* (Chicago: University of Chicago Press, 1969), chap. 5.

8. Mine Ener, *Managing Egypt's Poor and the Politics of Benevolence, 1800–1952* (Princeton, NJ: Princeton University Press, 2004), xi, 26.

9. Ener, *Managing Egypt's Poor*.

10. Ibid., 42–45, 155n81.

11. Ibid., 42, 155n82.

12. E. W. Lane, *An Account of the Manners and Customs of the Modern Egyptians* (London, 1842; rep. London: Ward, Lock and Co., 1890), 176.

13. Andrea B. Rugh, "Orphanages in Egypt: Contradiction or Affirmation in a Family-Oriented Society," in Fernea, ed., *Children in the Muslim Middle East*, 130.

14. Ener, *Managing Egypt's Poor*, 56–58.

15. Ibid., 57–58.

16. Iris Agmon, *Family and Court: Legal Culture and Modernity in Late Ottoman Palestine* (Syracuse, NY: Syracuse University Press, 2006), chap. 5.

17. Antoine K. Sabbagh, *Les Meglis Hasbys et la protection des biens des mineurs en Egypte* (Paris: A. Fabre, 1931), 11–20.

18. Baer, *Social History*, 83.

19. Victor Guerin, *La France catholique en Egypte* (Tours: Alfred Mame et Fils, 1894), 54–61; Ener, *Managing Egypt's Poor*, 103.

20. Guerin, *France catholique*, 169, 174–75.

21. Ibid., 208–9.

22. See Robert L. Tignor, *Modernization and British Colonial Rule in Egypt, 1882–1914* (Princeton, NJ: Princeton University Press, 1966); Roger Owen, *Lord Cromer: Victorian Imperialist, Edwardian Proconsul* (Oxford: Oxford University Press, 2004); Beth Baron, *Women's Awakening in Egypt: Culture, Society, and the Press* (New Haven, CT: Yale University Press, 1994), chap. 6.

23. See Baer, *Social History*, 83–84; Ener, *Managing Egypt's Poor*, 93–95.

24. Ener, *Managing Egypt's Poor*, 75, 95.

25. TNA, FO 371/3203/177595, Ali Labeeb, "Appendix: Ministry of Wakfs. The Medical Service," June 1918.

26. Beth Baron, "Liberated Bodies and Saved Souls: Freed African Slave Girls and Missionaries in Egypt," in *African Communities in Asia and the Mediterranean: Between Integration and Conflict*, ed. Ehud R. Toledano (Trenton, NJ: Africa World Press, 2012), 215–35.

27. Quote from TNA, FO 407/164, No. 82, Cromer to Lansdowne, Cairo, 15 March 1905, "Annual Report of 1904," 126; TNA, FO 407/161, No. 7, Cromer to Lansdowne, "Annual Report of 1902," 26 February 1903, 53; Balsam 'Abd al-Malik, "Malja' al-Atfal wa-l-Wilada," *al-Mar'a al-Misriyya* 1, no. 10 (December 1920): 353–57.

28. Jamila Bargach develops this idea in her *Orphans of Islam*, 181–84. See also Baron, "Women, Honour, and the State"; Ann Fessler, *The Girls Who Went Away: The Hidden History of Women Who Surrendered Children for Adoption in the Decades before Roe v. Wade* (New York: Penguin Press, 2006).

29. TNA, FO 371/1362/15421, Kitchener to Grey, "Annual Report for 1911," 6 April 1912, 37.

30. 'Abd al-Malik, "Malja' al-Atfal wa-l-Wilada," 353–57.

31. Minnie Goodnow, "In the Land of Egypt," *American Journal of Nursing* 25, no. 9 (September 1925): 756.

32. Rugh, "Orphanages in Egypt," 130–34.

33. TNA, FO 371/661/12738, Gorst to Grey, "Annual Report of 1908," 27 March 1909, 86.

34. Ener, *Managing Egypt's Poor*, 114–15.

35. NARA, SD 883.00/540, Howell to Sec. of State, 30 December 1924, "Note by Mrs. Russell Pasha on The Shoubra Waifs and Strays Home, for His Excellency Said Zulficar Pasha."

36. Ibid.

37. Ibid.; Balsam 'Abd al-Malik, "Malja' Abna' al-Sabil," *al-Mar'a al-Misriyya* 5, no. 6 (15 June 1924): 307.

38. NARA, SD 883.00/540, "Note by Mrs. Russell Pasha."

39. 'Abd al-Malik, "Malja' Abna' al-Sabil," 307; *al-Lata'if al-Musawwara*, 21 February 1921, cited in Ener, *Managing Egypt's Poor*, 118–22. The Shubra Home was called in Arabic "Malja' Abna' al-Shawari'a" or "Malja' Abna' al-Sabil," both connoting street children.

40. Beth Baron, "Islam, Philanthropy, and Political Culture in Interwar Egypt: The Activism of Labiba Ahmad," in *Poverty and Charity in Middle Eastern Contexts*, ed. Michael Bonner et al. (Albany: SUNY Press, 2003), 239–54.

41. Grace Thompson Seton, *A Woman Tenderfoot in Egypt* (New York: Dodd, Mead, 1923), 49.

42. TNA, FO 407/161, No. 7, Cromer to Lansdowne, "Annual Report of 1902," 26 February 1903, 53.

43. Minnie Goodnow, "In the Land of Egypt," *American Journal of Nursing* 25, no. 9 (September 1925): 756.

44. Fina Gued Vidal, *Safia Zaghloul* (Cairo: R. Schindler, 1946), 16–17.

45. Sonbol, "Adoption in Islamic Society," 60–61; for a discussion of secret adoption in Morocco, see Bargach, *Orphans of Islam*.

46. Ener, *Managing Egypt's Poor*, 102–3, 117–19; al-Jam'iyyat al-Khayriyya al-Islamiyya fi Thamanin 'Amm (Cairo: Dar al-'Ulum, 1979).

47. "Itmam 'Amal Jalil," *Tarqiyat al-Mar'a* 1 (1908): 76–77.

48. *Al-Lata'if al-Musawwara*, 4 April 1921, 11.

49. 'Abd al-Malik, "Malja' al-Atfal wa-l-Wilada," 356.

50. Ibid.; TNA, FO 371/1362/15421, Kitchener to Grey, "Annual Report for 1911," 6 April 1912, 37.

51. Ener, *Managing Egypt's Poor*, 117–19.

52. See Baron, "Islam, Philanthropy, and Political Culture in Interwar Egypt," 239–54.

53. Ibid.

54. Labiba Ahmad, "al-Malaji' wa-'Inayatuha," *al-Nahda al-Nisa'iyya* 4, no. 43 (June 1926): 240.

55. Beth Baron, "An Islamic Activist in Interwar Egypt," in *Iran and Beyond: Essays in Middle Eastern History in Honor of Nikki R. Keddie*, ed. Rudi Matthee and Beth Baron (Costa Mesa, CA: Mazda, 2000), 219.

56. "Attempts to Sell Her Child: Mother's Unnatural Action," *Egyptian Gazette*, 22 August 1933, 5.

57. Lucette Lagnado, *The Man in the White Sharkskin Suit: A Jewish Family's Exodus from Old Cairo to the New World* (New York: Harper, 2008), 58–59.

58. George Swan, *In Troublous Times: Sequel to "Lacked Ye Anything?"* (London: Egypt General Mission, 1923), 36.

59. TNA, FO 371/3203/177595, Ali Labeeb, "Appendix: Ministry of Wakfs. The Medical Service," June 1918.

60. L. E. Glenn, *A Shining Light: Viola Light Glenn* (n.p., n.d.), 31.

61. L. E. Glenn, *Missionary Life and Labors of Elder & Mrs. L.E. Glenn and Associates: Girls Orphanage Egypt* (c. 1934), 10–11.

62. Ibid., 5–6; see also Glenn, *A Shining Light*. Damanhur is notable as the town where Hasan al-Banna, founder of the Muslim Brotherhood, attended high school.

63. Glenn, *Missionary Life and Labors*, 29.

64. Ibid., 8; Glenn, *A Shining Light*.

65. Glenn, *Missionary Life and Labors*, 27; see also Marietta Simpson, "A New Step with the Lord!," in *Heralds of Light to Darkened Egypt: Missionary Work in Egypt*, compiled by Victor Glenn (Shoals, IN: Old Paths Tract Society, n.d.), 18–27.

66. Glenn, *Missionary Life and Labors*, 8; Glenn, *Heralds of Light to Darkened Egypt*.

67. Victor Glenn, *Crossing Continents with Christ: The Amazing Story of the Miracle Ministry of Faith Missions* (Bedford, IN: n.p., n.d.), 14.

Chapter 2: Winning Souls for Christ

1. "Egypt," *Women's Missionary Magazine*, September 1933, 108.

2. PHS, RG 209/2/30, Anna B. Criswell to Mildred Franklin, 26 June 1933.

3. Ibid.

4. PHS, RG 209/2/30, Anna B. Criswell to Friends of the Cleveland Presbyterial, 29 June 1933.

5. Heather J. Sharkey, *American Evangelicals in Egypt: Missionary Encounters in an Age of Empire* (Princeton, NJ: Princeton University Press, 2008); see also Khalid Na'im, *al-Judhur al-Tarikhiyya li-Irsaliyyat al-Tansir al-Ajnabiyya fi Misr, 1756–1986: Dirasa Watha'iqiyya* (Cairo: Kitab al-Mukhtar, 1988).

6. *History of the W.G.M.S. 1883–1933* (Pittsburgh: WMGS pamphlet, 1933), 23–25.

7. PHS, RG 404/1/2, "Miss Margaret Anna Smith"; Mrs. Ralph G. McGill, "Mararet [sic] A. Smith," *One Hundred Twenty Years of Service in Egypt: Anna Y. Thompson, Margaret A. Smith* (Pittsburgh: Women's General Missionary Society, n.d.), 8–9.

8. Elizabeth Kelsey Kinnear, *She Sat Where They Sat: A Memoir of Anna Young Thompson of Egypt* (Grand Rapids, MI: William B. Eerdmans Publishing Company, 1971), 28; Louisa Bond Moffitt, "Anna Young Thompson: American Missionary, Cultural Ambassador, and Reluctant Feminist in Egypt, 1872–1932" (PhD diss., Georgia State University, 2003).

9. Na'im, *al-Judhur al-Tarikhiyya*, 109–10.

10. PHS, RG 58/1/10, (microfilm 1009) Anna Young Thompson Papers, diary entry for 25 October 1877.

11. Ibid., diary entry for 26 October 1877.

12. See Heather J. Sharkey, "An Egyptian in China: Ahmed Fahmi and the Making of World Christianities," *Church History* 78, no. 2 (2009): 309–26; idem, *American Evangelicals in Egypt*, 78–81; Moffitt, "Anna Young Thompson," 135–51.

13. Sharkey, *American Evangelicals*, 42–43; Earl E. Elder, *Vindicating a Vision: The Story of the American Mission in Egypt, 1854–1954* (Philadelphia: Board of Foreign Missions of the United Presbyterian Church of North America, 1958), 72; Andrew Watson, *The American Mission in Egypt, 1854–1896* (Pittsburgh: United Presbyterian Board of Publication, 1898), 327.

14. PHS, RG 404/1/3, Margaret Smith Diary, entry for 5 December 1880.

15. Charles Watson quoted in McGill, *One Hundred Twenty Years of Service*, 12–13.

16. McGill, *One Hundred Twenty Years of Service*, 13.

17. Charles Watson quoted in McGill, *One Hundred Twenty Years of Service*, 13.

18. PHS, RG 404/1/3, Margaret Smith Diary, entry for 2 April 1880.

19. PHS, RG 404/1/3, Diary of Margaret Anna Smith, List of subscribers for Harit is Sakkaeen School Building, c. 1880; McGill, *One Hundred Twenty Years of Service*, 10; Kinnear, *She Sat Where They Sat*, 35–36.

20. Quote from Elder, *Vindicating a Vision*, 67; Sharkey, *American Evangelicals*, 89.

21. See FHL, RG 4/124, "The Fowler Orphanage," c. 1956.

22. J. S. Fowler, "Egypt," *The Friend*, 30 November 1901, 157; Rachel Cope, "Esther H. Fowler," *The Friend*, 22 June 1922, 602.

23. Quote from "The Fowler Orphanage"; see also "Items," *The Friend*, 3 August 1895, 15.

24. Mine Ener, *Managing Egypt's Poor and the Politics of Benevolence, 1800–1952* (Princeton, NJ: Princeton University Press, 2004), 113–24.

25. J. S. Fowler, "Egypt," *The Friend*, 30 November 1901, 157.

26. Letter from M. G. Kyle and C. S. Cleland to "Brethren in our Lord Jesus Christ everywhere" (12 July 1901), *The Friend*, 21 September 1901, 76.

27. M. G. Kyle and C. S. Cleland, "Articles of Agreement," *The Friend*, 21 September 1901, 76.

28. "Acknowledgments," *The Friend*, 27 December 1902, 192.

29. John S. Fowler, "The Egyptian Orphanage," *The Friend*, 21 May 1906, 346.

30. PHS, *Minutes of the Thirty Sixth Annual Meeting of the Egyptian Missionary Association, Cairo, February 1906* (Cairo: Les Pyramides, 1906), 34–35; PHS, *Minutes of the Summer Meeting of the Egyptian Missionary Association, Ramleh, July 1904*, 27–28; McGill, *One Hundred Twenty Years of Service*, 11–12.

31. PHS, *Minutes of the Summer Meeting of the Egyptian Missionary Association, Ramleh, July 1906*, 13–14.

32. PHS, *Annual Report of the American United Presbyterian Mission in Egypt and the Sudan, 1908–1909*, 47.

33. PHS, *Annual Report of the American United Presbyterian Mission in Egypt, 1906–1907*, 45.

34. PHS, *Annual Report of the American United Presbyterian Mission in Egypt and the Sudan for the Year 1909*, 54.

35. Beth Baron, "Liberated Bodies and Saved Souls: Freed African Slave Girls and Missionaries in Egypt," in *African Communities in Asia and the Mediterranean: Identities between Integration and Conflict*, ed. Ehud R. Toledano (Trenton, NJ: Africa World Press, 2012), 215–35.

36. PHS, *Minutes of the Fortieth Annual Meeting of the Egyptian Missionary Association, February–March 1910*, 36.

37. PHS, *Minutes of the Sixty-Second Annual Meeting of the Egyptian Missionary Association, Assiut, January 1932*, 103.

38. *Annual Report American Mission, 1909*, 55; PHS, *Minutes of the Fortieth Annual Meeting of the Egyptian Missionary Association, 1910*, 18.

39. FHL, RG 4/124, "Evangelical Church at Faggala, Cairo, Egypt," 4–5; Elder, *Vindicating a Vision*, 134–35.

40. "The Fowler Orphanage."

41. FHL, RG 4/124, Fowler Orphanage Association Minutes, 1926–1986.

42. PHS, *Minutes of the Egyptian Missionary Association, Ramleh, July 1923*, 405.

43. PHS, *Minutes of the Fifty-Third Annual Meeting of the Egyptian Missionary Association, Cairo, February 1923*, 299.

44. *Minutes of the Summer Meeting of the Egyptian Missionary Association, Ramleh, July 1920,* 12; *Minutes of the Fifty-Second Annual Meeting of the Egyptian Missionary Association, February 1922,* 139; *Minutes of the Fifty-Fifth Annual Meeting of the Egyptian Missionary Association, Assiut, January 1925,* 538; *Minutes of the Sixty-First Annual Meeting of the Egyptian Missionary Association, Assiut, January 1931,* 12; all in PHS.

45. *Annual Report American Mission, 1908–1909,* 50–51; *Minutes, EMA, January 1932,* 103.

46. *Annual Report American Mission, 1906–1907,* 44–45.

47. FHL, RG 24/124, see photo "First Moslem Convert—Fowler Orphanage" with details on back.

48. PHS, *Annual Report of the American United Presbyterian Mission in Egypt and the Sudan for the Year 1910,* 64.

49. *Annual Report American Mission, 1909,* 53.

50. *Annual Report American Mission, 1910,* 63–64.

51. Liat Kozma, *Policing Egyptian Women: Sex, Law, and Medicine in Khedival Egypt* (Syracuse, NY: Syracuse University Press, 2011).

52. *Annual Report American Mission, 1906–1907,* 45.

53. *Annual Report American Mission, 1910,* 64.

54. FHL, RG 4/124, Lucy Lightowler, Cairo, to Friends of John and Esther Fowler, 19 April 1950.

55. PHS, *Minutes of the Summer Meeting of the Egyptian Missionary Association, Ramleh, July 1909,* 7; *Annual Report American Mission, 1910,* 64.

56. PHS, *Annual Report of the American United Presbyterian Mission in Egypt and the Sudan for the Year 1920,* 34.

57. *Annual Report American Mission, 1909,* 53–54.

58. *Minutes, EMA, July 1923,* 406.

59. McGill, *One Hundred Twenty Years of Service,* 12.

60. Ibid., 13–14.

61. *Annual Report American Mission, 1909,* 55.

62. *Annual Report American Mission, 1910,* 64.

63. Ibid., 64.

64. *Annual Report American Mission, 1909,* 53–54.

65. PHS, *Minutes of the Fifty-Seventh Annual Meeting of the Egyptian Missionary Association, Assiut, January 1927,* 185.

66. *Annual Report American Mission, 1910,* 63–64.

67. Kinnear, *She Sat Where They Sat,* 28.

68. Beth Baron, "The Making and Breaking of Marital Bonds in Modern Egypt," in *Women in Middle Eastern History: Shifting Boundaries in Sex and Gender,* ed. Nikki R. Keddie and Beth Baron (New Haven, CT: Yale University Press, 1991), 281.

69. PHS, *Minutes of the Thirty Seventh Annual Meeting of the Egyptian Missionary Association, Assiut, February 1907,* 25.

70. PHS, *Minutes of the Summer Meeting of the Egyptian Missionary Association, Ramleh, July 1907,* 15.

71. PHS, *Annual Report of the American United Presbyterian Mission in Egypt, 1907–1908*, 59.

72. *Minutes, EMA, July 1907*, 15.

73. *Minutes, EMA, July 1923*, 406; *Minutes, EMA, January 1931*, 12.

74. *Annual Report American Mission, 1909*, 53.

75. *Annual Report American Mission, 1910*, 64.

76. *Annual Report American Mission, 1909*, 53.

77. See Selim Deringil, "'There Is No Compulsion in Religion': On Conversion and Apostasy in the Late Ottoman Empire: 1839–1856," *Comparative Studies in Society and History* 42, no. 3 (2000): 547–75; idem, *Conversion and Apostasy in the Late Ottoman Empire* (Cambridge: Cambridge University Press, 2012); Eyal Ginio, "Childhood, Mental Capacity and Conversion to Islam in the Ottoman State," *Byzantine and Modern Greek Studies* 25 (2001): 90–119; Sharkey, *American Evangelicals*, see esp. 63–71. See also idem, "Empire and Muslim Conversion: Historical Reflections on Christian Missions in Egypt," *Islam and Christian—Muslim Relations* 16, no. 1 (January 2005): 43–60.

78. PHS, *Minutes of the Fifty-Sixth Annual Meeting of the Egyptian Missionary Association, Assiut, January 1926*, 95.

79. *Minutes of the Fifty-Ninth Annual Meeting of the Egyptian Missionary Association, Assiut, December 1928–January 1929*, 394; *Minutes of the Sixtieth Annual Meeting of the Egyptian Missionary Association, Assiut, January 1930*, 505; both in PHS.

80. *Minutes, EMA, January 1931*, 12.

81. *Minutes, EMA, January 1927*, 185.

82. FHL, RG 24/124, see photo "First Moslem Convert—Fowler Orphanage" with details on back.

83. PHS, RG 209/2/30, Anna Criswell to Miss J. Sanford, 28 June 1933; RG 209/2/15, Ella Barnes to Mr. Taylor, 6 May 1937.

84. George Swan, *In Troublous Times: Sequel to "Lacked Ye Anything?"* (London: Egypt General Mission, 1923), 66–67, see photos following 80; idem, *"Lacked Ye Anything?": A Brief Story of the Egypt General Mission*, rev. ed. (London: Egypt General Mission, 1932), 51–52.

85. FHL, Lucy Lightowler, Cairo, to Friends of John and Esther Fowler, 19 April 1950.

86. Quote from *Programs and Needs of the Work of the American Mission in Egypt* (Cairo: Nile Mission Press, 1938), 28; see also PHS, *Minutes of the Sixty-Seventh Annual Meeting of the American Mission in Egypt, Assiut, January 1937*, 84–85.

87. PHS, RG 209/2/15, Barnes to Taylor, 6 May 1937, with "Fowler Orphanage, Abbassia, Cairo. Egypt. Record of Service 1906–1936."

88. Ibid.

89. PHS, RG 209/2/15, Barnes, "Fowler Orphanage, Abbassia."

90. PHS, RG 209/2/15, Barnes to Taylor, 6 May 1937.

91. PHS, *Findings of the General Conference of the American Mission Held at Schutz, Egypt, April 28th to May 5th 1912* (Cairo: Nile Mission Press, 1912), 14–15.

92. PHS, RG 209/26/12, "About the Baptism Event at Beni Suef," *Kawkab al-Sharq,*

22 June 1933; see also PHS, RG 209/26/38, Letter from C. C. Adams, Cairo, to Dr. Anderson, Philadelphia, 26 June 1933, 3.

93. PHS, RG 209/3/41, Lucy Lightowler, Mansura, Egypt, to Miss Grier, 30 March 1932.

94. Barnes, "Fowler Orphanage, Abbassia."

95. Ibid.

96. PHS, RG 209/2/15, Barnes to Taylor, 6 May 1937.

97. Ibid., with "Fowler Orphanage, Abbassia."

98. Jamila Bargach argues that missionary orphanages in Morocco left children feeling linguistically and religiously alienated from society. Bargach, "B-A-S-T-A-R-D Biographies: Inside an Invisible Space," paper presented at the conference on "Family History in Islamic and Middle East Studies," University of California, Berkeley, April 2000.

99. PHS, RG 209/5/38, Letter from Jane Smith, Cairo, 3 March 1933.

100. *Minutes, EMA, January 1932*, 103.

101. PHS, *Minutes of the Summer Commission of the Egyptian Missionary Association, Ramleh, July 1932*, 176.

Chapter 3: Speaking in Tongues

1. Lillian Trasher, *Letters from Lillian*, ed. Beverly Graham (Springfield, MO: Assemblies of God Division of Foreign Missions, 1983), letter dated 23 June 1933, 20–21. Trasher used the spelling "Assiout" for the orphanage; for consistency, I will use the more standard Arabic transliteration, Asyut.

2. Jerome Beatty, "Nile Mother," *American Magazine*, July 1939, 55; Lester Sumrall, *Lillian Trasher: The Nile Mother* (Springfield, MO: Gospel Publishing House, 1951); Beth Prim Howell, *Lady on a Donkey* (New York: E. P. Dutton, 1960); Trasher, *Letters from Lillian*; Janet and Geoff Benge, *Lillian Trasher: The Greatest Wonder in Egypt* (Seattle: YWAM Publishing, 2004).

3. Sharkey notes that Presbyterian evangelicals distinguished between conversions of Muslims, which entailed affirming Christian belief and accepting Evangelical doctrine, and accessions of Coptic Orthodox to Evangelicalism, which entailed shifting between Christian denominations. See Heather J. Sharkey, *American Evangelicals in Egypt: Missionary Encounters in an Age of Empire* (Princeton, NJ: Princeton University Press, 2008), 69.

4. Hanna F. Wissa, *Assiout—The Saga of an Egyptian Family* (Sussex, UK: Book Guild, 1994), 102–6.

5. Ibid., 117–22.

6. Ibid., 122.

7. Trasher, *Word and Witness*, 20 October 1913, 2.

8. Muhafazat Asyut, *Asyut fi 10 Sanawat* (Cairo: Matba'at Nahdat Misr, 1962), 9; Beth Baron, "Liberated Bodies and Saved Souls: Freed African Slave Girls and Missionaries in Egypt," in *African Communities in Asia and the Mediterranean: Identities between Integration and Conflict*, ed. Ehud R. Toledano (Trenton, NJ: Africa World Press, 2012), 215–35.

9. FPHC, Lillian Trasher Personal Papers, File cards, 0504 074.

10. Trasher, *Word and Witness*, 20 October 1913, 2.

11. "Notice," *Pentecost*, 1 November 1909, 4; Sarah Smith, "With the Women of Egypt," *Latter Rain Evangel*, October 1912, 11.

12. Wissa, *Assiout*, 175–76; Veronica Seton-Williams and Peter Stocks, *Blue Guide: Egypt* (New York: W. W. Norton, 1984), 475.

13. Florence Bush, "Florence I. Bush and Mother," *Weekly Evangel*, 24 April 1915, 4.

14. C. W. Doney, "C. W. Doney," *Weekly Evangel*, 31 July 1915, 4.

15. Ghali Hanni, "Among the Natives in Egypt," *Latter Rain Evangel*, October 1916, 14; Pastor Habeb Yousef, "The Pentecostal Work in Egypt," *Weekly Evangel*, 3 March 1917, 13; idem, "The Call of Egypt," *Weekly Evangel*, 19 May 1917, 13.

16. Trasher, "The Miracle of the Assiout Orphanage," *Latter Rain Evangel*, August 1924, 22. For background on women in the war, see Beth Baron, "The Politics of Female Notables in Postwar Egypt," in *Borderlines: Genders and Identities in War and Peace, 1870–1930*, ed. Billie Melman (New York: Routledge, 1998), 332–33.

17. Trasher, "When God Called and Equipped," *Latter Rain Evangel*, March 1919, 15.

18. Beth Baron, *Egypt as a Woman: Nationalism, Gender, and Politics* (Berkeley: University of California Press, 2005), chaps. 5–7.

19. Trasher, "God's Protection through a Reign of Terror," *Latter Rain Evangel*, September 1919, 16.

20. *Muhafazat Asyut: al-'Id al-Qawmi, 18 Abril 1982* (Cairo: Jumhuriyyat Misr al-'Arabiyya, al-Hay'a al-'Amma li-l-Isti'lamat, 1982), 7–8.

21. Ibid. After the 1952 Revolution, a square and a major thoroughfare coming out of it were named after Muhammad Kamil Muhammad.

22. Trasher, "God's Protection in Great Peril," *Latter Rain Evangel*, June 1919, 11; idem, "God's Protection through a Reign of Terror," 16; A. H. Post, "Alexandria, Egypt," *Christian Evangel*, 28 June 1919, 10.

23. See Beth Baron, "Islam, Philanthropy, and Political Culture in Interwar Egypt: The Activism of Labiba Ahmad," in *Poverty and Charity in Middle Eastern Contexts*, ed. Michael Bonner et al. (Albany: SUNY Press, 2003), 239–54; Mine Ener, *Managing Egypt's Poor and the Politics of Benevolence, 1800–1952* (Princeton, NJ: Princeton University Press, 2004), 121–24.

24. Trasher, "Notes from Africa," *Pentecostal Evangel*, 2 April 1921, 12.

25. FPHC, Lillian Trasher Personal Papers, Deeds, 0795 043.

26. Ibid., Explanation of Deeds, 0795 043.

27. Ibid., waqf document in Arabic and English translation, 0795 043.

28. Wissa, *Assiout*, 176; *Muhafazat Asyut*, map on 38.

29. Trasher, "The Miracle of the Assiout Orphanage," 21.

30. Wissa, *Assiout*, 176–79.

31. Trasher, "The Family Growing at Assiout," *Pentecostal Evangel*, 18 July 1925, 10.

32. Sumrall, *Lillian Trasher*, 22–23; Trasher, "The Assiout Orphanage," *Pentecostal Evangel*, 25 August 1923, 12.

33. Trasher, "Happy Hearts," *Pentecostal Evangel*, 14 March 1925, 10.

34. Lillian Trasher, *Extracts from My Diary: A Review of God's Gracious Provisions*

for the Needs of the Assiout Orphanage (1927–1931) (Springfield, MO: Foreign Missions Dept., n.d.), 15, letter dated 31 January 1928.

35. Trasher, "The Lord Will Provide," *Pentecostal Evangel*, 21 March 1931, 15.

36. Trasher, *Letters from Lillian*, letter dated 13 March 1933, 20.

37. Trasher, "Miss Lillian Trasher," *Pentecostal Evangel*, 25 June 1921, 13.

38. Trasher, *Extracts from My Diary*, letter dated 22 November 1927, 11.

39. Ibid., letter dated 24 February 1928, 17–18.

40. Andrea B. Rugh, "Orphanages in Egypt: Contradiction or Affirmation in a Family-Oriented Society," in *Children in the Muslim Middle East*, ed. Elizabeth Warnock Fernea (Austin: University of Texas Press, 1995), 130–31.

41. Trasher, "Happy Hearts," 10.

42. Trasher, *Extracts from My Diary*, letter dated 22 November 1927, 11.

43. Ibid., letter dated 24 February 1928, 18.

44. Ibid., letter dated 31 January 1928, 15.

45. Trasher, "The Assiout Orphanage," 12.

46. Florence Christie, *Called to Egypt* (Seal Beach, CA: Florence V. Christie Church School Services, 1997), 45–46.

47. Trasher, "Thou God Seest Me," *Pentecostal Evangel*, 13 December 1930, 11; see Beth Baron, "Women, Honour, and the State: Evidence from Egypt," *Middle Eastern Studies* 42, no. 1 (2006): 1–20.

48. Trasher, "Thou God Seest Me," 11.

49. Trasher, "The Assiout Orphanage," 12.

50. Christie, *Called to Egypt*, 53.

51. Trasher, "Suffer the Little Children to Come," *Latter Rain Evangel*, October 1919, 7.

52. FPHC, Lillian Trasher Personal Papers, Waqf, 0795 043.

53. Lillian Trasher, *Work of Faith and Labor of Love, The Assiout Orphanage: Gleanings from the Correspondence with Miss Lillian Trasher* (Springfield, MO: Foreign Missions Department, Assemblies of God in Foreign Lands, 1937), letter dated 8 March 1935, 29.

54. "A Big Revival in Egypt," *Pentecostal Evangel*, 27 March 1926, 11.

55. Ibid.

56. Quote from Trasher, *Letters from Lillian*, letter dated 7 April 1927, 17–18; see also idem, "Mighty Revival at Asyut Orphanage, Egypt," *Pentecostal Evangel*, 7 May 1927, 10; idem, "More About the Revival in Asyut, Egypt," *Pentecostal Evangel*, 14 May 1927, 10.

57. Trasher, "Great Pentecostal Outpouring in North and South Africa," *Latter Rain Evangel*, May 1927, 13, letter dated 9 April 1927.

58. H. E. Randall, "Asyut Orphanage Revival—A Wonderful Work of God," *Pentecostal Evangel*, 4 June 1927, 6.

59. The history of disabled people in Egypt is a topic deserving greater study. For a brief overview in a book that focuses on the contemporary situation, see Lesley Lababidi in collaboration with Nadia El-Arabi, *Silent No More: Special Needs People in Egypt* (Cairo: American University in Cairo Press, 2002).

60. Christie, *Called to Egypt*, 54–55.

61. Trasher, "Another Wonderful Revival at Asyut, Egypt," *Pentecostal Evangel*, 18 March 1933, 8; idem, "Continued Revival in Asyut, Egypt," *Pentecostal Evangel*, 8 April 1933, 11.

Chapter 4: Nothing Less Than a Miracle

1. Founded as the Swedish Mission to Mohammedans, the mission took the name Salaam Mission in the 1920s when it became internationalized. For background on Nordic missionaries, see Inger Marie Okkenhaug, "Gender and Nordic Missions in the Nineteenth and Twentieth Centuries," *Scandinavian Journal of History* 28 (2003): 73–82; idem, ed., *Gender, Race and Religion: Nordic Missions 1860–1940* (Uppsala: Studia Missionalia Svencana XCI, 2003).

2. YDS-Salaam, Maria Ericsson, *The Swedish Mission Story: Egypt* (n.p., [1924]), quote from 16–17; see also Helmi Pekkola, *Jumalan Poluilla Islamin Eramaassa* (Porvoo: Werner Soderstrom Osakeyhitio, 1934). Merja Jutila translated parts of this book from Finnish to English for me; the translations throughout are hers.

3. Ericsson, *Swedish Mission Story*, 3.

4. Personal communication from Inger Marie Okkenhaug, History Institute, Volda University College, 23 November 2011; F. Fris Berg, "The Share of Scandinavia in Christian Missions to Moslems," *Moslem World* 14, no. 1 (January 1924): 30–36; David Bundy, *Visions of Apostolic Mission: Scandinavian Pentecostal Mission to 1935* (Uppsala: Uppsala Universitet, 2009), 110–13, 129, 131.

5. Pekkola, *Jumalan Poluilla*, 11–12; Berg, "Share of Scandinavia," 30–36. On Swedish missions in the Middle East, see Inger Marie Okkenhaug, "Signe Ekblad and the Swedish School in Jerusalem 1922–1948," *Swedish Missiological Themes* 94, no. 2 (2006): 147–61.

6. Ericsson, *Swedish Mission Story*, 4–6, quote on 6.

7. Ibid., 6; Pekkola, *Jumalan Poluilla*, 29.

8. Ericsson, *Swedish Mission Story*, 6.

9. Ibid., 6–7.

10. Personal communication from Okkenhaug, 23 November 2011.

11. Ericsson, *Swedish Mission Story*, 7.

12. Pekkola, *Jumalan Poluilla*, 18–40, esp. 20, 38. Personal communication from Seija Jalagin, Department of History, University of Oulu, Finland, drawing on Anu-Elina Veakevainen, "Suomen Nuorten Naisten Kristillisen Yhdistyksen lahetit 1901–1949" (The Missionaries of the YMCA in Finland, 1901–1949) (master's thesis, University of Helsinki, 1995).

13. Pekkola, *Jumalan Poluilla*, 41–45; quote from 44; on missions to Arabia, see Eleanor Abdella Doumato, *Getting God's Ear: Women, Islam, and Healing in Saudi Arabia and the Gulf* (New York: Columbia University Press, 2000).

14. Pekkola, *Jumalan Poluilla*, 41–45.

15. Dia al-Din Hassan al-Qadi, *Historical Encyclopadeia of Bur Sa'id*, 2 vols. (Port Said: al-Mustaqbal, 2002).

16. Sylvia Modelski, *Port Said Revisited* (Washington, D.C.: Faros, 2000), 51–54. Consular records contain multiple cases detailing conflicts between prostitutes, pimps,

and clients. See, e.g., TNA, FO 846/29, Bint Abdulla vs. Pollet et al., Port Said, 6 September 1909.

17. Dia el Dine Hassan Al Kady, "Port Said between Its Past and Unique Origins," in al-Qadi, *Historical Encyclopadeia of Bur Sa'id*, G–J.

18. Ericsson, *Swedish Mission Story*, 31.

19. Al Kady, "Port Said," H.

20. Victor Guerin, *La France catholique en Egypte* (Tours: Alfred Mame et Fils, 1894), 201–10; Al Kady, "Port Said," J.

21. TNA, FO 371/452/38684, Eldon Gorst to Edward Grey, 30 October 1908. On British missions in Palestine, see Inger Marie Okkenhaug, *The Quality of Heroic Living, of High Endeavour and Adventure: Anglican Mission, Women and Education in Palestine, 1888–1948* (Leiden: Brill, 2002).

22. Antoine K. Sabbagh, *Les Meglis Hasbys et la protection des biens des mineurs en Egypte* (Paris: A. Fabre, 1931), 20.

23. TNA, FO 371/452/38684, Eldon Gorst to Edward Grey, 30 October 1908.

24. Ibid.

25. Ibid.; see also Selim Deringil, "'There is No Compulsion in Religion': On Conversion and Apostasy in the Late Ottoman Empire: 1839–1856," *Comparative Studies in Society and History* 42, no. 3 (July 2000): 547–75; idem, *Conversion and Apostasy in the Late Ottoman Empire* (Cambridge: Cambridge University Press, 2012).

26. Maria Ericsson, "The Christian's Debt to the Moslem World," *Latter Rain Evangel*, March 1926, 2.

27. Ibid., 2.

28. Ericsson, *Swedish Mission Story*, 9.

29. Ericsson, "Christian's Debt," 2.

30. Pekkola, *Jumalan Poluilla*, 63–65.

31. See Heather J. Sharkey, *American Evangelicals in Egypt: Missionary Encounters in an Age of Empire* (Princeton, NJ: Princeton University Press, 2008).

32. Najiya Rashid, "Khatir al-Madaris al-Ajnabiyya," *Tarqiyat al-Mar'a* (1908): 89; see also Beth Baron, *The Women's Awakening in Egypt: Culture, Society, and the Press* (New Haven, CT: Yale University Press, 1994), 140.

33. PHS, *The Annual Report of the American United Presbyterian Mission in Egypt and the Sudan for the Year 1910*, 63.

34. Ericsson, *Swedish Mission Story*, 9; Samuel M. Zwemer, *Childhood in the Moslem World* (New York: Fleming H. Revell Company, 1915), 254–55; Baron, *Women's Awakening in Egypt*, chap. 6.

35. Ericsson, "Christian's Debt," 3.

36. Ericsson, *Swedish Mission Story*, 16–17.

37. Ibid., 10–149; Zwemer, *Childhood in the Moslem World*, 254–55.

38. Al-Qadi, *Bur Sa'id*, 1:192–216; Dia el Dine Hassan Al Kady, "Port Said between Its Past and Unique Origins," in *Port Said*, G–J; Ericsson, *Swedish Mission Story*, 13–16, 29.

39. Ericsson, *Swedish Mission Story*, 16; Berg, "Share of Scandinavia," 32.

40. Ericson, *Swedish Mission Story*, 20–24; Guerin, *La France catholique en Egypte*, 201–10; Al Kady, "Port Said," J; al-Qadi, *Bur Sa'id*, 2:183–84.

41. Ericsson, *Swedish Mission Story*, 20–24.

42. Ibid., 23.

43. PHS, RG 209/26/12, "Conditions Imposed by the Missionaries for the Reception of Children into Their Orphanages," trans. from *al-Balagh*, 2 July 1933.

44. Ericsson, *Swedish Mission Story*, 21–23.

45. Pekkola, *Jumalan Poluilla*, 222.

46. Ericsson, *Swedish Mission Story*, 21–22.

47. Ericsson, "Christian's Debt," 4.

48. Ericsson, *Swedish Mission Story*, 31–32. See also, e.g., TNA, FO 846/29, Bint Abdulla vs. Pollet et al., Port Said, 6 September 1909.

49. Ericsson, *Swedish Mission Story*, 8, 16–17, 31.

50. Ibid., 19–20.

51. Ibid., 30.

52. Ericsson, *Swedish Mission Story*.

53. George Swan, *In Troublous Times: Sequel to "Lacked Ye Anything?"* (London: Egypt General Mission, 1923), 66–67, see photos following 80; idem, *"Lacked Ye Anything?" A Brief Story of the Egypt General Mission*, rev. ed. (London: Egypt General Mission, 1932), 51–52; Sharkey, *American Evangelicals*, 259n151; Ericsson, *Swedish Mission Story*, 8, 28.

54. Ericsson, *Swedish Mission Story*, 26–27.

55. Ibid., 25–26, quote from 25.

56. Quote from ibid., 29, see picture of workers on 2; Pekkola, *Jumalan Poluilla*, 7, see picture of mission workers from 1927.

57. See Sharkey, *American Evangelicals*, 90–95, 108–15.

58. YDS-Salaam, Brochure, *Salaam Mission to Mohammedans*, n.d. [1920s]; Zwemer, *Childhood in the Moslem World*, 254–55.

59. *Conferences of Christian Workers among Moslems 1924* (New York: Chairman of the International Missionary Council, 1924), 77.

60. *Salaam Mission to Mohammedans*; Passenger Record for Maria Ericsson, Statue of Liberty, Ellis Island Foundation, www.ellisisland.org/search/passRecord, accessed 17 April 2008; Pekkola, *Jumalan Poluilla*, 15, 195.

61. Ericsson, "Christian's Debt," 2.

62. Pekkola, *Jumalan Poluilla*, 107, 195–200; *Salaam Mission to Mohammedans*; Ericsson, *Swedish Mission Story*; Stella C. Dunkelberger, *Crossing Africa: Being the Experiences of a Home Secretary in Primitive Parts of the Black Continent* (Philadelphia: Mission Offices, 1935), 92.

63. Pekkola, *Jumalan Poluilla*, 16, 196–200.

64. Ibid., 189; NARA, RG 84, 350/37/13/04, Egypt, 1931–1935, Port Said Consulate, Strictly Confidential Files, Vol. 98, Horace Remillard, American Consul, Port Said, to William Jardine, American Minister, Cairo, 26 June 1933, "The So-Called 'Missionary Incident' at Port Said," 3–4.

65. *Directory of Foreign Missions*, ed. Esther Boorman Strong and A. L. Warshuis (New York: International Missionary Council, 1933), 148–49; NARA, RG 59, SD 883.404/43, Jardine to Secretary of State, 8 July 1933, 3; Maria Ericsson, *The Egypt Salaam Mission Story* (Port Said: Egypt Salaam Mission, 1930), 39.

66. Al-Qadi, *Bur Sa'id*, 2:120–21; Modelski, *Port Said Revisited*.

67. See Prologue.

Chapter 5: Fight Them with Their Own Weapons

1. "Jam'iyyat al-Ikhwan al-Muslimin wa-l-Tabshir," *Jaridat al-Ikhwan al-Muslimin* 1, no. 3 (6 Rabi' I, 1352/29 June 1933): 15–18. On the history of the Society of Muslim Brothers, see Richard P. Mitchell, *The Society of the Muslim Brothers* (Oxford: Oxford University Press, 1969; repr. 1993); Brynjar Lia, *The Society of the Muslim Brothers in Egypt: The Rise of an Islamic Mass Movement 1928–1942* (Reading, UK: Ithaca Press, 1998); Gudrun Kraemer, *Hasan al-Banna* (Oxford: One World, 2010).

2. Lia, *Muslim Brothers*, 21–27.

3. Hasan al-Banna, *Mudhakkirat al-Da'wa wa-l-Da'iya*, 2nd ed. (Cairo: n.p., 1966), 14. Al-Banna's memoirs were written in the late 1940s after an internal crisis in the organization. Lia, *Muslim Brothers*, 21, 27. For a translation, see *Memoirs of Hasan Al Banna Shaheed*, trans. M. N. Shaikh (Karachi: International Islamic Publishers, 1981).

4. Al-Banna, *Mudhakkirat*, 14.

5. Ibid., 14, 41. Heather Sharkey suggests that al-Banna may have been referring to Florence Lillian White, a member of the American Mission from Grove City, Pennsylvania, who had joined the Presbyterians in Egypt in 1919 at the age of twenty-two. White headed the mission's school for girls in Tanta, a hub of American evangelical activity from which missionaries and Bible women fanned out to provincial villages. Assigned to help administer mission accounts in Delta stations, White may have found her way to al-Mahmudiyya; she retired or was let go by the American Mission after only seven years of service, having been deemed "unacceptable as a worker." See Heather J. Sharkey, *American Evangelicals in Egypt: Missionary Encounters in an Age of Empire* (Princeton, NJ: Princeton University Press, 2008), 107–8, 254n48.

6. George Swan, *"Lacked Ye Anything?" A Brief Story of the Egypt General Mission*, rev. ed. (London: Egypt General Mission, 1932), 67.

7. Ibid., 20.

8. Ibid.; George Swan, *In Troublous Times: Sequel to "Lacked Ye Anything?"* (London: Egypt General Mission, 1923); Earl E. Elder, *Vindicating a Vision: The Story of the American Mission in Egypt, 1854–1954* (Philadelphia: Board of Foreign Missions of the United Presbyterian Church of North America, 1958), 163; Sharkey, *American Evangelicals*, 82.

9. Swan, *In Troublous Times*, 60.

10. YDS-EGM, Pamphlet: *A Run Round the Stations* (London: Egypt General Mission, [c. 1934]), 4.

11. YDS-EGM, "Who's Who: Miss E. A. Langford," *Egypt General Mission News* 31, no. 175 (September–October 1931): 127.

12. *A Run Round the Stations*, 4; "Who's Who: Miss E. A. Langford," 127. While

EGM records indicate the presence of only two missionaries, al-Banna mentions three. Bible women were not counted by the missionaries but may have been by al-Banna. See al-Banna, *Mudhakkirat*, 14.

13. *A Run Round the Stations*, 4–5.

14. Lia, *Muslim Brothers*, 27–30; Beth Baron, *Egypt as a Woman: Nationalism, Gender, and Politics* (Berkeley: University of California Press, 2005), 208–10.

15. Charles C. Adams, *Islam and Modernism in Egypt: A Study of the Modern Reform Movement Inaugurated by Muhammad 'Abduh* (New York: Russell and Russell, 1933), 195–98. Missionaries such as Adams saw in the Islamic reform movement parallels to the Protestant Reformation and established a scholarly tradition for understanding it through this lens. Umar Ryad, "Muslim Responses to Missionary Activity in Egypt: With a Special Reference to the Al-Azhar High Corps of 'Ulama (1925–1935)," in *New Faith in Ancient Lands: Western Missions in the Middle East in the Nineteenth and Early Twentieth Centuries*, ed. Heleen Murre-van den Berg (Leiden: Brill, 2006), 301; Lia, *Muslim Brothers*, 57, 87n9.

16. Al-Banna, *Mudhakkirat*, 64; Lia, *Muslim Brothers*, 29–30, 54–56.

17. Al-Banna, *Mudhakkirat*, 66; Mitchell, *Muslim Brothers*, 8; Lia, *Muslim Brothers*, 36.

18. Lia, *Muslim Brothers*, 40–42.

19. Swan, *"Lacked Ye Anything?"*; *A Run Round the Stations*; YDS-EGM, Pamphlet: Mrs. A. C. King, *A School Story* (Belfast: Graham & Heslip, Ltd., [193-]), see back page.

20. Swan, *"Lacked Ye Anything?,"* 26, 48; idem, *In Troublous Times*, 59–60.

21. King, *A School Story*, 5–6.

22. King quoted in Swan, *In Troublous Times*, 61.

23. Swan, *In Troublous Times*, 60; idem, *"Lacked Ye Anything?,"* 48; King, *A School Story*, 9–12; *A Run Round the Stations*, 10–12.

24. King, *A School Story*, 17–18.

25. "Jam'iyyat al-Ikhwan al-Muslimin wa-l-Tabshir," *Jaridat al-Ikhwan al-Muslimin* 1, no. 6 (27 Rabi' I, 1352/20 July 1933): 20.

26. Al-Banna, "Hawadith al-Takfir wa-Khatar al-Mubashshirin," *Jaridat al-Ikhwan al-Muslimin* 1, no. 3 (6 Rabi' I, 1352/29 June 1933): 1–3.

27. Al-Banna, *Mudhakkirat*, 85–87; Lia, *Muslim Brothers*, 40.

28. "Jam'iyyat al-Ikhwan al-Muslimin wa-l-Tabshir," *Jaridat al-Ikhwan al-Muslimin* 1, no. 6 (27 Rabi' I, 1352/20 July 1933): 20.

29. Al-Banna, "Hawadith al-Takfir," 3.

30. *A Run Round the Stations*, 12. See also B. E. Nott, "Ismailia Girls' School," *Egypt General Mission News* 26, no. 146 (November–December 1926): 160.

31. Quote from "Jam'iyyat al-Ikhwan al-Muslimin wa-l-Tabshir," *Jaridat al-Ikhwan al-Muslimin* 1, no. 6 (27 Rabi' I, 1352/20 July 1933): 20; al-Banna, *Mudhakkirat*, 97–98; Lia, *Muslim Brothers*, 40–41; Mitchell, *Muslim Brothers*, 175.

32. Al-Banna, *Mudhakkirat*, 98, 140–41, 154–55; Baron, *Egypt as a Woman*, 209–10.

33. "Jam'iyyat al-Ikhwan al-Muslimin wa-l-Tabshir," *Jaridat al-Ikhwan al-Muslimin* 1, no. 6 (27 Rabi' I, 1352/20 July 1933): 20.

34. "Ismailia Women's Work," *Egypt General Mission News* 33, no. 184 (March–April 1933): 51.

35. Swan, *"Lacked Ye Anything?,"* 47.

36. "Jam'iyyat al-Ikhwan al-Muslimin wa-l-Tabshir," *Jaridat al-Ikhwan al-Muslimin* 1, no. 6 (27 Rabi' I, 1352/20 July 1933): 20.

37. Swan, *"Lacked Ye Anything?,"* 54.

38. Al-Banna, *Mudhakkirat*, 133–34. The starting date al-Banna gives, 28 Safar 1352, converts to June, although he mentions May in the text. Lia, *Muslim Brothers*, 97.

39. Quote from al-Banna, *Mudhakkirat*, 94; Lia, *Muslim Brothers*, 43, 60–72.

40. Al-Banna, *Mudhakkirat*, 91–93.

41. Quote from "Jam'iyyat al-Ikhwan al-Muslimin wa-l-Tabshir," *Jaridat al-Ikhwan al-Muslimin* 1, no. 3 (6 Rabi' I, 1352/29 June 1933): 15; Lia *Muslim Brothers*, 43.

42. "Jam'iyyat al-Ikhwan al-Muslimin wa-l-Tabshir," *Jaridat al-Ikhwan al-Muslimin* 1, no. 3 (6 Rabi' I, 1352/29 June 1933): 15–16. For background on the school, see YDS-Salaam, Maria Ericsson, *The Swedish Mission Story: Egypt* (n.p., [1924]): 25–26.

43. "Jam'iyyat al-Ikhwan al-Muslimin wa-l-Tabshir," *Jaridat al-Ikhwan al-Muslimin* 1, no. 3 (6 Rabi' I, 1352/29 June 1933): 16–17.

44. Ibid., 17.

45. Ibid., 17–18.

46. Ibid., 18. See also al-Banna, *Mudhakkirat*, 141–45.

47. "Jam'iyyat al-Ikhwan al-Muslimin wa-l-Tabshir," *Jaridat al-Ikhwan al-Muslimin* 1, no. 3 (6 Rabi' I, 1352/29 June 1933): 18. See also al-Banna, *Mudhakkirat*, 141–45.

48. See *Jaridat al-Ikhwan al-Muslimin* 1, no. 1 through 1, no. 6 (1352); on the publication of letters, see, e.g., PHS, RG 209/26/12, "Preaching by Letters," *al-Balagh*, 16 June 1933.

49. Lia gives the date of the first annual conference as May (65), June (94), and May–June (122n26), generally referring to *Jaridat al-Ikhwan al-Muslimin* as his source; Mitchell places the meeting in May (13), giving a later publication of al-Banna as a reference; the date given for the meeting in the General Advisory Council's petition to the king is 22 Safar 1352, which is also the date Hasan al-Banna gives in his memoirs, but which converts to 16 June 1933. The June date makes more sense than a May date given the topic of discussion. Hasan al-Banna et al., "Surat al-'Arida," *Jaridat al-Ikhwan al-Muslimin* 1, no. 3 (6 Rabi' I, 1352/29 June 1933): 19–20; al-Banna, *Mudhakkirat*, 140; Mitchell, *Muslim Brothers*, 13; Lia, *Muslim Brothers*, 65, 94, 122n26.

50. "Insha' Lijan Far'iyya li-Jam'iyyat al-Ikhwan al-Muslimin," *Jaridat al-Ikhwan al-Muslimin* 1, no. 3 (6 Rabi' I, 1352/29 June 1933): 18.

51. Salama Khatir, "Lajnat Muqawamat al-Tabshir fi al-Isma'iliyya," *Jaridat al-Ikhwan al-Muslimin* 1, no. 5 (20 Rabi' I, 1352/13 July 1933): 24.

52. Ibid.

53. "Jam'iyyat al-Ikhwan al-Muslimin wa-l-Tabshir," *Jaridat al-Ikhwan al-Muslimin* 1, no. 6 (27 Rabi' I, 1352/July 20, 1933): 20.

54. Ibid., 20–21.

55. Swan, *"Lacked Ye Anything?,"* 49, see also 59–61 for the story of a Suez convert; "Suez," *Egypt General Mission News; A Run Round the Stations*, 9–10; YDS-EGM, Pamphlet: L. Kathleen Hamilton, *"But Prayer"—The Story of a Great Deliverance* (London: Egypt General Mission, 193–).

56. *A Run Round the Stations*, 10.

57. Hamilton, *"But Prayer,"* quote from 10.

58. Ibid., 5–9, quote from 9.

59. Ibid., 11–14, quote from 11.

60. TNA, FO 141/760/19, Keown-Boyd, 22 June 1933, "Note on the case of Kawkab Ibrahim alias Hayat Ibrahim Zeidan, of the Egypt General Mission School for Girls at Suez."

61. Hamilton, *"But Prayer,"* 14–15.

62. Jam'iyyat al-Ikhwan al-Muslimin wa-l-Tabshir," *Jaridat al-Ikhwan al-Muslimin* 1, no. 6 (27 Rabi' I, 1352/July 20, 1933): 21. The Brothers identified the girl, who had gone home with her father on a visit and not returned, as Fatima 'Abd al-Ghali. This is probably the same girl the missionaries had identified as "F," showing the intense fight between missionaries and Muslim Brothers over specific children.

63. "Jam'iyyat al-Ikhwan al-Muslimin wa-l-Tabshir fi al-Mahmudiyya Buhayra," *Jaridat al-Ikhwan al-Muslimin* 1, no. 5 (20 Rabi' I, 1352/13 July 1933): 23.

64. *A Run Round the Stations*, 4; "Mahmudiyya," *Egypt General Mission News* 31, no. 172 (March–April 1931): 30–31; "Mahmudiya," *Egypt General Mission News* 32, no. 178 (March–April 1932): 31; "Mahmudiya," *Egypt General Mission News* 33, no. 186 (July–August 1933): 37–38.

65. Swan, *"Lacked Ye Anything?,"* 49.

66. "Jam'iyyat al-Ikhwan al-Muslimin wa-l-Tabshir fi al-Mahmudiyya Buhayra," *Jaridat al-Ikhwan al-Muslimin* 1, no. 5 (20 Rabi' I, 1352/13 July 1933): 23.

67. Ibid.

68. Ibid. Mitchell noted the tie between missionary economic activities and that of the Muslim Brotherhood. See Mitchell, *Muslim Brothers*, 274.

69. "Jam'iyyat al-Ikhwan al-Muslimin wa-l-Tabshir," *Jaridat al-Ikhwan al-Muslimin* 1, no. 3 (6 Rabi' I, 1352/29 June 1933): 15.

70. Al-Banna, *Mudhakkirat*, 94.

Chapter 6: Combating Conversion

1. PHS, RG 209/26/38, Letter from C. C. Adams to Dr. Anderson, 26 June 1933, 4; PHS, RG 209/26/12, *Kawkab al-Sharq*, 23 June 1933.

2. TNA, FO 141/760/19, Suez Canal Police, Special Branch, Daily Report No. 428, Port Said, 24 June 1933; TNA, FO 141/760/19/84–86, Special Section, Port Said, 25 June 1933.

3. PHS, RG 209/26/12, "Aggression for the Sake of Belief: What Turkia Hassan Says," *al-Siyasa*, 23 June 1933; see also "Miss Turkiya Youssef in the Offices of Assiyassa," *al-Kawkab al-Sharq*, 23 June 1933; PHS, RG 209/26/38, Letter from C. C. Adams to Dr. Anderson, 26 June 1933, 4; TNA, FO 141/760/19, Suez Canal Police, Special Branch, Daily Report No. 428, Port Said, 24 June 1933.

4. TNA, FO 141/760/19, Suez Canal Police, Special Branch, Daily Report No. 428, Port Said, 24 June 1933; TNA, FO 141/760/19/84–86, Special Section, Port Said, 25 June 1933. For background on the league, see Khalid Na'im, *Tarikh Jam'iyyat Muqawamat al-Tansir al-Misriyya (1933–1937)* (Cairo: Kitab al-Mukhtar, n.d.).

5. Labiba Ahmad in *Nahda Nisa'iyya* 10 (December 1932): 398.

6. Arthur Goldschmidt, Jr., *Historical Dictionary of Egypt* (Metuchen, NJ: Scarecrow Press, 1994): 264; Beth Baron, *Egypt as a Woman: Nationalists, Gender, and Politics* (Berkeley: University of California Press, 2005), 203, 208.

7. Labiba Ahmad, "Fi Sabil I'zaz al-Din," *al-Nahda al-Nisa'iyya* 11, nos. 8–9 (August 1933): 253; for more on Labiba Ahmad, see Baron, *Egypt as a Woman*, chap. 8.

8. Ahmad, "Fi Sabil I'zaz al-Din," 253.

9. Ibid.

10. See Baron, *Egypt as a Woman*, 208; Brynjar Lia, *The Society of the Muslim Brothers in Egypt: The Rise of an Islamic Mass Movement 1928–1942* (Reading, UK: Ithaca Press, 1998), 55; Heather J. Sharkey, *American Evangelicals in Egypt: Missionary Encounters in an Age of Empire* (Princeton, NJ: Princeton University Press, 2008), 120.

11. Hasan al-Banna, *Mudhakkirat al-Da'wa wa-l-Da'iya*, 2nd ed. (Cairo: n.p., 1966), 154.

12. For Labiba Ahmad's message to my "sisters and daughters," see ibid., 155; see also Baron, *Egypt as a Woman*, 208–10.

13. Hasan al-Banna et al., "Surat al-'Arida," *Jaridat al-Ikhwan al-Muslimin* 1, no. 3 (6 Rabi' I, 1352/29 June 1933): 19–20; al-Banna, *Mudhakkirat*, 140; Richard P. Mitchell, *The Society of the Muslim Brothers* (Oxford: Oxford University Press, 1969; repr. 1993), 13; Lia, *Muslim Brothers*, 65, 94, 122n26.

14. Al-Banna et al., "Surat al-'Arida," 19–20.

15. Ibid., 20–21.

16. Ibid., 21.

17. Ibid.

18. NARA, RG 59, SD 883.404/45, W. M. Jardine to Secretary of State, "Anti-Missionary Agitation in Egypt," 29 July 1933, 6–8; "Defence of Islam Against Missionaries," *Egyptian Gazette*, 24 June 1933, 8; "Nahda Mubaraka wa-Ijtima'i Hafil bi-Dar," *Jaridat al-Ikhwan al-Muslimin* 1, no. 3 (6 Rabi' I, 1352/29 June 1933): 22; Rainer Brunner, "Education, Politics, and the Struggle for Intellectual Leadership: Al-Azhar between 1927 and 1945," in *Guardians of Faith in Modern Times: 'Ulama' in the Middle East*, ed. Meir Hatina (Leiden: Brill, 2008), 109–40; Umar Ryad, "Muslim Responses to Missionary Activity in Egypt: With a Special Reference to the Al-Azhar High Corps of 'Ulama (1925–1935)," in *New Faith in Ancient Lands: Western Missions in the Middle East in the Nineteenth and Early Twentieth Centuries*, ed. Heleen Murre-van den Berg (Leiden: Brill, 2006), 281–307.

19. Dr. 'Abd al-Hamid Sa'id, "Mas'alat al-Tabshir fi Majlis al-Nuwwab," *al-Fath* 8, no. 351 (6 Rabi' I, 1352/29 June 1933): 20.

20. "A Moslem Meeting in Cairo," *Egyptian Gazette*, 20 June 1933, 5; Baron, *Egypt as a Woman*, 208; "Nahda Mubaraka wa-Ijtima'i Hafil bi-Dar," 22.

21. Quoted in Israel Gershoni and James P. Jankowski, *Redefining the Egyptian Nation 1930–1945* (Cambridge: Cambridge University Press, 1995), 66, see also 56–59.

22. "Nahda Mubaraka wa-Ijtima'i Hafil bi-Dar," 22; PHS, RG 209/26/12, "Fighting Evangelization: Defending Islam and Propagating It," *Kawkab al-Sharq*, 23 June 1933; "Defence of Islam against Missionaries," *Egyptian Gazette*, 24 June 1933, 8; "Anti-

Missionary Agitation in Egypt," 6–8; TNA, FO 141/760/19, A. S. (Abdel Salam) to D. G. (Director General), 23 June 1933.

23. TNA, FO 141/760/19/104, Keown-Boyd, "Note on an Interview with Sheikh Maraghi," Cairo, 27 June 1933.

24. "Nahda Mubaraka wa-Ijtima'i Hafil bi-Dar," 22; NARA, RG 59, SD 883.404/45, W. M. Jardine to Secretary of State, 29 July 1933, 6–8; "Defence of Islam Against Missionaries," *Egyptian Gazette*, 24 June 1933, 8; TNA, FO 141/760/19, A. S. to D. G., 23 June 1933.

25. "Defence of Islam Committee at Work," *Egyptian Gazette*, 26 June 1933, 6.

26. Quote from "The Anti-Missionary Campaign: Petition Submitted to King Fuad," *Egyptian Gazette*, 28 June 1933, 6; PHS, RG 206/26/12, Maraghi, "League of Defense of Islam Begs H.M. the King to Defend the Religion of the Country from Missionaries," *al-Siyasa*, 28 June 1933; TNA, FO 141/760/19, A. S. to D. G., 27 June 1933.

27. Quote from "The Anti-Missionary Campaign: Appeal to Government," *Egyptian Gazette*, 29 June 1933, 6; PHS, RG 206/26/12, Maraghi, "A Petition to the Prime Minister," *al-Jihad*, 29 June 1933; PHS, RG 209/26/37, al-Maraghi, "Petition by the League for Defending Islam Addressed to the Egyptian Government," *al-Ahram*, 29 June 1933; TNA, FO 141/760/19/111, Abdel Salam to D. G., 28 June 1933.

28. Al-Maraghi, "Kitab Jama'at al-Difa' 'an al-Islam," *al-Fath* 8, no. 353 (20 Rabi' I, 1352/13 July 1933): 12; NARA, SD 883.404/43, Enclosure No. 8, M. Moustafa El Maraghi to Minister, quote is translation from the French, 3; "Defence of Islam League: Appeal to Foreign Powers," *Egyptian Gazette*, 3 July 1933: 6.

29. "Appeal for Funds: A Violent Manifesto," *Egyptian Gazette*, 6 July 1933, 6.

30. Al-Maraghi, "Nida' min Jama'at al-Difa' 'an al-Islam," *al-Fath* 8, no. 353 (20 Rabi' I, 1352/13 July 1933): 13; PHS, RG 209/26/12, al-Maraghi, "A Proclamation to the Nation by the Society for the Defense of Islam," *al-Siyasa*, 30 June 1933.

31. "Appeal for Funds: A Violent Manifesto," 6.

32. "Qursh al-Islam," *al-Fath* 8, no. 353 (20 Rabi' I, 1352/13 July 1933): 14.

33. James P. Jankowski, *Egypt's Young Rebels: "Young Egypt," 1933–1952* (Stanford, CA: Hoover Institution Press, 1975), 9–25.

34. TNA, FO 141/760/19/103, Keown-Boyd, "Note on an Interview with Sheikh Maraghi," Cairo, 27 June 1933; Sharkey, *American Evangelicals*, 128.

35. TNA, FO 141/760/19/104–5, Keown-Boyd, "Note on an Interview with Sheikh Maraghi," Cairo, 7 June 1933.

36. *Ruz al-Yusuf*, no. 277 (1933): cover.

37. NARA, RG 59, SD 883.404/8, "The Zwemer Incident," 21 April 1928, Letter from North Winship to Secretary of State; Enclosure No. 1, *Return to the Old Qibla*; Enclosure No. 5, S. M. Zwemer to North Winship, 20 April 1928; Ryad, "Muslim Responses to Missionary Activity in Egypt," 286–89; Sharkey, *American Evangelicals*, 90–95, 108–16.

38. NARA, RG 59, SD 883.404/8, "The Zwemer Incident," 21 April 1928, Letter from North Winship to Secretary of State; Enclosure No. 1, *Return to the Old Qibla*; Enclosure No. 5, S. M. Zwemer to North Winship, 20 April 1928; Ryad, "Muslim Responses to Missionary Activity in Egypt," 286–89; Sharkey, *American Evangelicals*, 90–95, 108–16.

39. NARA, RG 59, SD 883.404/12, George Wadsworth to Secretary of State, 28 Au-

gust 1929; Graves to Wadsworth, 16 July 1929; Wadsworth to Graves, 27 July 1929; Graves to Wadsworth, 29 July 1929.

40. Quote from "Qarar," *Nur al-Islam* 4, no. 3 (Rabi' I, 1352/1933): 203; "Ulemas Appeal to Government Drastic Measures Wanted," *Egyptian Gazette*, 27 June 1933, 5. See Brunner, "Education, Politics, and the Struggle for Intellectual Leadership," 109–40; Ryad, "Muslim Responses to Missionary Activity in Egypt," 281–307.

41. TNA, FO 141/760/19/78–80, Keown-Boyd to Campbell, 26 June 1933, 2–3.

42. TNA, FO 141/752/1, Campbell, "Anti-Missionary Campaign and Missionary Activities," Minute Sheet, 30 June 1933.

43. "Bayan," *Nur al-Islam* 4, no. 3 (Rabi' I, 1352/1933): 207; see also Ryad, "Muslim Responses to Missionary Activity in Egypt," 295.

44. "Resolutions of the Body of Grand Ulema," *Nur al-Islam* 4, no. 4 (Rabi' II, 1352/1933): 8; "Ulemas Appeal to Government," *Egyptian Gazette*, 27 June 1933, 5.

45. TNA, FO 141/760/19/93, Keown-Boyd to Campbell, 27 June 1933.

46. Ibid.

47. As quoted in "The Anti-Missionary Campaign: Mufti of Egypt Counsels Caution," *Egyptian Gazette*, 8 July 1933, 5.

48. "Anti-Missionary Agitation," *Egyptian Gazette*, 7 July 1933, 5.

49. "Al-Jam'iyyat al-Khayriyya al-Islamiyya," *al-Fath* 8, no. 351 (6 Rabi' I, 1352/29 June 1933): 15.

50. Mine Ener, *Managing Egypt's Poor and the Politics of Benevolence, 1800–1952* (Princeton, NJ: Princeton University Press, 2003), 102–3; *al-Jam'iyyat al-Khayriyya al-Islamiyya fi Thamanin 'Aman* (Cairo: Dar al-'Ulum li-l-Tiba'a, 1979), 5–8; 'Abd al-Salam 'Abd al-al-Halim 'Amir, "al-Jam'iyyat al-Khayriyya al-Islamiyya mundhu Ta'sisiha hatta al-Harb al-'Alamiyya al-Thaniyya min 1892–1939," in *al-Majallat al-Tarikhiyya al-Misriyya* (1995): 419–55; Hilmi Ahmad Shalabi, *Harakat al-Islah al-Ijtima'iyya fi Misr* (Cairo: n.p., 1988).

51. "Al-Jam'iyyat al-Khayriyya al-Islamiyya," 15.

52. "Mustashfa Harmil wa-l-Tabshir," *al-Fath* 8, no. 353 (20 Rabi' I, 1352/13 July 1933): 10.

53. "Al-Jam'iyyat al-Khayriyya al-Islamiyya," 15.

54. Ibid.

Chapter 7: Crackdown

1. "Anisa Turkiyya Hasan Yusuf fi Dar al-Jihad," *al-Jihad*, 24 June 1933, 5; PHS, RG 209/26/12, "Aggression for the Sake of Belief: What Turkia Hassan Says," *al-Siyasa*, 23 June 1933; "Miss Turkiya Youssef in the Offices of Assiyassa," *Kawkab al-Sharq*, 23 June 1933; "Miss Torkya Hassan Youssef in al Jahad's Offices: Comprehensive Information about the Evangelists," *al-Balagh*, 24 June 1933; TNA, FO 141/760/83, Suez Canal Police, Special Branch, Daily Report No. 428, Port Said, 24 June 1933; TNA, FO 141/760/19/84–86, Special Section, 25 June 1933; PHS, RG 209/26/38, Letter from C. C. Adams to Dr. Anderson, 26 June 1933, 4.

2. TNA, FO 141/752/1, Rachad to D. G., 4 July 1933.

3. "Sada Hawadith al-Tabshir al-Akhira," *Jaridat al-Akhwan al-Muslimin* 1, no. 3 (29 June 1933): 9.

4. Malak Badrawi, *Isma'il Sidqi, 1875–1950: Pragmatism and Vision in Twentieth Century Egypt* (Richmond, Surrey: Curzon, 1996), 92.

5. *Al-Lata'if al-Musawwara*, 3 July 1933, 28.

6. TNA, FO 141/752/1, R. C. "Anti-Missionary Campaign and Missionary Activities," Minute Sheet, 30 June 1933; NARA, RG 59, SD 883.404/43, Enclosure 4, A. W. Keown Boyd to George Swan, 1 July 1933, 1.

7. "A Missionary Article: Arabic Newspaper Editors Interrogated," *Egyptian Gazette* 23 June 1933, 6. On the Press Law of 1931, see Ami Ayalon, *The Press in the Arab Middle East: A History* (New York: Oxford University Press, 1995), 120, 239.

8. "Egyptian Magazine Libel Action: Parquet Search Offices," *Egyptian Gazette*, 24 June 1933, 2.

9. "The Anti-Missionary Campaign: A Parquet Enquiry," *Egyptian Gazette*, 28 June 1933, 6.

10. "Defense of Islam Committee: Editor of 'Al Wadi' Interrogated," *Egyptian Gazette*, 3 July 1933, 6.

11. TNA, FO 141/752/1, R. C., "Anti-Missionary Campaign and Missionary Activities," Minute Sheet, 30 June 1933.

12. NARA, RG 59, SD 883.404/43, Enclosure 6, W. M. Jardine, "Memorandum of a Conversation between the Acting High Commissioner, Mr. R. I. Campbell, and the Minister, Regarding the Religious Controversy," 1 July 1933, 2; see also Jardine to Secretary of State, "Foreign Missionary Activities in Egypt," 8 July 1933, 10–11.

13. TNA, FO 141/752/3, Acting Judicial Adviser to the Residency, "Attaques dirigées contre des missionnaires," 14 August 1933.

14. NARA, RG 59, SD 883.404/43, Enclosure 4, A. W. Keown-Boyd to George Swan, 1 July 1933, 1.

15. "Journalists in Trouble: Cairo Parquet Questions Seven," *Egyptian Gazette*, 22 July 1933, 4; TNA, FO 141/752/1, D. G. to Smart, with copy of cartoon, 16 July 1933.

16. "Journalists in Trouble: Cairo Parquet Questions Seven," 4.

17. "Arabic Newspapers in Trouble: Cabinet Ministers Libelled," *Egyptian Gazette*, 14 August 1933, 6.

18. "German Press and Missionary Incidents," *Egyptian Gazette*, 4 July 1933, 5; "The Anti-Missionary Campaign: Repercussion Abroad," *Egyptian Gazette*, 6 July 1933, 6.

19. Quote from NARA, RG 59, SD 883.404/45, Enclosure 9, Translation of *Il Giornale d'Oriente*, 5 July 1933; see also NARA, RG 59, SD 883.404/43, Jardine to Secretary of State, 8 July 1933, 9.

20. "Attacks on Missionaries: Café Owner Arrested for Assault," *Egyptian Gazette*, 26 June 1933, 6; "Missionaries Attacked in Cairo: Coptic Priest Beaten," *Egyptian Gazette*, 27 June 1933, 5.

21. TNA, FO 141/752/1, Ronald Campbell, Residency, 13 July 1933; NARA, RG 59, SD 883.404/45, Jardine to Secretary of State, 29 July 1933; "The Anti-Missionary Campaign: Serious Incidents at Kafr El Zayat, Sisters of Mercy Attacked by Hooligans," *Egyptian*

Gazette, 13 July 1933, 6; "Attacks on Missionaries," *Egyptian Gazette*, 14 July 1933, 5; PHS, RG 209/26/37, *al-Balagh*, 13 July 1933, and "The Causes Why the Meeting of Tantah Was Banned," *al-Ahram*, 14 July 1933.

22. TNA, FO 141/752/1, Campbell, Residency, 13 July 1933; NARA, RG 59, SD 883.404/45, W. M. Jardine to Secretary of State, 29 July 1933; "The Anti-Missionary Campaign: Serious Incidents at Kafr El Zayat, Sisters of Mercy Attacked by Hooligans"; "Attacks on Missionaries: Agitation Continues," *Egyptian Gazette*, 14 July 1933, 5; PHS, RG 209/26/37, *al-Balagh*, 13 July 1933, and *al-Ahram*, 14 July 1933.

23. TNA, FO 141/752/1, Campbell, Residency, 13 July 1933.

24. NARA, RG 59, SD 883.404/45, Jardine to Secretary of State, 29 July 1933; "The Anti-Missionary Campaign: Serious Incidents at Kafr El Zayat, Sisters of Mercy Attacked by Hooligans"; "Attacks on Missionaries: Agitation Continues."

25. "Ma'a al-Shaytana wa-Wakilatiha," *al-Fath* 8, no. 351 (6 Rabi' I, 1352/29 June 1933): 12.

26. "Anti-Missionary Meeting in Tanta," *Egyptian Gazette*, 13 July 1933, 6.

27. "Attacks on Missionaries: Damanhour Meeting Banned," *Egyptian Gazette*, 14 July 1933, 5.

28. "The Anti-Missionary Campaign: Official Statement," *Egyptian Gazette*, 15 July 1933, 5.

29. "Attaques dirigées contre des missionnaires."

30. "The Anti-Missionary Campaign: Official Statement," 5; see also NARA, RG 59, SD 883.404/45, Jardine to Secretary of State, 29 July 1933, 2, 5.

31. "The Anti-Missionary Campaign: Official Statement," 5.

32. "Hay'at Kubar al-'Ulama," *al-Nur al-Islam* 4 (Rabi' II, 1352/1933): 276–80, quote from 276; see also "Resolutions of the Body of Grand Ulema," *Nur al-Islam* 4, no. 4 (Rabi' II, 1352/1933): 5–8.

33. "Attacks on Missionaries: Sheikh Maraghi's Protest," *Egyptian Gazette*, 14 July 1933, 5–6; TNA, FO 141/752/1, Keown-Boyd to Residency, 15 July 1933; Campbell, Minute Sheet, "Anti-Missionary Campaign."

34. *Al-Siyasa* article translated in "Missionaries Still the Main Topic: 'Al-Siyasa' Impenitent," *Egyptian Gazette*, 17 July 1933, 4.

35. *Al-Balagh* article translated in "'Al Balagh' and Religion: The Kafr El Zayat Affair," *Egyptian Gazette*, 15 July 1933, 4.

36. TNA, FO 141/752/1, Official Communiqué; see also Campbell, Minute Sheet, "Anti-Missionary Campaign," 15 July 1933.

37. Campbell, Minute Sheet, "Anti-Missionary Campaign."

38. TNA, FO 141/752/2, Campbell, Minute Sheet, "Missionaries," 19 July 1933.

39. Labiba Ahmad, "Fi Sabiq I'zaz al-Din," *al-Nahda al-Nisa'iyya* 11, no. 8–9 (August 1933): 254; Khalid Na'im, *Tarikh Jam'iyyat Muqawamat al-Tansir al-Misriyya (1933–37)* (Cairo: Kitab al-Mukhtar, 1987), 51–54.

40. "'Ashara Alafi Junayhin," *al-Fath* 8, no. 354 (27 Rabi' I, 1352/20 July 1933): 8; NARA, RG 59, SD 883.404/45, Jardine to Secretary of State, 29 July 1933, 7–8; Na'im, *Tarikh Jam'iyyat Muqawamat al-Tansir al-Misriyya*, 51–54.

41. "'Ashara Alaf Guinea," *al-Fath* 8, no. 354 (27 Rabi' I, 1352/20 July 1933): 8.

42. PHS, RG 209/26/37, "The Government and Evangelization: An Interview with the Minister of Wakfs," *al-Siyasa*, 10 July 1933.

43. "2,500 Mitr min al-Ard," *al-Fath* 8, no. 34 (27 Rabi' I, 1352/20 July 1933): 13; "Site for Waifs' Home Given at Giza," *Egyptian Gazette*, 15 July 1933, 5.

44. NARA, RG 59, SD 883.404/43, Enclosure 4, Keown-Boyd to Swan, 1 July 1933, 2.

45. "The Anti-Missionary Campaign: Al Siyassa's Reply to Coptic Protest," *Egyptian Gazette*, 13 July 1933, 8.

46. Ibid., 8.

47. NARA, RG 59, SD 883.404/43, Enclosure 6, Jardine, "Memorandum of a Conversation between the Acting High Commissioner, Mr. R. I. Campbell, and the Minister, Regarding the Religious Controversy," 1 July 1933, 3.

48. NARA, RG 59, SD 883.404/43, Enclosure 4, Keown Boyd to Swan, 1 July 1933, 3.

49. TNA, FO 141/752/3, Campbell, note in margin of Communication, 6 September 1933.

50. "Questions in House of Commons," *Egyptian Gazette*, 6 July 1933, 6.

51. "Anti-Missionary Agitation: Sir J. Simon's Denies Forcible Conversion," *Egyptian Gazette*, 7 July 1933, 5; "Egypt Will Not Be Subdued," *Egyptian Gazette*, 10 July 1933, 4.

52. "Memorandum of a Conversation between the Acting High Commissioner, Mr. R. I. Campbell, and the Minister, Regarding the Religious Controversy," 3.

53. NARA, RG 59, SD 883.404/43, Enclosure 4, Keown-Boyd to Swan, 1 July 1933.

54. NARA, RG 59, SD 883.404/43, Enclosure 3, Swan to Keown-Boyd, 26 June 1933.

55. NARA, RG 59, SD 883.404/43, Enclosure 4, Keown-Boyd to Swan, 1 July 1933, 2–3.

56. On the policy, see TNA, FO 141/742/4, "The Policies of the Missionary Societies of the Egypt Inter-Mission Council," 18 October 1933.

57. "Mufawadat al-Tabshir," *al-Fath* 8, no. 355 (4 Rabi' II, 1352/27 July 1933): 3; "al-I'ana bi-Madaris al-Tabshir," *al-Fath* 8, no. 353 (20 Rabi' I, 1352/13 July 1933): 10; "Ulemas Appeal to Government: Drastic Measures Wanted," *Egyptian Gazette*, 27 June 1933, 5.

58. "Israr al-Mubashshirin 'ala Khittatihim," *al-Fath* 8, no. 358 (25 Rabi' II, 1352/17 August 1933): 19.

59. Ibid.

60. "20,000 Junayhin," *al-Fath* 8, no. 354 (27 Rabi' I, 1352/20 July 1933): 19.

61. "Mu'tamar li-l-Mubashshirin fi Dahiyya al-Zaytun," *al-Fath* (11 Rabi' II, 1352/3 August 1933): 3; "A Missionary Conference: 'Defence of Islam' Committee Seeks Ban," *Egyptian Gazette*, 1 August 1933, 5.

Chapter 8: The Battle for Egypt's Orphans

1. Quote from PHS, RG 209/26/37, *al-Balagh*, 1 July 1933; TNA, FO 141/752/1, Abdel Salam to D. G., 2 July 1933.

2. "Turkiyya Hasan," *al-Fath* 8, no. 353 (20 Rabi' I, 1352/13 July 1933): 3; TNA, FO 141/752/1, Abdel Salam to D. G., Press Summary from *al-Ahram*; "Anti-Missionary Agitation: Turkiya Hassan Becomes a Nurse," *Egyptian Gazette*, 7 July 1933, 5.

3. "Anisa Turkiyya Hasan Yusuf fi Dar al-Jihad," *al-Jihad*, 24 June 1933, 5

4. Ibid.; TNA, FO 141/752/1, "Ibrahim Nohman Mohammed"; PHS, RG 209/26/12, "al-Balagh Investigation in Port Said Incident," *al-Balagh*, 16 June 1933; Muhammad Ahmad Shirdi, "The Calamity of a Moslem Family Dispersed by the Evangelists in Port Said," *Kawkab al-Sharq*, 21 June 1933.

5. TNA, FO 141/760/19, Martha Boulos to Booth, 17 June 1933 (translation of Arabic original); see also "The Government and Missionaries," *Egyptian Gazette*, 23 June 1933, 2.

6. TNA, FO 141/760/19, A. W. Keown-Boyd, "Note on the Case of Martha Bouloss, alias Aida Mohammed Neman, of the Salaam Institution, Port-Said," 22 June 1933. For Arabic press coverage of this case, see, e.g., PHS, RG 209/26/12, *al-Jihad*, 27 June 1933, *al-Balagh*, 27 June 1933, *Kawkab al-Sharq*, 10 July 1933; PHS, RG 209/26/37, *al-Ahram*, 13 July 1933, *al-Balagh*, 17 July 1933.

7. TNA, FO 141/760/88, Keown-Boyd to Labiba Bey Atia, Cairo, 25 June 1933.

8. TNA, FO 141/760/87, Keown-Boyd, Case of Martha Boulos of the Salaam Institution, Port Said, Cairo, 26 June 1933.

9. TNA, FO 141/760/98, Keown-Boyd, Case of Martha Boulos, No. 3, Cairo, 27 June 1933.

10. TNA, FO 141/752/1, Case of Martha Boulos (Aida Mohammed Neiman), Note No. 5, Cairo, 7 July 1933; PHS, RG 209-26-12, "Court Decision on the Cases of Nazla Ghoneim and Ayda and Nabaweya Nahman," *al-Balagh*, 7 July 1933; "Concerning the Cases of the Missionaries and the Judgments Which Were Delivered Concerning Them," *al-Jihad*, 4 July 1933.

11. TNA, FO 141/760/19, W. J. Ablitt, Commandant, Suez Canal Police, 24 June 1933; see PHS, Pam Fol HV866.E4 Q2d, "Graduates of Boys' Orphanage, Qaliub, Egypt," where orphanage records list an Abdu Basalious as a merchant's assistant in 1930; PHS, RG 209/26/12, "Evangelisation by Aggression at Port Said," *Kawkab al-Sharq*, 22 June 1933, 21.

12. TNA, FO 141/752/1, Case of Martha Boulos (Aida Mohammed Neiman), Note No. 5, Cairo, 7 July 1933; PHS, RG 209/26/12, "In the Missionary's Incidents: A Question to the Cabinet," *Kawkab al-Sharq*, 29 June 1933, 51.

13. PHS, RG 209/26/37, "Report by Abbas El Gamal and Mahmoud Sayem, Mohammedan Lawyers to the Advocate General," *al-Balagh*, 17 July 1933.

14. TNA, FO 141/752/2, Telephone message from Ablitt Bey on 21 July 1933 at 1:10 p.m.; TNA, FO 141/760/19, Ablitt, Suez Canal Police, 24 July 1933.

15. "Fada'ih al-Mubashshirin," *al-Jihad*, 21 June 1933; see front-page photo, *al-Jihad*, 22 June 1933; "The Government and Missionaries: 'Al Siyassa's' Tireless Attack," *Egyptian Gazette*, 23 June 1933, 2; PHS, RG 209/26/38, Letter from C. C. Adams to Dr. Anderson, 26 June 1933, 2; NARA, RG 59, SD 883.404/43, Jardine, 8 July 1933, 3.

16. TNA, FO 141/760/19, Ablitt, Commandant, Suez Canal Police, 15 June 1933.

17. "Fada'ih al-Mubashshirin," *al-Jihad*, 21 June 1933; NARA, RG 59, SD 883.404/43, Jardine, 8 July 1933, 3.

18. TNA, FO 141/760/19, Ablitt, Commandant, Suez Canal Police, 15 June 1933.

19. "The Government and Missionaries: 'Al Siyassa's' Tireless Attack," 2; "Jam'iyyat

al-Ikhwan al-Muslimin wa-l-Tabshir," *Jaridat al-Ikhwan al-Muslimin* 1, no. 3 (6 Rabi' I, 1352/29 June 1933): 18.

20. PHS, RG 209/26/12, *al-Jihad*, 1 July 1933.

21. PHS, RG 209/26/37, *al-Balagh*, 17 July 1933.

22. "Taslim Fatat Thalatha," *al-Fath* 8, no. 355 (4 Rabi' II, 1352/27 July 1933): 18.

23. "Taslim Fatatayn min Dahaya al-Tabshir," *al-Fath* 8, no. 355 (4 Rabi' II, 1352/27 July 1933): 17.

24. Ibid.

25. "Jam'iyyat al-Ikhwan al-Muslimin wa-l-Tabshir fi al-Mahmudiyya Buhayra," *Jaridat al-Ikhwan al-Muslimin* 1, no. 5 (20 Rabi' I, 1352/13 July 1933): 23.

26. TNA, FO 141/752/3, Ablitt to Roche, 23 July 1933, Attachment: Petition from Ali Mohamed El Alfi to H. E. the Governor of the Canal.

27. TNA, FO 141/752/3, Tomlyn to Roche, 30 July 1933.

28. PHS, *Minutes of the Sixty-Fourth Annual Meeting of the Egyptian Missionary Association, Assiut, 1934* (Alexandria: Whitehead Morris Ltd., 1934), 298.

29. Ibid.

30. PHS, *Minutes of the Sixty-Third Annual Meeting of the Egyptian Missionary Association, Assiut, 1933* (Alexandria: Whitehead Morris Ltd., 1933), 215.

31. PHS, RG 209/26/12, "Investigation of the 'Balagh' Regarding the Missionary Incidents," *al-Balagh*, 2 July 1933.

32. "Graduates of Boys' Orphanage, Qaliub, Egypt."

33. *Minutes of the Sixty-Fourth Annual Meeting of the Egyptian Missionary Association*, 299.

34. PHS, RG 209/26/38, Letter from C. C. Adams, American Mission in Egypt, Cairo, to Dr. Anderson, Philadelphia, 26 June 1933, 3; Renate Lunde, "Building Bonny Babies—Missionary Welfare Work in Cairo, 1920–1950," in *Interpreting Welfare and Relief in the Middle East*, ed. Nefissa Naguib and Inger Marie Okkenhaug (Leiden: Brill, 2008), 83–106.

35. PHS, RG 209/26/12, "About the Baptism Event at Beni Suef," *Kawkab al-Sharq*, 22 June 1933; PHS, RG 209/26/38, Letter from C. C. Adams to Dr. Anderson, 26 June 1933, 3.

36. TNA, FO 141/752/4, "Summary of Miss McCrory's Statement," 15 September 1933.

37. Ibid.

38. PHS, RG 209/2/30, Anna B. Criswell to Friends of the Cleveland Presbyterial, 29 June 1933.

39. TNA, FO 141/752/4, Mamur of Markaz Benha to Mudir of Qalioubia, "Fatma Hassanein," 21 August 1933.

40. TNA, FO 141/752/4, "Rev. A. A. Thompson's Statement," 15 September 1933.

41. "Egypt," *Women's Missionary Magazine*, October 1934, 107–8.

42. "Egypt," *Women's Missionary Magazine*, September 1933, 108.

43. There are three published accounts of events in the wake of the Turkiyya Hasan affair based on Trasher's letters of 23 June 1933 and/or 20 July 1933. A brief account paraphrased from Trasher's 20 July 1933 letter appeared in the *Pentecostal Evangel*, 26 August 1933, 9; the two letters were fused into one under the title "Clouds of Trouble" in *Work*

of Faith and Labor of Love, The Assiout Orphanage: Gleanings from the Correspondence with Miss Lillian Trasher (Springfield, MO: Foreign Missions Department, Assemblies of God in Foreign Lands, 1937), 18–20; and slightly different versions of the two letters appeared in *Letters from Lillian*, ed. Beverly Graham (Springfield, MO: Assemblies of God Division of Foreign Missions, 1983), 20–23. Editors have taken liberties, including shortening or excluding some material, editing the English, and using different appellations—Mohammedan and Muslim—for the native population. The quote here is from *Work of Faith*, 18, and *Letters from Lillian*, 21.

44. Trasher, *Work of Faith*, 18–19.

45. Ibid., 18; in *Letters from Lillian*, the editor changes the "me" to "us" (21).

46. PHS, RG 209/26/37, *al-Jihad*, 3 July 1933; see also PHS, RG 209/26/12, "Scandal of the Evangelists in Suez and Assiout," *Kawkab al-Sharq*, 23 June 1933.

47. Trasher, *Work of Faith*, 19; idem, *Letters from Lillian*, letter dated 20 July 1933, 22; "Officials Commend Assiout Orphanage," *Pentecostal Evangel*, 26 August 1933, 9.

48. Trasher, *Work of Faith*, 18–19.

49. Ibid., 19; idem, *Letters from Lillian*, letter dated 20 July 1933, 22; "Officials Commend Assiout Orphanage," 9.

50. "Al-Malaji' li-Abna' al-Muslimin," *al-Fath* 8, no. 353 (20 Rabi' I, 1352/13 July 1933): 14.

51. PHS, RG 209/26/37, "Removal of the 64 Moslem Children from Miss Lillian's Orphanage at Assiout," *al-Jihad*, 10 July 1933.

52. Trasher, *Work of Faith*, 20; idem, *Letters from Lillian*, 22–23.

53. PHS, RG 209/26/37, *al-Jihad*, 10 July 1933; "al-Malaji' li-Abna' al-Muslimin," 14. The dispute over the exact number may have been related to the disabled girl left behind or the chaos of the moment.

54. PHS, RG 209/26/37, *al-Jihad*, 10 July 1933.

55. "Inqadh Atfal Radi'," *al-Fath* 8, no. 355 (4 Rabi' II/27 July 1933): 4.

56. PHS, RG 209/26/37, *al-Jihad*, 10 July 1933.

57. "Wakf Home for Cairo Orphans," *Egyptian Gazette*, 21 June 1933, 6.

58. PHS, RG 209/26/12, "The Government and Evangelization," *al-Balagh*, 10 July 1933.

59. Ibid.

60. Ibid.; "Orphanages Opened at Assiut," *Egyptian Gazette*, 31 August 1933, 6.

61. "2,500 Mitr min al-Ard," *al-Fath* 8, no. 34 (27 Rabi' I, 1352/20 July 1933): 13; "Site for Waifs' Home Given at Giza," *Egyptian Gazette*, 15 July 1933, 5.

62. "Homes for Moslem Orphans," *Egyptian Gazette*, 10 July 1933, 2; "al-Malaji' li-Abna' al-Muslimin," 14; "Enlargement of Asile Abbassi," *Egyptian Gazette*, 21 July 1933, 5.

63. "Al-Malaji'," *al-Fath* 8, no. 357 (18 Rabi' II, 1352/10 August 1933): 19.

64. "Insha' Malja' fi Bur Sa'id," *al-Fath* 8, no. 353 (20 Rabi' I, 1352/14 July 1933): 18.

65. "Homes for the Destitute," *Egyptian Gazette*, 29 July 1933, 5; "Homes for Alexandria Waifs," *Egyptian Gazette*, 24 August 1933, 5.

66. "Al-Malaji'," 19.

67. Ibid.

68. Ibid.

69. "Harakat al-Insha' fi Misr," *al-Fath* 8, no. 360 (10 Jumadi I, 1352/31 August 1933): 3.

70. "Progress at Tanta: Many Improvements," *Egyptian Gazette*, 1 July 1933, 2.

71. "New Orphanage Opened at Minia," *Egyptian Gazette*, 29 August 1933, 2.

72. "Orphanages Opened at Assiut," 6.

73. Ibid.

Epilogue

1. Malak Badrawi, *Isma'il Sidqi, 1875–1950: Pragmatism and Vision in Twentieth Century Egypt* (Richmond, Surrey: Curzon, 1996), 92.

2. Heather J. Sharkey, *American Evangelicals in Egypt: Missionary Encounters in an Age of Empire* (Princeton, NJ: Princeton University Press, 2008), 133–48.

3. Helmi Pekkola, *Jumalan Poluilla Islamin Eramaassa* (Porvoo: Werner Soderstrom Osakeyhitio, 1934), 222.

4. Maria Ericsson, *The Egypt Salaam Mission Story* (Port Said: Egypt Salaam Mission, 1930), 40; NARA, RG 59, SD 883.404/43, Jardine to Secretary of State, 8 July 1933, 3.

5. Pekkola, *Jumalan Poluilla*, 222.

6. Esther Boorman Strong and A. L. Warnshuis, ed., *Directory of Foreign Missions: Missionary Boards, Societies, Colleges, Cooperative Councils, and Other Agencies of the Protestant Churches of the World* (New York: International Missionary Council, 1933), 148–49; Charles Edwin Jones, *A Guide to the Study of the Pentecostal Movement* (Metuchen, NJ: Scarecrow Press, 1983), 1:626; John Thomas Nichol, *Pentecostalism* (New York: Harper and Row, 1966), 167–68; *Pentecostal Evangel*, 19 June 1955, 7.

7. PHS, *Minutes of the Sixty-Fifth Annual Meeting of the Egyptian Missionary Association, Assiut, Winter Meeting 1935* (Alexandria: Whitehead Morris, Ltd., 1935), 391.

8. FHL, Fowler Orphanage Association Papers, Elizabeth M. Nilson to Miss Smith, 21 August 1953.

9. On the final decades of the mission, see Sharkey, *American Evangelicals in Egypt*.

10. Jerome Beatty, "Nile Mother," *American Magazine*, July 1939, 5.

11. For details on developments in the home after 1933, see Beth Baron, "Nile Mother: Lillian Trasher and Egypt's Orphans," in *Competing Kingdoms: Women, Mission, Nation, and the American Protestant Empire, 1812–1960*, ed. Barbara Reeves-Ellington et al. (Durham, NC: Duke University Press, 2010), 255–62.

12. Veronica Seton-Williams and Peter Stocks, *Blue Guide: Egypt* (New York: W. W. Norton, 1984), 475.

13. FPHC, Lillian Trasher Personal Papers, Scrapbook; *Al-Ahram*, 25 March 1953; *al-Akhbar*, 25 March 1953; Florence Christie, *Called to Egypt* (Seal Beach, CA: Florence V. Christie Church School Services, 1997), 142–43; "General Naguib's Visit to Assiut," *Pentecostal Evangel*, 13 February 1955, 2.

14. FPHC, Lillian Trasher Personal Papers, 1094 247, Gamal Abdel Nasser to Lillian Trasher, 13 October 1959, and Lill to Jen, 20 October 1959.

15. Trasher, "News from Lillian Trasher," *Pentecostal Evangel*, 10 March 1957, 23.

16. Baron, "Nile Mother," 260.

17. "Jama'at al-Sayyidat lil-Difa' 'an al-Islam," *Jaridat al-Ikhwan al-Muslimin* 1, no. 8 (11 Rabi' II, 1352/3 August 1933): 23.

18. Khalid Naʻim, *Tarikh Jamʻiyyat Muqawamat al-Tansir al-Misriyya (1927–1933)* (Cairo: Kitab al-Mukhtar, n.d.).

19. Umar Ryad, "Muslim Responses to Missionary Activity in Egypt: With a Special Reference to the Al-Azhar High Corps of ʻUlama (1925–1935)," in *New Faith in Ancient Lands: Western Missions in the Middle East in the Nineteenth and Early Twentieth Centuries*, ed. Heleen Murre-van den Berg (Leiden: Brill, 2006), 298; B. L. Carter, "On Spreading the Gospel to Egyptians Sitting in Darkness: The Political Problem of Missionaries in Egypt in the 1930s," *Middle Eastern Studies* 20 (October 1984): 26–27; Sharkey, *American Evangelicals in Egypt*, 130.

20. Rainer Brunner, "Education, Politics, and the Struggle for Intellectual Leadership: Al-Azhar between 1927 and 1945," in *Guardians of Faith in Modern Times: ʻUlama' in the Middle East*, ed. Meir Hatina (Leiden: Brill, 2008), 131–34.

21. Brynjar Lia, *The Society of the Muslim Brothers in Egypt: The Rise of an Islamic Mass Movement, 1928–1942* (Reading, UK: Ithaca Press, 1998), 94.

22. See, e.g., Charles C. Adams, *Islam and Modernism in Egypt: A Study of the Modern Reform Movement Inaugurated by Muhammad ʻAbduh* (New York: Russell and Russell, 1933).

23. PHS, RG 209/26/28, "The Swedish Salaam Orphanage at Port Said," *al-Jihad*, 18 March 1936.

24. Lillian Trasher, *Letters from Lillian*, ed. Beverly Graham (Springfield, MO: Assemblies of God Division of Foreign Missions, 1983), letter dated 26 April 1935, 29.

25. Beth Baron, *Egypt as a Woman: Nationalism, Gender, and Politics* (Berkeley: University of California Press, 2005), 210–11.

26. Leila Ahmed, *A Border Passage: From Cairo to America—A Woman's Journey* (New York: Farrar, Straus and Giroux, 1999), 132.

27. Andrea B. Rugh, "Orphanages in Egypt: Contradiction or Affirmation in a Family-Oriented Society," in *Children in the Muslim Middle East*, ed. Elizabeth Warnock Fernea (Austin: University of Texas Press, 1995), 130–31; Amira al-Azhary Sonbol, "Adoption in Islamic Society: A Historical Survey," in *Children in the Muslim Middle East*, 60–61.

28. Rugh, "Orphanages in Egypt," 133–34; Sonbol, "Adoption in Islamic Society," 61–62.

29. Nancy Gallagher, *Egypt's Other Wars: Epidemics and the Politics of Public Health* (Syracuse, NY: Syracuse University Press, 1990), 171; Afaf Marsot, "The Revolutionary Gentlewomen in Egypt," *Women in the Muslim World*, ed. Louis Beck and Nikki Keddie (Cambridge, MA: Harvard University Press, 1978), 272–74; Rugh, "Orphanages in Egypt," 133–35.

30. Muhammad ʻAzmi Salih, *al-Riʻaya al-Ijtimaʻiyya li-l-Yaytama fi al-Islam* (Cairo: Maktaba Wahba, 1977).

31. Kamal Fahmi, *Beyond the Victim: The Politics and Ethics of Empowering Cairo's Street Children* (Cairo: American University in Cairo Press, 2007).

32. Amira El-Noshokaty, "Home Alone," http://weekly.ahram.org.eg/2004/685/feature .htm, accessed 12 May 2008.

33. Ibid.

34. Sarah El-Rashid, "Egyptian Orphans Still Suffering on Their National Day," http://english.ahram.org.eg/NewsContent/1/64/68132/Egypt/Politics-/Egyptian-or phans-still -suffering-on-their-National.aspx, accessed 13 September 2013. For more on orphans in contemporary Egypt, see Reymon Adly Ethnasios, "Describing the Care and Treatment of Orphans in Egypt through the Perspectives of Residents, Caretakers and Government Social Workers" (EdD diss., University of Southern California, 2012); Jacqueline Gibbons, "Orphanages in Egypt," *Journal of Asian and African Studies* 40 (2005): 261–85.

35. TNA, FO 141/760/19/85, Suez Canal Police, Special Branch, Commandant's Office, Port Said, 24 June 1933, Daily Report No. 428 (Rashad); TNA, FO 141/752/1, Copy of letter from Commandant, Suez Canal Police, to Director General European Department, 2 July 1933.

INDEX